WITHDRAWN BY THE
UNIVERSITY OF MICHIGAN

Public Opinion, Party Competition, and the European Union in Post-Communist Europe

Edited by
Robert Rohrschneider
and
Stephen Whitefield

PUBLIC OPINION, PARTY COMPETITION, AND THE EUROPEAN
UNION IN POST-COMMUNIST EUROPE
© Robert Rohrschneider and Stephen Whitefield, 2006.

All rights reserved. No part of this book may be used or reproduced in any manner whatsoever without written permission except in the case of brief quotations embodied in critical articles or reviews.

First published 2006 by
PALGRAVE MACMILLAN™
175 Fifth Avenue, New York, N.Y. 10010 and
Houndmills, Basingstoke, Hampshire, England RG21 6XS
Companies and representatives throughout the world.

PALGRAVE MACMILLAN is the global academic imprint of the Palgrave Macmillan division of St. Martin's Press, LLC and of Palgrave Macmillan Ltd. Macmillan® is a registered trademark in the United States, United Kingdom and other countries. Palgrave is a registered trademark in the European Union and other countries.

ISBN-13: 978–1–4039-7526–3
ISBN-10: 1–4039-7526–4

Library of Congress Cataloging-in-Publication Data

Public opinion, party competition, and the European Union in post-communist Europe / edited by Robert Rohrschneider and Stephen Whitefield.
    p. cm.
  Includes bibliographical references and index.
  ISBN 1–4039-7526–4
   1. European Union—Public opinion. 2. Political parties—Europe—Public opinion. 3. Europe—Economic integration—Public opinion. 4. Public opinion—Europe. 5. Europe—Politics and government—1989– I. Rohrschneider, Robert. II. Whitefield, Stephen

JN30.P9315 2006
341.242′2—dc22   2006041575

A catalogue record for this book is available from the British Library.

Design by Newgen Imaging Systems (P) Ltd., Chennai, India.

First edition: August 2006

10 9 8 7 6 5 4 3 2 1

Printed in the United States of America.

To Sarah

CONTENTS

List of Tables and Figures   vi
Acknowledgments   viii

Introduction: A Theoretical Backdrop   1
Robert Rohrschneider and Stephen Whitefield

Part I   The Policy Context

Chapter 1   European Union Policies toward Accession Countries   19
Beate Sissenich

Part II   The Party Context

Chapter 2   Party Systems and EU Accession: Euroskepticism in East Europe   43
Jack Bielasiak

Chapter 3   Party Ideology and European Integration: An East–West Comparison   65
Gary Marks, Liesbet Hooghe, Moira Nelson, and Erica Edwards

Part III   Public Opinion about European Integration

Chapter 4   Support Based on Values? Attitudes toward the EU in Eleven Postcommunist Societies   85
Jörg Jacobs and Detlef Pollack

Chapter 5	The Grass is Always Greener . . . : Mass Attitudes toward the European Union in the Czech and Slovak Republics *Petr Kopecký and Joop van Holsteyn*	105
Chapter 6	Knocking on Europe's Door: Public Opinion on the EU Accession Referendum in Poland *Krzysztof Jasiewicz*	121
Chapter 7	Determinants of Support for EU-Membership in Hungary *Attila Fölsz and Gábor Tóka*	145
Chapter 8	East of Vienna, South of the Drina: Explaining the Constituencies for Europe in Southeastern Europe *Alina Mungiu-Pippidi*	165
Chapter 9	Support for the European Union in the Baltic States *Stephen Whitefield, Robert Rohrschneider, and Rasa Alisauskiene*	187
Chapter 10	Attitudes toward European Integration and NATO in Hungary, Bulgaria, and the Ukraine *Matthew Loveless and Robert Rohrschneider*	203
Chapter 11	Between East and West: Attitudes toward Political and Economic Integration in Russia and Ukraine, 1993–2001 *Stephen Whitefield*	217
	Conclusion: The Political Consequences of Postcommunist Accession *Robert Rohrschneider and Stephen Whitefield*	241

Notes on Contributors 253
References 259
Index 275

LIST OF TABLES AND FIGURES

Tables

1.1	Accession conditions and controversial policy issues	27
2.1	Party systems and percentage of votes and seats of Euroskeptic parties	51
2.2	Characteristics of Euroskeptic parties at last elections	56
3.1	West versus East: Left/right, Gal/tan, and party position on European integration	72
3.2	Mean Standard Deviations of Expert Evaluations	81
4.1	Support for joining the EU, 1990–2003	87
4.2	Regression of attitudes toward the EU on social structure, economic situation, political cues, and value orientations	96
5.1	Expectations of EU opportunities in the Czech Republic and Slovakia	111
6.1	Support for Poland's accession to the EU, 1994–2002	122
6.2	Determinants of participation in the EU referendum	136
6.3	Determinants of vote choice in the EU referendum	138
7.1	Support for Hungary's EU-accession over time	150
7.2	Positions attributed to the four parliamentary parties regarding EU membership, March 2003	154
7.3	Dependence of support for EU membership in 10 different surveys on available cues: Sociodemographic group membership, policy and performance evaluations, and party preference	158

8.1	Nationalism as a Broad Regional Phenomenon	178
9.1	Support for European integration in the Baltic states, 1999–2003	191
9.2	Regression of EU support onto attitudinal factors, 2002 and 2003	195
9.3	Multinomial logistic regression of party vote intention onto EU support (unstandardised betas), 2001, 2002, 2003	197
10.1	OLS regression on support for membership in the European Union	210
10.2	OLS regression on support for foreign investment	212
11.1	Support for forms of integration in Russia (1995–2003) and Ukraine (1995–1998)	223
11.2	Russia: Regression of support for Western integration onto social characteristics and attitudes toward alternative integration, political, and economic norms, and economic experience	227
11.3	Russia: Multinomial logit regressions of intended party choice onto views of integration, political and economic norms, and evaluations	233
12.1	Mean scores on integration issues by accession wave and region	246
12.2	Party polarization on integration issues by accession wave	249

Figures

1	Conceptualizing integration dimensions	4
3.1	Dimensions of party competition in Western Europe. Cases weighted by vote percentage in most recent national election. $N = 98$ parties	67
3.2	Dimensions of party competition in Central and Eastern Europe. Cases weighted by vote percentage in most recent national election. $N = 73$ parties	68
3.3	Left/right and general position on European integration in Western Europe. N in dataset = 98 parties	70
3.4	Left/right and general position on European integration in Central and Eastern Europe. N in dataset = 73 parties	74
5.1	Voting in hypothetical referendum on EU accession	108
8.1	NATO and EU confidence compared	174

ACKNOWLEDGMENTS

It gives us pleasure to acknowledge the generous support of various institutions that made possible the conference at Indiana University in Bloomington where the first draft of the chapters was presented. We are grateful to the Friedrich-Ebert Foundation and its former Washington director, Dieter Dettke, for supporting the conference with enthusiasm from the very beginning. At Indiana University, we appreciate the support of the Center for Participation and Citizenship, College of Arts & Sciences, dean of Faculties, International Programs, Law School, Political Science Department, Polish Studies Center, Research & the University Graduate School, Russian & East European Institute, and West European Studies Institute. And at Oxford University, we appreciate the support of the Department of Politics and International Relations. We are grateful to Denise Gardiner (Russian and East European Studies), Karen Boschker (West European Studies), and Scott Feickert (Political Science) for taking care so effectively of the administrative aspects of the conference, and Daniel Beers for his meticulous work in preparing the final manuscript.

We appreciate the intellectual contributions of various discussants at the conference: Michael Dauderstädt, Dieter Dettke, Dieter Fuchs, Matthew Gabel, Henry Hale, Edeltraud Roller, and Charles Wise.

Finally, Robert Rohrschneider would like to acknowledge the hospitality of the German Marshall Fund's Transatlantic Center in Brussels where the final editing took place. Stephen Whitefield is grateful to the Leverhulme Trust for its support in awarding him a Major Research Fellowship. Both of them would also like to thank the Nuffield Foundation for supporting their study of party stances on European integration and Matt Loveless for his superb research assistance on that project.

Introduction: A Theoretical Backdrop

Robert Rohrschneider and Stephen Whitefield

The accession of 10 new countries to the European Union (EU) on May 1, 2004 marks the beginning of a new era for Europe. For the eight new members from postcommunist states, accession is the culmination of a monumental transformation barely 15 years after they began to institutionalize market-based democracies in their nations after the demise of socialist regimes. In contrast with the euphoria of 1989, however, the moment of accession itself in Eastern Europe was characterized by widespread uncertainty, lack of enthusiasm, and growing public and elite skepticism about the consequences of EU membership. A central concern of this book is to investigate why this change of mood has occurred.

How citizens and parties respond to integration questions is affected clearly by their economic, social, institutional, and historical circumstances. Moreover, just as parties take public preferences into account when deciding how to compete, so are citizens likely to be influenced in their views and political behavior by ways in which integration issues are taken up by political elites. Surprisingly few studies in any context, however, have systematically investigated citizens' or parties' responses to integration. Almost none has considered how parties frame European integration in domestic political debates. Collectively, the contributions to this volume address these questions.

The inclusion of postcommunist states in the European Union is likely to have dramatic consequences for the EU itself. Virtually every aspect of the evolving EU polity must be shaped and reshaped in the years to come, including its market institutions and political systems, both at the nation-states level and at the supranational level. Importantly, the character of popular opinion and party competition in

Eastern Europe is likely to have a distinct and new impact on how the EU evolves, that may lead to far greater and more ideologically divided policy contestation in EU institutions.

Existing integration scholarship, however, does not provide an adequate theoretical framework to deal with the consequences of eastward expansion. This is because postcommunist societies have characteristics that differentiate them from states that were involved in the previous stages of European integration. Indeed, it is our belief that the inclusion of postcommunist states in the EU may lead us to rethink our understanding of the dynamics and consequences of the integration process as a whole. This book is centrally concerned, therefore, with exploring these theoretical issues.

This volume brings together a group of leading EU and postcommunist scholars to consider these questions. The immediate impetus for the project came from surprising results of an analysis that we undertook into support for the EU and foreign ownership among citizens in 13 postcommunist states in the first half of the 1990s (Rohrschneider and Whitefield 2004a). Even in the early 1990s, we had already encountered a strong kernel of Euroskepticism in a twofold pattern of growing opposition to integration.

First, although publics and elites strongly supported in principle the idea of integration with the West and the EU, they were already considerably more skeptical about specific *integration instruments*, such as the presence of foreign companies in their nations. Second, more often than not, citizens opposed aspects of integration because they disagreed with the *normative premises* underlying the integration process, particularly the market values upon which the EU's common market is based.

Subsequently, in the latter half of the 1990s and increasingly up to the moment of accession, political parties began to channel this growing dissatisfaction into the political arena. The growth of Euroskeptic parties in the region attests to the crumbling consensus among elites as to the desirability of EU enlargement (Taggart and Szczerbiak 2004). This combination of public and elite Euroskepticism, which is based on distinct normative commitments as well as calculations about costs and benefits, is not likely to disappear. Rather, with accession the particular features of postcommunist politics have now been incorporated into EU governance.

But exactly how do citizens and parties in the region frame the debates over accession? What are the dimensions over which integration may be contested, and which, in the postcommunist context, are most likely to be activated politically? We consider next how the issues of political and economic integration should be conceptualized theoretically.

What Shapes the Politics of European Integration?

How can we explain support for, and growing opposition to, EU enlargement and other supranational economic and political institutions among citizens in postcommunist Eastern Europe? What are the most relevant dimensions on which integration is likely to be contested? This chapter considers each of these questions and seeks to develop a broader model of the politics of European integration in postcommunist states.

Conceptualizing Integration

First, we consider the range of integration issues facing citizens and political parties in postcommunist Europe. What are the dimensions of the integration process itself that publics are faced with, and which ones are more or less likely to be politicized and contested?

Our view of the structure of integration issues is presented in figure 1. We distinguish two dimensions: economic versus political and ideal-typical versus performance. We are guided in making these distinctions by transition research that indicates the importance of separating politics from economics and the ideal-typical from the actual performance of institutions (Evans and Whitefield 1995; Fuchs and Klingemann 2002; Rohrschneider 1999). Consequently, political and economic integration ideals are distinguished from the existing institutional arrangements of the EU. By keeping these dimensions distinct, we are able to focus theoretically on the various bases on which citizens may make judgments about integration or on which parties may choose to position themselves.

Specifically, we note that the European Union has developed on the basis of a commitment to a set of broad economic and political normative ideals: in economic terms, this means support for liberal markets, which includes migration of workers and of capital; in political terms, it means that the EU involves a transfer (or pooling) of sovereignty to a supranational government, via new parliamentary, executive, and judicial institutions. Support for the EU should, therefore, reflect attitudes toward these political and economic ideals.

Dimension	Economy	Polity
Ideals	Liberal markets	Supranational institutions
Evaluations	Economic benefits	Democratic and institutional performance

Figure 1 Conceptualizing integration dimensions.

At the same time, the EU involves a set of expectations about outcomes in both the political and the economic spheres. As a project to create a single economic market, the EU promises to improve economic performance and social welfare. Similarly, its political arrangements, including subsidiarity and supranational regulation of some aspects of domestic policy, promise to improve citizens' sense of the quality of governance.

To understand support for the EU in postcommunist states, therefore, we need to examine what kind of ideals and expectations citizens and parties envisage at the EU level (e.g., the contributions by Jacobs and Pollack, and Marks et al.). There is plenty of evidence that citizens are often quite supportive of a new and unknown order, both in the market (Duch 1993; Rohrschneider 1996) and political contexts (Evans and Whitefield 1995; Whitefield and Evans 2001). But when markets and democracies are implemented, the rough-and-tumble of these institutions may create a harsh reality that could lead to a decline of mass support for them. That this dynamic appears to work in the context of supranational regional integration may be consistent with the growing skepticism about the EU in accession countries (see also chapter 10 by Loveless and Rohrschneider, this volume).

Public Support for Integration

Importantly, the distinctions between politics and economics and between ideals and performance evaluations help illuminate why some of the central premises pervading Western-based research may be unlikely to apply in Eastern Europe. Most studies of support for international integration have focused on Western Europe and North America, where market economies were already in place. In Eastern Europe, in contrast, elites and many members of the public saw

European integration as a mechanism for the consolidation of new market structures that continued, in important respects, to be contested by significant sections of public opinion. In our view this difference of context has important implications, for understanding public attitudes and requires a shift away from much of the existing literature developed on the two most prominent cases in international integration—the EU and North American Free Trade Agreement NAFTA.

The evolution of the European Union in Western Europe in particular has stimulated intense theorizing and debate about the motivations and dynamics of how citizens evaluate the supranational framework. Competing schools within this literature explain the drive to integration in different ways—the push of state interests (intergovernmentalism), the need to remove market distortions between sectors at different stages of integration (functionalism), or the dynamics of interest group pressure, including political parties (neofunctionalism) (George 1996). Despite differences among these theories, they operate on a shared assumption that liberal-democratic and market values underlie the integration process (Hooghe 2001).

But the normative premises of the process have seldom been questioned. It is widely assumed that both citizens and parties share commitments to market *norms*, so that the case for and against integration is made with reference to market *benefits*. Instrumental reasoning, in these contexts, has dominated the scholarship, and the success of European integration has resulted from the excess of (perceived) winners over losers. While some analysts in the West have pointed at the role of party elites in generating public resistance to integration (Anderson 1998; Franklin and Marsh 1994), postmaterial values and left–right ideology (Inglehart 1977), or the quality of national institutions (Rohrschneider 2002; Sanchez–Cuenca 2000), none of these examines how normative commitments to market and liberal-democratic ideals affect citizens' perception of integration.

The literature on integration and enlargement in Eastern Europe to date has usually followed the standard West European/North American model. It has been generally assumed that EU enlargement to Central East Europe would be relatively easy to achieve politically because it was based on strong elite and mass commitments to market values and, even more so, on favorable economic calculations, at least for the potential entrants. Any contradictions or difficulties in the European project are normally situated to the East, particularly in the former Soviet Union, where market values were thought to be weakly embedded and market calculations less favorable. These parts of postcommunist Eastern

Europe have been correspondingly discounted as potential integration partners. Consequently, most analyses of EU support in Eastern Europe stress economic winners and losers of integration (Cichowski 2000; Tucker, Pacek, and Berinsky 2002).

The practice of democratic politics in Eastern Europe, however, shows that this neat picture is difficult to support. Our own research, for example, suggests that this "instrumental" view of integration does not apply to postcommunist publics (Rohrschneider and Whitefield 2004a). In particular, East Europeans are much more likely to make judgments about foreign ownership based on their underlying economic values than on expected material pay-offs. And, unlike in the West, transition research informs us that citizens' economic and political values in Eastern Europe are often incompatible with markets and, to some degree, with liberal democracies (Fuchs and Roller 1998; Gibson 1993).[1] However, because of the prevailing consensus in Western-based scholarship, value-based predictors of integration are, with a few exceptions, largely ignored by this research (Inglehart 1990; Wessels 1995). It is therefore possible, indeed likely, that public opinion in the postcommunist context about integration is driven by factors that were irrelevant in the context of Western Europe's stable democracies and affluence.

There is a clear need, therefore, to broaden the range of possible factors that may account for how the public responds. In the postcommunist context where system-level transition is at stake, these would include not just economic benefits but also regime ideals, both economic and political. Moreover, in Eastern Europe, where in many cases state structures are themselves relatively new and contested both internally and externally, views of national independence may also be important determinants.

We therefore consider a range of possible factors shaping public opinion and argue that citizens' individual economic experiences *and* ideological values (of various sorts) affect public views about integration in the postcommunist context.

Regime Ideals

Our analysis of support for foreign ownership and EU support suggested that ideological values matter enormously in evaluating the aspects of the integration process. An account of mass views that takes values seriously would start from the premise that these define individuals' ideal-typical orders and reflect the preferred procedures through which these ideals ought to be accomplished (Almond and Verba 1963). As such, they are likely to be of greatest relevance in the circumstances of revolutionary political and economic transformation experienced in Eastern Europe. Importantly, ideological values also help individuals to evaluate issues in situations where information is not readily available, experience is limited, and societal phenomena are transient (Sniderman, Brody, and Tetlock 1991). This is precisely the context in Eastern Europe that, we would suggest, creates a situation where values should become most relevant to citizens. Publics in these highly volatile contexts, in all likelihood, lack information and experience in evaluating market-based issues purely on the basis of their costs and benefits. Instead, in a new and transient environment, citizens are likely to resort to their long-term predispositions in sorting out the pros and cons of supranational markets and political regimes.

From this perspective, it is important that much evidence suggests that, to a surprising degree, citizens in postcommunist societies continue to endorse economically socialist ideals (Fuchs and Roller 1998; Miller, Hesli, and Reisinger 1995). Thus, citizens may apply their views about the domestic economy, which, to a considerable degree, represent socialist views, in appraising various aspects of the emerging international markets as well. If socialist values matter, it may well reduce public support for economic integration. For if one rejects the idea of a market economy, one is not likely to endorse economic integration justified by a desire to strengthen market relationships. Socialist ideals (for an egalitarian society, for instance) may also reduce support for a future Europe-wide polity if it does not secure egalitarian outcomes. Conversely, those who support market reforms may welcome the involvement of international corporations in the domestic economy. There are good conceptual and empirical reasons to argue that citizens rely on their (often socialist) values when they appraise emerging supranational markets as is documented by the chapters in this volume, particularly by Jacobs and Pollack, Fölsz and Tóka, and Whitefield.

Regime Performance

This set of predictors focuses on citizens' experience with new democracies and markets in Central Europe. The expectations here are premised on the idea that evaluations of the EU will in part be influenced by how well national markets and democratic regimes are perceived to work. Transition research indicates that public evaluations of national market institutions and democratic regimes are heavily shaped by their current performance (Evans and Whitefield 1995; Hofferbert and Klingemann 1999; Mishler and Rose 2001). Prior research also informs us that publics compare the current regime with the performance of a collapsed communist regime (Mishler and Rose 1997). Given this insight from transition research, we expect that mass support for integration depends, in part, on how well national regimes work.

Surprisingly, there are few analyses in the literature that consider how postcommunist publics view a second transition within their lifespan. Consider that integration entails national institutions to be partly replaced with a supranational framework. That is, a little over a decade after communist regimes were replaced with markets and liberal democracies, publics now face another transition. In turn, we expect that the performance of national regimes influences views about the EU. The better national systems perform, the more reluctant citizens will be to abandon national institutions for the EU. Ironically, this expectation may magnify the degree of opposition to integration in first-wave accession countries since these are also the ones that are the most democratic and the most successful in implementing market reforms. The extent to which citizens compare the current regime with the potential gains from the EU beyond economic benefits is an area largely ignored by integration research in the area. Nearly all the chapters in this volume consider instrumental factors—but find surprisingly little support for them.

Economic Experience

We argued above that the literature to date on this subject has emphasized the economically instrumental character of reasoning about these questions. Because of the value consensus, support is presumably generated from expected gains from developing markets or, once the integration process has begun, to redress advantages accorded to lead sectors. Public support—and obviously opposition from the losers in the process—is expressed through interest groups and political parties.

A broad version of this sort of explanation (Anderson 1998; Eichenberg and Dalton 1993; Gabel 1998c) suggests that citizens make decisions about economic policy based on an extrapolation from past economic conditions to what the future may bring. In principle, the logic here is straightforward. When citizens evaluate economies positively, the idea of integration is more appealing than when they assess market reforms negatively. If they also blame (or credit) the incumbent government for the economic conditions, then they react accordingly. This process is not limited to national governments. When citizens believe that the common market brings about affluence, support for the EU increases because, as Eichenberg and Dalton put it, "if the EC has promised anything, it has promised the enhancement of member states' economic welfare" (Eichenberg and Dalton 1993, 510).

Another microlevel model favored by the political economy literature emphasizes (1) the individual capacities of citizens to engage with the international economy, which is particularly influenced by age and education levels, and (2) the sectoral locations of citizens (Gabel 1998c; Scheve and Slaughter 2001). Age and education matter because of the relative flexibility that each is expected to impart to individuals in adapting to new working and labor market conditions. Education also matters because of the cognitive skills it involves, not only greater knowledge of global markets but also language and technical skills.

A final variant in this group emphasizes how the vulnerability of individuals' occupations to economic fluctuations affects their views about economic structures. The more one expects to benefit (suffer) from economic changes in economic systems, the more likely one is to support (oppose) such changes. As one EU analyst put it, "EU membership provides significant economic gains and losses to skilled and unskilled workers depending on their position in the EU labor market" (Gabel 1998c, 938). Likewise, workers in those industries adversely affected by NAFTA are less inclined to support the free trade zone in North America (Scheve and Slaughter 2001).

Nationalism

Two other social and attitudinal factors may also be expected to play an important role in Eastern Europe. Although nationalism and ethnicity are rarely considered as independent factors in motivating support for the EU in Western Europe (e.g., they are not even mentioned in the indexes of two important contributions to EU analyses: George 1996; Moravcsik 1998), there are reasons to believe that their effects are more powerful in Eastern Europe (Zielonka 2002).

First, by comparison with Western Europe (Hooghe and Marks 2004), postcommunist states are highly ethnically diverse. All except

Hungary, Poland, and Slovenia have significant minorities. The effect of this may be to shift views of the EU away from economic concerns to focus on the ways in which supranational bodies may support minorities' political aspirations—which will therefore also produce consequences for the politics of majorities.

Second is the factor that concerns the recent history of supranational rule in states in the region. All accession countries—with the exception of Slovenia, which was in any case arguably subordinate within Yugoslavia—were formally part of the Soviet bloc or the Soviet Union itself and were more (Czechoslovakia) or less (Romania) dominated by it politically and economically. Political mobilization against communist power in every state discussed in this book—including Russia—was to a significant degree nationalist in character, though the form of nationalism varied in terms of the push to inclusion in broader international economic and especially political structures, including the EU and North Atlantic Treaty Organization (NATO). We may therefore expect support for nationalism to have a complex and possibly independent relationship with EU enlargement and integration. In some cases, especially in East Central Europe, integration may be seen as a means of consolidating national independence. In other cases, particularly in Russia, Moldova, and Ukraine, the integration of neighboring states in the EU or NATO may be seen as threatening to national independence. The effects of nationalism and ethnic division, therefore, need to be considered separately.

The Role of Political Parties

We noted earlier that the literature on economic integration in Eastern Europe and elsewhere has, with a few exceptions, paid little systematic analytical attention to the effects of party competition on public support. This lacuna is surprising given the theory and evidence of party effects in other areas, such as globalization (Garrett 1998), the cleavage literature, and the considerable literature on party identification (Dalton, Flanagan, and Beck 1984; Dalton and Wattenberg 2000; Franklin 1992). The lack of attention to party effects is perhaps more surprising given that one of the most developed studies of the effects of parties is to be found in an analysis of the varying issue bases of politics in postcommunist Eastern Europe (Kitschelt et al. 1999). We therefore consider a variety of ways in which the structure of party competition and the characteristics of parties themselves may have an impact on how integration issues are framed for citizens.

First, the comparative literature points to the existence of distinctive party "families" (Duverger 1954; Mair and Mudde 1998), which divide socially and ideologically—social-democratic, communist, liberal, agrarian, religious, nationalist, etc.—in ways that may have consequences for how integration matters to voters. Supporters of a particular party family, regardless of country, may be expected to relate integration issues to the ideological and social characteristics of the party. More generally, party systems as a whole differ in the extent to which they focus on economic, social, ethnic, or other issues. These differences need not result exclusively from public preferences, but from characteristics of the mode of transition (Kitschelt et al. 1999) that become institutionalized in the parties. Parties may also choose to highlight issues in order to avoid competing on questions of central concern to parts of the electorate (McLean 2001).

The effect of party presentation, however, may be to change the ways in which integration and enlargement issues are packaged with other ideological dimensions. Where economic issues dominate party competition, for example, integration is likely to be principally an economic question. Where nationalist issues dominate, integration and enlargement will to a greater extent take on these ideological clothes. Because the postcommunist public is divided on economic values, however, when economic issues dominate party competition and structure discussion of integration and enlargement, the activation of economic values is likely to be more pronounced.

Similarly, parties (and party systems) differ in the extent to which they are based, if at all, on ideological appeals, as opposed to clientelistic or charismatic relations with the electorate (Kitschelt et al. 1999). The causes of such differences are probably mainly cultural and historical, but their consequences for the structure of public support are likely to be distinct and independent of the forms of programmatic competition. Because programmatic party competition of any sort (economic, social, or nationalist) involves justification of policy in terms of collective benefits, it is likely to produce greater focus on structured issue division. Clientelistic competition, by contrast, operates through distribution of particular benefits and is thus less ideological, whereas charismatic competition, at the extreme, personalized politics void of issue content. Parties (and party systems) with programmatic competition, therefore, are much more likely to be based on values. Parties are more likely to polarize on integration and enlargement, and as a consequence, support for integration and enlargement is likely to be lower and values more mobilized than is the case in patronage-based or charismatic conditions.

Second, parties may be differentiated based on organization type, the relationships among members, activists, and leaders (Duverger 1954). Such organizational differences at the level of membership involvement are likely to affect the breadth of a party's appeal—with catch-all parties appealing broadly and less ideologically to the electorate than mass parties—and, as a result, differences are to be expected in the extent to which integration issues are connected to other attitude dimensions and in levels of polarization and consequently in support.

Third, research in many contexts has shown that party identifiers are more likely, by comparison with others, to adapt their position to that taken by their party leadership. We note in this regard that partisan identification among many East European electorates is now similar to that found in more established democracies (Dalton and Wattenberg 2000). We should expect, therefore, to find significant differences between party identifiers and others in the ways in which they view integration issues, both in the salience attached to issues, the extent of overall structure in their attitudes derived from greater awareness of party stances, and in the direction of their support.

A Cost Mobilization Model

The points made above about the dimensions of integration issues facing postcommunist Eastern Europe, the sources of citizens' support and opposition, and the impact of parties and the party system on the framing of integration come together in what we call a "cost mobilization" model of the politicization of European integration.

The premise of the cost-mobilization model is that the integration issues may be affected by ways in which citizens become acquainted with the policy via the democratic process—and, in line with the discussion above, with how this interacts with their underlying values. In Eastern Europe, this may entail political entrepreneurs, who oppose market reforms, mobilizing mass sentiments against integration especially during elections; market supporters in turn will mobilize their camp. EU opponents may mobilize opposition to accession criteria that include deepening of the integration process. These debates, in turn, may entail that citizens are exposed to competing elite cues about such issues as foreign ownership, free migration of workers, or the degree to which nation-states yield decision-making authority to the EU.

In turn, elite competition often mobilizes mass sentiments on both sides of an issue (McClosky and Zaller 1984; Zaller 1992) and may increase uncertainty about the benefits of the policy and therefore reduce support for it. We are not suggesting that party competition entirely determines how citizens think about the EU. Obviously, economic experiences and ideological predispositions in part affect how parties frame the issue in the first place. But this book also assumes that the specific manifestation that party systems give to latent societal conflicts influences how much weight citizens attach to various experiences and predispositions. Consequently, party competition may directly affect how publics evaluate the EU and may mediate the salience of individual level factors on how citizens view the EU.

Structure of the Book

The chapters in this book address different aspects of the issues raised above. The contributions emerged out of an initial two-day conference that was organized at Indiana University in April 2004 where we brought together a diverse group of scholars who shared our interest in how citizens evaluate regime transitions, and who, like us, believe that one also must examine the party and policy context of a nation in order to understand how citizens relate to political issues.

Given our theoretical aims, we structured this volume into three parts.

Part I, which consists of Sissenich's study, examines the policy issues that EU accession created for the new member-states. Her chapter discusses how the EU's negotiations with applicants defined the EU-related policy framework for domestic political debates in accession countries. The study highlights the policy issues the EU identified as relevant for each country, and how these issues set the stage for policy debates within new member-states.

Sissenich's broad overview is followed by part II, consisting of two chapters, which examines how political parties channeled EU accession criteria into domestic political debates. (The relationship between accession and party positions and divisions is also considered in chapter 12 by Rohrschneider and Whitefield, this volume.) First, Bielasiak's chapter (chapter 2) argues that integration issues—especially opposition to accession—are used by peripheral parties as part of an effort to improve their fortunes in elections, particularly by mobilizing those citizens who stand to lose most from integration. Second, an analysis by Marks, Hooghe, Nelson, and Edwards (in chapter 3) shows how parties' stances about integration are closely linked to a left–right dimension in postcommunist countries, in contrast to Western Europe. Cumulatively, although the studies disagree to some degree over the precise correlates of party positions on integration, they converge on documenting that (1) integration is indeed a polarizing issue at the level of parties in most countries; (2) party debates over integration are linked to other domestic conflict dimensions; and (3) these controversies occur especially in countries that first joined the EU.

The third, and largest, section analyzes how publics evaluate various integration aspects and their sources.

Part III begins with a broad, cross-national study by Jacobs and Pollack (chapter 4). Their analysis portrays the growing skepticism about integration in those nations that recently joined the EU and also shows that these attitudes are linked to whether citizens support the ideological values underlying European integration, such as promarket and prodemocratic values.

Chapter 5 by Kopecký and van Holsteyn examines attitudes to integration and EU referenda in the Czech Republic and Slovakia and places the contrasting views of these publics in the European context. They argue that the lower enthusiasm in the Czech Republic can be explained, in part, by the more intense controversies among parties in the Czech Republic.

Next, the analyses of the Polish case by Jasiewicz (in chapter 6) provide a detailed profile of the decisions underlying the choices made by Polish citizens in the 2003 accession referendum. His study points to the role of ideological values and structural factors in shaping the referendum behavior of the Polish public.

The Hungarian pattern, examined in chapter 7 by Fölsz and Tóka, also documents growing skepticism among Hungarians as well as the importance of ideological values in shaping these attitudes. Contrary to the Czech and Slovakian cases, however, they argue that Hungarians are less influenced by party elites than is commonly assumed.

Chapter 8 by Mungiu-Pippidi examines why publics in Romania and Bulgaria staunchly support the EU even when most of the cultural elites in these countries are skeptical about it. She points in particular to the positive "role model" that NATO plays in generating positive views about the EU in many countries.

In chapter 9, Whitefield, Rohrschneider, and Alisauskiene consider the particularities of EU integration politics in the Baltic States where recent history of incorporation into the Soviet Union and the presence of significant Russian minorities, particularly in Estonia and Latvia, lead to a strongly ethnic and nationalist component to mass attitudes and partisan choices. The chapter also notes the difficulties that may arise for EU politics more generally from the association between opposition to integration in the Baltic States and opposition to democracy per se.

In chapter 10, Loveless and Rohrschneider examine whether the experience with a country's membership in NATO contributes to support for the EU. The study argues that the positive effect of NATO is limited to the most general aspects of European integration but does not extend to specific integration instruments.

Chapter 11 by Whitefield broadens the scope of this volume by examining how publics in Russia and Ukraine evaluate international integration. He again points to the central importance of ideological values in shaping attitudes toward Western integration but notes that in addition to normative contestation over the value of markets, Russians and Ukrainians also divide over their relationship to the West, on the one hand, and the historic space of the Soviet Union, on the other.

In their concluding chapter, Rohrschneider and Whitefield return to the implications of the cost mobilization model for the political contestation of European accession in postcommunist states. They argue that as accession becomes a reality, so does the intensity of skepticism and partisan division across the whole party political spectrum. The conclusion, therefore, highlights the central theoretical themes and empirical evidence considered in the book: the importance of distinguishing elements of the integration process, the importance of distinguishing normative from instrumental bases of support and opposition, and the importance of considering the effects of political elites and parties on the mobilization of public opinion.

As with all empirical social science, particularly as it addresses new issues and problems, this book raises many questions requiring further investigation. We believe, however, that it demonstrates the need to take seriously the accession of postcommunist states whose citizens have quite distinct normative commitments and whose parties may operate in a political space that is quite different from that found in Western Europe.

Note

1. A consistent pattern in transition research is that while publics in postcommunist systems support liberal-democratic rights in the abstract, citizens also hold societal ideals that are to some degree incompatible with liberal democracies.

PART I
The Policy Context

CHAPTER 1

European Union Policies toward Accession Countries

Beate Sissenich

Introduction

The Union's recent jumbo-enlargement concluded a decade or more of rigorous preparations during which the countries of Central and Eastern Europe were pursuing a moving target. Despite some candidates' tough negotiating positions on issues such as agricultural subsidies, land sales, and visa policies, the EU was able to set the preaccession conditions largely unilaterally. This was due to the asymmetric interdependence between candidates and the EU in which each candidate stood to gain disproportionately from accession (and lose by nonaccession) compared with the benefits accruing to the EU as a whole. As the EU took its time to commit to an accession date, candidates grew less and less patient with fulfilling unilateral conditions when the benefits seemed to become intangible. Nevertheless, governments of both the left and the right remained committed to the reforms stipulated by the EU, even though they regularly paid for this commitment by not being reelected. Government elites, it appears, were willing to set aside short-term electoral considerations for the expected long-term benefits of EU membership and/or domestic reform. Where this was not the case, the EU responded with delayed entry—witness the pressure on Slovakia under Mečiar and on Romania up to the present.

This chapter analyzes the framework under which accession preparations took place, providing a backdrop for the subsequent chapters on public opinion in the new member-states. I begin by highlighting the asymmetric interdependence between the EU and candidates, which allowed the former to impose accession conditions unilaterally. Thus, I describe the formal policies of the EU toward the candidates and the instruments it used to transfer its rules to the transformation countries. I then spell out some of the implications of those policies, notably risks and benefits of externalizing reform, the strengthening of national executives relative to parliaments, the likely gap in implementation resulting from hasty legal harmonization, and a poor fit of some EU policies in the transformation countries of the east. Finally, I examine some of the most controversial negotiating issues between the EU and candidate countries as these are likely to remain important for domestic debates on EU membership.

Asymmetric Interdependence and Unilateral Accession Conditions

Despite euphoric proclamations by West European leaders about Europe's impending unity, the relationship between the EU and aspirant members in the east was one of asymmetric interdependence (Moravcsik and Vachudova 2003). Although both old and new members are likely to draw economic and political benefits from an enlarged Union, the EU was able to define and alter accession conditions unilaterally. This is because the opportunity cost of nonaccession was disproportionately greater for any single candidate country than for the EU as a whole (Moravcsik and Vachudova 2003). One incentive for Central and Eastern European Countries (CEECs) seeking membership was precisely the prospect of gaining bargaining power relative to their current status. As nonmembers, they were already affected by EU policies on a wide range of issues (Rabkin 2000); as members, they can now help shape these policies.

Asymmetric interdependence was reflected in the institutional framework of negotiations between candidates and the Union. The Association Agreements with Poland and Hungary, signed in December 1991 and effective since 1994, are a case in point.[1] Also called "Europe Agreements," they established bilateral institutions for accession negotiations and a legal framework for political and economic relations between the EU and CEECs, focusing on political dialogue, trade, movement of workers, and economic, financial, and cultural cooperation. The trade component, in particular, revealed the power asymmetry and the real economic gains the EU derived from relations with Central and Eastern Europe (CEE) (Inotai 1995, 1999). The agreements contained a formal commitment to establish a free trade area between the community and each CEEC and also obliged the community to reduce trade barriers faster than the CEECs. However, the agreements restricted access to the community market in sectors in which CEECs had a comparative advantage, notably agriculture, textiles and clothing, and coal and steel. Trade, therefore, generated much political dispute (Duponcel 1998; Kaminski 1995; Mayhew 1998; Williams, Balaz, and Zajac 1998).[2]

The asymmetry of the CEECs' relationship with the EU was also evident in the latter's ability to unilaterally determine and revise accession conditions. While the absence of a ready-made script for the biggest enlargement in EU history was hardly surprising, the piecemeal fashion in which the Union developed its approach kept candidates uncertain about ever-more stringent conditions piled up on top of earlier ones (Nicolaides et al., 1999).[3] At its Copenhagen meeting in June 1993, the European Council formulated three broad criteria for accession, the so-called Copenhagen criteria: (1) *Politically*, an acceding country needs to have stable democratic institutions and rule of law, respect human rights, and protect minorities. (2) *Economically*, a country must demonstrate the existence of a functioning market economy and its ability to withstand the competitive pressures resulting from its internal market. (3) *Legally* and *administratively*, a country must adopt and implement the entire body of community law and policy. The last is clearly the most demanding criterion as it requires accession countries to rewrite national laws and policies to accommodate the nearly 100,000 pages of community law. As Iankova and Katzenstein have noted, this criterion contains an element of "hypocrisy" (Iankova and Katzenstein 2003). On the one hand, given member-states' considerable variation in complying with community law, it is in the EU's best interest to utilize its ability to control accession unilaterally in order to enforce the *acquis* before countries gain membership. On the other hand, the implementation gap among member-states is a widely discussed problem (Börzel 2001; Jordan 1999; Levy 2000; Majone 2000; Peters 2000).[4] Hence, making full implementation an accession prerequisite asks candidates to show greater conformity than is effectively achieved among those states that actually shaped the policies in question. Consequently, the Commission's enforcement mandate is greater for the candidate countries than for the member-states. By making full implementation of the *acquis* an entry condition, the Union wields a crude enforcement mechanism in which delayed entry is a threat against noncompliance in *any* sector. This contrasts with the more differentiated enforcement mechanisms used against member-states, which target *specific* cases of implementation shortfalls.

More accession requirements were elaborated in subsequent years. Underlining the double standard implicit in EU demands was the repeated call for improved implementation capacity. The 1995 Madrid European Council emphasized the importance of adequate administrative capacity in the candidate countries without specifying what such capacity would look like and whether it could be found in the member-states, which had never been subject to this criterion at all (Dimitrova 2002). Administrative capacity was further highlighted at the European Council meetings in Santa Maria da Feira (June 2000), Nice (December 2000), and Göteborg (June 2001).

Thus, the EU developed its approach to the 2004 enlargement in stops and starts (see table A1 in the Internet appendix)[5] (Grabbe 2001). Certainly, the undertaking was complex. Previous enlargements consisted of no more than three countries at a time and the socioeconomic variance between old and new member-states has never been as wide as now. This complexity partly explains the Union's vacillations—the refusal until 2001 to commit to any clear dates of accession, the vague and all-encompassing Copenhagen criteria that hold applicants to higher standards than member-states, and the wavering between political commitments to European unity and utilitarian considerations of economic benefits. Asymmetric interdependence left candidate countries at the receiving end of unilateral conditions with only occasional verbal posturing to suggest that such unilateralism should not be taken for granted.[6]

Instruments for EU Policy Transfer

Asymmetric interdependence allowed the EU to develop increasingly demanding unilateral accession conditions. The period 1996–2004, roughly speaking, was therefore filled with frenzied efforts by the candidates to conform to EU demands. How has the EU actually gone about transmitting its policies to candidate countries? The transfer instruments build on the logic of rational cost–benefit calculations in a context of asymmetric interdependence. Candidates have abided by them because they expected to be rewarded with full membership in the EU. The Union's enhanced preaccession strategy has had three explicit components: increased preaccession aid, accession partnerships, and participation in community programs, agencies, and committees. Additional transfer tools have included regular reports on candidate progress, the national programs for the adoption of the *acquis*, nonbinding opinions from various EU institutions, and joint consultative committees. Let me elaborate on two of these instruments: financial assistance and regular reports. Financial assistance allowed the EU to direct accession preparations at the micro- and mesolevel; at the same time, it served to prepare candidates for absorbing considerably larger funds after accession. The regular reports were widely publicized (and hotly debated) gauges for the state of preparations on both sides. They constituted the principal source of information on enlargement preparations for EU actors outside the Commission.

Financial Assistance

Financial assistance has taken three forms: Phare, Instrument for Structural Policies for Pre-Accession (ISPA), and Special Accession Program for Agriculture and Rural Development (SAPARD). The last two began in 2000; SAPARD assists preparations in agriculture (EUR 520 million/year),[7] whereas ISPA supports investments in environmental and transportation infrastructure (EUR 1.1 billion/year)[8] (Commission of the European Communities 2002). Phare[9] was first established in 1989 to assist the postcommunist transformation in East Central and Southeastern Europe. The program has been partly focused on accession preparations since 1993 and was revamped in 1998 to concentrate on two accession-related priorities. The first priority is investments, accounting for 70 percent of the annual budget[10] and targeting the "regulatory infrastructure needed to ensure compliance with the *acquis* and direct, *acquis*-related investments" (Commission of the European Communities 1999) as well as economic and social cohesion in preparation for future Structural Fund participation. The second is institution building; it has made up 30 percent of Phare's annual budget and focused on the political and administrative accession criteria. Aside from legal harmonization and administrative capacity, Phare institution-building programs have supported public authorities and NGOs in securing democratic institutions, the rule of law, respect for human rights, and protection of minorities (Commission of the European Communities 2001b).[11] Hence, institution-building assistance has been paid out not only to governments but also to nonstate actors at the local, regional, and national level. Phare has comprised both national and multinational programs. The latter have often supported cross-border cooperation. Critics of the EU's financial assistance to CEE have pointed out several problems: First, its overly complicated bureaucracy increased transaction costs and made it difficult for CEE actors to access the funds. Second, contracting rates were low and processing speeds slow. Ironically, the CEECs most in need of assistance were least able to absorb the funds because they lacked the requisite administrative capacity (Bailey and De Propris 2004). Third, candidate countries pointed out that a sizeable share of the funds goes back to the old member-states, either to government actors (as in the case of twinning) or private contractors (as in the case of infrastructural investments).

Regular Reports

The regular reports have been an important signaling device for the Commission since 1997. The reports measure compliance with the Copenhagen criteria, focusing in particular on applicants' ability to implement the *acquis* in all fields. They have informed EU institutions, member-states, and the general public on the state of preparations in each country, indicating Commission approval and disapproval to the candidate countries in a widely publicized and detailed format. The reports have been designed to permit comparison and encourage competition among countries in each policy field. Though there is no uniform matrix in which qualitative language corresponds exactly to a certain level of preparedness, the wording within each chapter has been calibrated to allow detection of a scale of progress among countries.[12] Furthermore, the reports are the culmination of constant monitoring and graduated rule enforcement. Rounds of questions, meetings at various levels of authority, and formal inquiries in negotiation subcommittees have preceded negative assessments in the reports. Although such close monitoring may be burdensome for the candidates, it has allowed for instant feedback. Thus, both sides have tried to preempt overt criticism by resolving disagreements out of public sight.[13] Producing the reports has involved wide-ranging, day-to-day communications among Commission and candidate country officials, member-state civil servants, representatives of other international organizations (notably IMF, World Bank, and OECD), and nongovernmental organizations. Commission officials have canvassed societal representatives for views on their governments' adoption of EU rules. This active solicitation has afforded nonstate actors the opportunity to provide valuable information to Commission officials as a means of generating pressure on their own governments. For the countries of the 2004 wave, the Commission published a Composite Report to indicate remaining shortcomings (see table A2 in the Internet appendix for a summary by country).

In sum, asymmetric interdependence has enabled the EU to enforce its rules in the candidate countries not by coercion but by granting and withholding rewards (Schimmelfennig, Engert, and Knobel 2003). But there are potential costs associated with the insistence that candidates conform to the full set of EU laws right from the get-go. The next section explores the implications of the ways in which the EU has handled enlargement preparations.

Implications of Asymmetric Interdependence and Unilateral Conditionality

All exclusive clubs set their membership rules unilaterally and have the prerogative of screening would-be members using criteria that are often less than transparent and exceed expectations for existing members. This is no different in the case of the EU. But although many sound arguments speak in favor of stringent accession criteria, what often vexed CEE governments and observers was the EU's mix of utilitarian considerations with high-minded rhetoric of European solidarity and historic justice. Furthermore, observers increasingly point to the drawbacks of the wholesale transfer of EU policies at breakneck speed. Potential long-term problems include the crumbling of public support for policies devised elsewhere and for different circumstances, weak legislatures compared with national executives, a lasting implementation gap as preparations focused on legal harmonization, and a poor fit of EU policies to CEE economies. Let me address each of these concerns in turn.

Externalization of Reform

Many of the reforms imposed by the EU have been changes that elites in the CEECs would most probably have seen fit to undertake at any rate, with or without EU membership. From this perspective, accession merely provided added impetus for a necessary reform process in order to turn command economies into capitalist democracies. This is most obviously true for the first Copenhagen criterion of democracy and respect for human rights, as well as for those areas of the EU *acquis* that are directly related to the single market. Where governments were less than fully committed to liberal democracy, as was the case in Slovakia under Mečiar, the EU's leverage strengthened domestic actors supporting political reform (Vachudova 2004). Restrictive minority policies have undergone significant changes as a result of EU scrutiny (Tesser 2003).

A remarkable aspect of the political transformation in CEE accession has been the wide agreement among leading political parties on the need for radical economic and political reforms. This reform commitment predated the formal accession preparations, which accelerated in the late 1990s. Yet, CEE governments have consistently paid for their reform commitment by being voted out of office. The fact that CEE governments on both sides of the political spectrum have tended to follow broadly similar reform policies suggests a general consensus on the long-term goals of democracy, the market, and integration in Western alliances. In this perspective, CEE voters are inclined to share these long-term goals and vote against incumbents to express their dissatisfaction with short-term effects of the reform process. CEE's most successful parties, furthermore, have tended to be catch-all parties with heterogeneous constituencies, a professional apparatus, and no mass membership. In an environment in which cleavages remain fluid, a catch-all strategy is eminently reasonable but cuts down on policy options (Lewis 2001; Szczerbiak 2003).

Despite general elite agreement on the necessity of reforms, one may ask the counterfactual question of whether the same reforms would have happened without EU pressure. Without the promise of EU membership as a reward, mobilizing the needed political support for sweeping changes would have been much more difficult. EU conditionality allowed CEE governments to assign responsibility for painful reforms to an outside actor. The benefits of this strategy go beyond mere blame-shifting. Reform externalization allows elites to make credible commitments by voluntarily entering a contract with external actors to limit domestic policy options.[14] Yet there may be a political liability attached to this approach. The closer the CEECs came to the accession date, the less their governments were able to rely on a broad societal consensus about the fundamental benefits of EU membership.

Where CEE electorates saw their governments as having settled for unfavorable accession conditions, some perceptions of domestic reforms changed from necessary alterations to undesirable foreign dictates (as the various public opinion chapters in this volume make plain). Some parties have responded by increasing their Euroskeptic rhetoric. Examples include the Czech Republic's Civic Democratic Party under Vaclav Klaus and Hungary's FIDESZ under Viktor Orbán. In general, party-based Euroskepticism in CEE tends to cluster on the political right, even though it certainly occurs on both sides of the spectrum (Taggart and Szczerbiak 2004).[15] Furthermore, as countries have moved closer to accession, they have been more likely to have parties that were opposed to European integration in principle, rather than specific EU policies.[16]

It is impossible to ascertain which reforms would or would not have occurred without EU accession requirements. Nor is it useful to speculate about the direction of reforms in the absence of EU pressure. There are a number of issues in which the EU has little or no jurisdiction, notably defense, taxation, education, and social security systems (Moravcsik 2002).[17] Table 1.1 lists the policy areas under negotiation in the run-up to accession and highlights elements that generated considerable domestic controversy. The list of controversial items should not be seen as exhaustive. Rather, it documents the most important sources of disagreement between the EU and CEECs. On many of these issues, candidate governments found it difficult to accept EU stipulations due to domestic pressure. In a few cases, such as land and real estate sales, the candidates prevailed, but usually in exchange for concessions elsewhere (labor mobility and agricultural subsidies). I discuss the substance of the most important disagreements in the negotiations in the fourth section of this chapter.

Table 1.1 Accession conditions and controversial policy issues

Copenhagen criterion	Issue	Country
Democracy, rule of law, human rights, and minority protection	Minority rights	Bulgaria, Czech Republic, Estonia, Hungary Latvia, Lithuania, Romania, Slovakia
	Human rights (orphanages and child adoptions)	Romania
	Rule of law	Romania

Continued

Table 1.1 Continued

Copenhagen criterion	Issue	Country
Functioning market economy and ability to withstand competitive pressures of the Common Market		
Adoption and implementation of the entire body of EU laws and policies		
Note: Madrid criterion of institutional and administrative capacity		
Acquis chapter:		
1. Free movement of goods		
2. Free movement of persons	Transition periods imposed by most old member-states	All except Malta and Cyprus
3. Freedom to provide services		
4. Free movement of capital	Land and real estate sales/secondary residences	Cyprus, Czech Republic, Hungary, Lithuania, Latvia, Estonia, Poland, Malta, Slovenia
5. Company law		
(a) Competition policy	Competition policy (fiscal state aids, steel, shipbuilding, etc.)	All
6. Agriculture	Subsidies, reference quantities, production standards	All
7. Fisheries		
8. Transport policy	Miscellaneous	Czech Republic, Slovakia, Poland, Estonia, Latvia, Lithuania, Malta, Cyprus
9. Taxation		
10. EMU		
11. Statistics		
12. Social and employment affairs		
13. Energy		
14. Industrial policy		
15. Small and medium enterprises		
16. Science and research		
17. Education and training		
18. Telecommunications and information technology		
19. Culture and audiovisual policy		
20. Regional policy and coordination		
21. Environment	Nuclear power plants and other issues	Bulgaria, Czech Republic, Estonia, Latvia, Lithuania, Poland, Slovakia, Slovenia

Continued

Table 1.1 Continued

Copenhagen criterion	Issue	Country
22. Consumer and health protection		
23. Justice and home affairs	Visa policy	Estonia, Hungary, Latvia, Lithuania, Poland, Romania, others
24. Customs union		
25. External relations		
26. Common foreign and security policy		
27. Financial control		
28. Finance and budget provisions		
29. Institutions (no national legal approximation required)	Representation of new member-states in EU institutions—Nice Treaty versus Constitution	All, but especially Poland
30. Other		

Strengthening Executives at the Expense of Legislatures

By requiring the full adoption of the nearly 100,000 pages of EU law, the Union has effectively turned CEE parliaments into conveyor belts for legal harmonization. Parliaments have lacked both time and resources to devote significant attention to the *quality* of legal harmonization. Admittedly, current member-states face similarly devalued legislatures and enhanced executives. This is because policy negotiations in Brussels are carried out by national executives, leaving legislators at the receiving end of EU policies (Moravcsik 1994, 2002). Though actual measurement is difficult, the bulk of legislative acts now passed in the member-states originates in Brussels, where it has been negotiated by national executives (Töller 1995).[18] But the problem is compounded in CEE, where the speed of legal harmonization was vastly accelerated *and* the starting point lay elsewhere. Williams has aptly characterized this effect as the EU's "exporting [its] democratic deficit" (Williams 2001). Even if we agree with Moravcsik's argument that distributive conflicts continue to be fought by legislators at the domestic level, where the bulk of spending policies originates, we may find the shifting balance between executives and legislatures in terms of regulatory authority a troubling development for democratic control (Moravcsik 2002).[19]

Conceivably, this weakening of the legislature is only a temporary effect of accession preparations and a small price to pay for the long-term benefits of full membership (including the ability to shape future EU policies). However, the devaluation of parliaments has coincided with the political transformation of the region. At a time when the new democratic institutions were supposed to unfold their full potential, parliaments saw their ability to control the executive curtailed almost from the get-go (Commission of the European Communities 2001a).[20]

Implementation Gap

We can expect the EU's existing implementation gap to widen as a consequence of the 2004 enlargement. Changes in the caseload of the European Court of Justice (ECJ) after previous enlargements provide a good gauge for the actual implementation of EU laws and policies. Thus, in 1973 (the year Denmark, Ireland, and the United Kingdom joined), the number of new cases multiplied by a factor of 2.34 over the previous year, with direct actions accounting for most of the increase. Subsequent enlargements have triggered lesser spikes (15 percent in 1981 and 19 percent in 1995) (European Court of Justice 2001).[21] The 2004 enlargement wave is likely to cause an upsurge in the court's caseload that will exacerbate the existing backlog and slow processing times (European Court of Justice 2004).[22] True, national courts in the new member-states may initially be reluctant to refer cases to the ECJ (European Court of Justice 2004, 223).[23] But the Commission has announced its intention to use all available means to pursue infringements, which include direct actions (Commission of the European Communities 2003a).

Why should we expect the Union's implementation gap to widen? Also, should this be a cause for concern? First, we can expect a deteriorating implementation deficit because the administrative capacity of the new entrants lags behind that of current members (Cameron 2003; Sissenich 2003). This is true even when notorious violators of community law (such as Greece and Italy) are taken into account. Second, the conveyor-belt-style transposition of community law in the run-up to accession means that less attention has been given to questions of compatibility with existing laws and administrative practices. A widening implementation gap is indeed worrisome because it undermines the credibility of EU policy making altogether (Majone 2000). Whatever the benefits of integration, they are unlikely to materialize when jointly agreed policies cannot be implemented. In the long run, therefore, the widening implementation gap may undercut the legitimacy of EU policy making.

Inadequate Policy Fit

Contrary to the argument that EU accession speeds up necessary reforms in CEE, critics of the wholesale transfer of EU laws and policies point to the incongruity between the needs of advanced capitalist democracies and those of transformation economies. By this account, the widening implementation gap is not merely due to the speed of legal harmonization and the inadequate preparation of administrative institutions. Rather, the EU's imposition of policies designed for advanced capitalist democracies on transformation countries means a loss of flexibility and the diversion of precious resources from where they are most needed for economic modernization.

Few observers have spelled out this argument in detail thus far. Three areas come to mind in which differences in economic structures between old and new members may affect the relevance of existing community law:

1. *Legislation relevant to the single market.* The share of small and medium enterprises of the overall national economy is far greater in the new member-states than it is in the old ones. Single market legislation is often costly, especially for small firms. Existing surveys show that entrepreneurs in the new member-states are barely informed about their obligations under the single market and have difficulty translating the legal requirements into their own context (Eurochambres 2004).
2. *Agriculture.* Once again, economic units are far smaller than in the old member-states though there are important variations among CEECs. Subsistence farming is widespread, raising the question of not only how farmers are to finance adherence to new production standards, but also whether production standards apply to these units at all.
3. *Environmental policy.* Undoubtedly, when they are mature capitalist economies, the CEECs will benefit from the Union's extensive environmental legislation. But in order to get there, candidates may

have to pursue different strategies than those contained in existing community law. As Ellison has recently argued, for instance, point source pollution concentrated in specific regions or firms is more widespread in CEE than in Western Europe (Ellison 2004b). This type of pollution calls for legislation targeting specific producers rather than aggregate pollution levels. Yet, the bulk of EU environmental law focuses on aggregate levels, benefiting countries where pollution is distributed relatively evenly across firms and regions. The problem of poorly fitting policies is compounded by the sheer cost of compliance, which Ellison puts at between 7 and 70 percent of 2001 GDP, depending on the country (Ellison 2004b, 42). Hence, for a decade or more, resources will have to be diverted from more pressing policy needs, such as the upgrading of environmentally advantageous forms of transportation, for example, railways, buses, and subways. Similarly, CEECs have been led to abandon some of their most positive policy legacies, such as extensive recycling and energy-efficient district heating, as they seek to comply with EU policies instead (Ellison 2004b, 26).

None of these dilemmas is easy to resolve. What seems clear is that the character of the EU is likely to change with 10 new members. Institutional changes will follow. The current framework, which had its origins in Franco-German reconciliation after World War II, may well have outlived its usefulness for Europe. But there are more immediate issues that are likely to dominate public discourse in the EU, most of them stemming from accession negotiations. The next section examines these potential sources of discord.

The Accession Treaty and Controversial Negotiations

Despite asymmetric interdependence and unilateral accession conditionality, there are some policy areas in which intense preferences led candidates to adopt tough negotiating positions and achieve a number of permanent derogations or transition arrangements from existing EU law. The controversy between old and new members also extended to the draft EU Constitution. See table 1.1 for the key areas of controversies.

The 10 new member states differ considerably in the number of transition arrangements achieved.[24] Malta (with 76 arrangements) and Poland (with 43 arrangements) lead the count. Certain transition arrangements apply to most or all accession countries (Commission of the European Communities 2003b).[25] These include intellectual property rights for pharmaceuticals, state aids in specific sectors, agricultural subsidies, veterinary and phytosanitary standards, access to national transport markets in road haulage, and value-added taxation and excise duties. By the same token, there are certain policies in which absolutely no transition periods have been obtained by either side: economic and monetary union,[26] statistics, industrial policy, small and medium enterprises, science and research, education and training, culture and audiovisual policy, consumer and health protection, external relations, common foreign and security policy, and financial control. In justice and home affairs, the CEECs will bear a disproportionate burden in providing the public good of internal security and border management due to their geographic location. Hence they must comply with the bulk of the *acquis* upon accession. But as in previous enlargements, internal border controls between the old and new member-states will not be lifted until later. Thus, only at that point will laws pertaining to internal border controls have to be implemented in the new member-states. A number of transition arrangements are highly idiosyncratic in that they involve peculiarities of certain accession countries and member-states. For instance, Lithuania obtained legal and financial guarantees in order to implement the Union's transit regime to Kaliningrad, concluded with Russia. A number of nuclear power plants will have to be closed in the near or medium term at the insistence of neighboring member-states.[27] Finally, the most controversial areas of negotiations overall were agricultural subsidies, the free movement of persons, land and real estate sales, and visa policies toward third-country nationals. With respect to agriculture and the free movement of persons, the demand for restrictions of the *acquis* came from the member-states. By contrast, it was the candidate countries who insisted on transitional restrictions on land and real estate sales to foreigners (following the example of Denmark in the Maastricht Treaty). No derogations were granted in visa policies forcing CEECs to impose visa restrictions on countries with which they maintain close economic and societal relations. The following sections elaborate on these highly controversial issues.

Common Agricultural Policy

To begin with agriculture, the Accession Treaty specifies that direct payments to farmers will be extended only gradually to the new member-states, moving from a level of 25 percent in 2004 to 100 percent in 2013. There are several justifications for what must undoubtedly seem a rather unfair approach that distorts the market in favor of the current member-states. First, the direct payments were introduced in 1992 to compensate farmers for the loss of income they experienced after the community radically curtailed its reliance on price guarantees. Seeing as the CEECs were never the beneficiaries of EU price guarantees, the EU argued that there was no reason to compensate them for any lost income. Second, the CAP is widely seen as inefficient and in dire need of reform. Extending it to the new member-states would have further reduced the chances for fundamental restructuring by creating a new set of stakeholders in the status quo. Third, extending the subsidies in full would have removed an important incentive for economic rationalization of CEE agriculture whose productivity lags behind that of current member-states. Fourth, applying the direct payments in full would quite simply have led to the implosion of the EU budget. Additional controversies pertained to the administration of production quotas, specifically to the question of how to determine the appropriate base year. The EU promoted quotas based on production levels just prior to accession; candidates, by contrast, favored 1989 as the base year, that is, before their production collapsed in the transition process. Overall, the Union missed an excellent opportunity to get its own house in order and restructure a flawed policy before the entry of additional veto players. The need for reform is underlined not only by the accession negotiations but also by the increasing pressure from developing countries on the EU and North America to abandon agricultural subsidies. The collapse of the WTO negotiations in Cancún in 2003 made it clear that the existing system is untenable and external reform pressure mounting.

Limited Access to the Labor Markets of Current Members

The EU's restriction of the free movement of persons has symbolic significance far beyond its practical implications. The derogation gives current member-states the option of limiting access to their national labor markets for up to seven years (subject to reviews after the second and fifth year). A standstill clause ensures that labor market access cannot be more limited than at the time the Accession Treaty was signed.[28]

Migration experts tend to agree that the actual potential for Westward migration from the CEECs is very low, in particular given the minimal internal mobility in these countries (Boeri and Brückner 2001). Thus, the derogation caters to populist sentiments in the current member-states. It signals to the new member-states a second-class version of Union membership in ways that are highly visible to the individual voter.

Restrictions on Land and Real Estate Sales to Foreigners in the New Member-States

On the free movement of capital, candidates have obtained transition periods during which they can limit the sale of real estate,[29] or more specifically, the acquisition of secondary residences by foreigners.[30] Also covered by this derogation is the sale of agricultural land and forest to nationals of current member-states. The Czech Republic, Slovakia, Hungary, and the Baltics may apply such restrictions on land sales for 7–10 ten years whereas Poland has secured a 12-year transition period. Candidates used this issue as their strongest bargaining chip against EU restrictions of labor mobility.

Visa Requirements for Neighboring Countries

Although no transition periods were requested in the field of justice and home affairs, certain requirements were highly controversial in the candidate countries. The imposition of visas on countries with which candidates have traditionally had close relations means a disruption in the flow of people and goods. Regular cross-border commutes are common between Poland and Ukraine, between the Baltics and Russia (note in particular their large Russian minority populations), and between Hungary and Romania (also due to the large Hungarian minority in the latter). In this context, it is worth noting also the protracted dispute over the Hungarian Status Law, which grants ethnic Hungarians in neighboring countries financial and economic benefits (Dunai 2003; Gal 2003). The EU and the Council of Europe objected to the law because of its positive discrimination on ethnic grounds. Slovakia and Romania protested against what they viewed as extraterritorial policy making.

The Constitution and Institutional Reform

Finally, an issue separate from the Accession Treaty is the draft EU Constitution. Though a compromise was reached in June 2004, the negotiations on this document collapsed earlier at the European Council in Brussels in December 2003. The conflict over voting rights in the Council divided the largest member-states, notably Germany and France, against the two medium-sized states, namely Spain and Poland (Grabbe 2004). Under the Nice Treaty, the latter have 27 votes each in the Council compared with 29 for the four largest member-states. The Constitution called for new voting rules (a "double majority") that would have devalued the status of medium-sized countries and upgraded that of the most populous countries. Several candidates, most notably Poland, resisted this change, arguing that their electorates had voted for EU accession on the basis of the Nice Treaty. Changing the rules after the referenda of 2002–2003 would not only delegitimize the accession process but also require a new set of referenda that might further delay accession. Under the Irish presidency and with the help of a new government in power in Madrid and a rapprochement between Berlin and Warsaw, the issue has been resolved but only after considerable antagonism between certain old and new members.

In sum, the EU was able to enforce its preferences in the bulk of the accession negotiations, with the notable exceptions of land and real estate sales and the institutional reforms pursued by the draft Constitution. The free movement of persons, agricultural subsidies, and relations with third countries are likely to remain at the center of public debate in the new member-states in the foreseeable future.

Conclusion

I have argued that asymmetric interdependence has allowed the EU to pursue enlargement in a rather heavy-handed way. Though both sides clearly benefit from the enlargement, CEECs individually benefit more from joining than does the EU as a whole. By the same token, the costs of nonaccession are greater for any individual country thus concerned than they are for the EU. As a consequence, the EU's ability to unilaterally set accession conditions has intersected in awkward ways with the rhetoric of European unification and the righting of historic wrongs.

It is moot at this point to speculate about alternative approaches that could have been taken, such as membership in stages that could have started earlier but would not have required full implementation of the *acquis* until later. The CEECs themselves pushed for speedy accession. Many elite actors have seen the wholesale transfer of EU policies as an opportunity to accelerate domestic reform while insulating the government against domestic criticism. But there may be long-term drawbacks to this reform method, notably the weakening of national legislatures. The effect of policies designed for entirely different circumstances than those of CEE remain to be seen in the decades to come. In the more immediate future, we are likely to see a heated debate on what voters are likely to see as the unfavorable entry conditions of their countries. This is particularly true in agriculture and the free movement of labor. Whether this will permanently damage the EU's legitimacy is uncertain. There is a possibility that the benefits of membership, notably participation in decision making, will offset the bad feelings surrounding the accession process.

Notes

1. Hungary and Poland were the first CEECs to apply for membership in March and April 1994, respectively. Romania, Slovakia, Latvia, Estonia, Lithuania, and Bulgaria followed in 1995, and the Czech Republic and Slovenia applied in 1996.
2. Duponcel points to the underutilization of narrowly defined agricultural quotas due to high transaction costs. Nevertheless, the Europe Agreements, combined with the collapse of Eastern markets, shifted the international economic relations of the CEECs from the former Soviet Union toward the EU.
3. See the timetable on p. 21.
4. The Union's implementation gap results from the mismatch between regulatory and enforcement capacity of EU institutions; see Börzel (2001) for a dissenting view.
5. The Internet appendix can be found at www.indiana.edu/~iupolsci/ rrohrsch/PalgraveTables+Figures.pdf
6. In 2000, complaining that Hungary "has always been five years away from accession," then prime minister Orbán suggested that his country could "have a future outside the EU" and "will be obliged to look for alternatives" if the pace of negotiations did not pick up (Radio Free Europe-Radio Liberty 2000).
7. Based on 1999 terms.
8. In 2001 terms.
9. "Phare" is the French acronym for "Poland and Hungary Assistance for Economic Restructuring" and also means "lighthouse."
10. Since 1998, Phare's annual budget has been approximately EUR 1.5 billion.

11. Between 1990 and 2000, the EU committed EUR 179.26 million to civil society and democratization (1.5 percent of total Phare commitments during that period), EUR 559.83 million to social development and employment (4.7 percent of total commitments), and EUR 113.39 million to public health (1 percent of total commitments). In addition, during the same period, it committed EUR 1,265.19 million (10.6 percent) to administration and public institutions and EUR 141.47 million (1.2 percent) to the approximation of legislation.
12. Evaluative terms in the reports are consistent within each policy area but not across negotiation chapter. Nor does the language permit assessment of a country's progress relative to previous years. Thus, a country that has undertaken great effort in a given field may still find itself at the lower end of the scale of progress, whereas a country with few changes in one field during the evaluation period may nevertheless come out at the upper end of the scale. The author's interview with Commission official, March 7, 2001 (Brussels).
13. The author's interview with Commission official, March 7, 2001 (Brussels).
14. Note that the externalization of reform is not limited to Eastward enlargement. It has long operated in the integration process among the old member-states as well. For instance, in the run-up to Economic and Monetary Union, countries with a notorious lack of budgetary discipline were able to impose stringent rules on unwilling domestic actors by claiming a lack of maneuvering space. Austerity measures were dictated by the EU Stability Pact, which the member governments had entered voluntarily. Whereas existing member-states can agree to reform externalization on a case-by-case basis, prospective entrants have to adopt the entirety of EU policies as a condition for entry and with no ability to shape these policies beforehand.
15. Taggart and Szczerbiak attribute this to the tendency of nationalist parties in CEE to be situated on the right of the political spectrum and of parties on the right to use nationalist discourse.
16. See Taggart and Szczerbiak's (2004) distinction of "hard" versus "soft" Euroskepticism.
17. These are precisely the areas that make up the bulk of the state budget of the new members. To the extent that the EU sought to influence these policies, it did so under the requirement of budget stabilization (the second Copenhagen criterion). However, other external actors, notably the World Bank, did exert some influence on the reform of social security systems, often in cooperation with the EU.
18. Töller provides a study of Germany's legislative activities resulting from EU membership. The difficulty of measuring the EU's impact on domestic legislative activity is due to the fact that few parliaments actually classify their acts by whether they originate in Brussels or elsewhere. Furthermore, legal transposition often proceeds through ministerial decrees rather than parliamentary acts.
19. Because party mobilization takes place primarily on the basis of distributive and redistributive policies, we would not necessarily expect it to be affected by the shift of regulatory authority to national executives.

20. Note the Commission's expression of disapproval with Slovenia's "slow" legislative procedures that require three plenary readings for every bill.
21. When Spain and Portugal joined in 1986, the number of new cases actually declined by 24 percent only to rise by 20 percent the following year.
22. The average duration of proceedings has increased steadily over the past five years. In 2003, direct actions took an average of 24.7 months (up from 23 months in 1999) whereas preliminary references by national courts took 25.5 months (up from 21.2 months in 1999).
23. Whether national courts refer cases to the ECJ depends on their own institutional capacity and EC-specific caseload. We can suspect that overall lower administrative capacity translates into less likelihood to engage the preliminary reference mechanism (thanks to Matt Gabel for pointing this out). Preliminary references have traditionally been the main source of ECJ proceedings but have declined and made up an average of 43 percent of cases from 1999 to 2003. Direct actions have been on the rise, accounting for an average of 42 percent of cases in the same period.
24. Of course, countries had their individual strategic reasons for requesting transition arrangements in any given area. The number of derogations a country requested need not reflect its actual ability to implement EU law. In some cases, requesting few derogations served to exaggerate a country's level of preparedness for membership; in other cases, requesting a large number of transition arrangements allowed countries to withdraw some of these requests later as a bargaining move.
25. This section relies heavily on the Commission's explanatory report to the European Parliament.
26. New members will not share the new currency yet but will participate in all the rules associated with EMU.
27. See the bilateral agreement between the Czech Republic and Austria on the Temelin power plant, concluded separately in advance of the Accession Treaty. Lithuania and Slovakia have negotiated transition arrangements for their nuclear power plants (Ignalina and Bohunice, respectively) with the EU as a whole.
28. Cyprus and Malta are not covered by this arrangement. On the contrary, Malta achieved the right to impose restrictions on its labor market for the first seven years after accession.
29. This concerns Slovenia which may impose restrictions for up to seven years.
30. The Czech Republic, Hungary, Poland, and Cyprus may limit sales for up to five years. Malta has the right to maintain its current legislation indefinitely.

PART II

The Party Context

CHAPTER 2

Party Systems and EU Accession: Euroskepticism in East Europe

Jack Bielasiak

Introduction

What is the political relevance of EU accession to party system contestation in the East European (EE) states? Previous studies considering the issue are divided on the place of "Europe" as a competitive dimension of party politics. With regard to the pre-2004 member-states, one analysis finds "little evidence of any direct impact" of the Europe question on domestic party structure (Mair 2000, 28). In contrast, another study claims that the "permissive consensus" of earlier times has given way to political conditions that necessitate parties to take into account the European question (Sitter 2002). Concerning accession countries, one popular view is that integration issues have attained greater saliency for domestic politics (Kopecký and Mudde 2002) and that party systems are critical in explicating parties' stance on European integration (Taggart and Szczerbiak 2004, 2–3). However, an opposing view stresses on the long-standing policy consensus on the "return to Europe" that renders the integration question a valence issue with little impact on political contestation in East Europe (Grabbe and Hughes 1999; Grzymala–Busse and Innes 2003).

This chapter examines the tension between these two outlooks by exploring competing explanatory models on the place of Europe as an issue in the party politics of the EE states during the candidacy period.

Most of the theoretical perspectives applied to East Europe are derived from the insights gained in the analysis of integration in West Europe, but the evidence here shows that such models do not travel well. The transitional nature of postcommunist politics presents specific challenges that affect party positions on integration that result in different party alignment dynamics than in the "old" Europe.

This chapter examines the explanatory relevance of models based on two primary paradigms on the role of Europe in domestic party politics: (1) the relationship between public opinion and party partisanship on accession, and (2) the linkage between party system properties and party positions on integration. Each of these perspectives offers distinct models in explaining the genesis of Europe as an issue in competitive politics:

1. *Public opinion model.* Partisan politics are driven primarily by mass opinions with political parties aligning or mobilizing positions to correspond with public preferences. There is congruence between mass and party standings on European integration; that is, countries with more pronounced skeptic views among the population make possible the greater success of parties advocating Euroskeptic platforms.
2. *Valence model.* Broad agreement among political elites on integration precludes the penetration of the accession issue as a partisan cleavage in electoral politics. The effect is low saliency of the Europe question that diminishes the relevance of public opinion in party contestation; that is, the extent of public Euroskepticism does not affect party Euroskepticism due to the high consensus on integration.
3. *Institutionalization model.* The transitional inchoate nature of postcommunist party systems provides opportunities for party entrepreneurs to engage new issues as partisan agendas to advance their political standing. The greater volatility of EE party systems signifies an electorate less captured by partisan identities so that a more pronounced visibility of the Europe issue makes it an appealing agenda for parties seeking electoral advance.
4. *Competitive model.* The nature of party preferences on Europe is determined by the competitive environment of domestic politics with ideology or strategy as alternatives driving political partisanship. Ideology is viewed as a long-standing political identity that defines preferences on Europe. The contrary postulate looks to strategic opportunities to win offices and votes as explanations for Euroskeptic positions.

5. *Power model.* The focus is on government participation as the primary determinant of parties' positions on Europe. Parties in power are constrained by the hegemony of the integration agenda to act as advocates of accession and are forced to take on responsibilities to bring their country to comply with the *acquis.* Parties in opposition are not bound as much by the integration valence and have greater flexibility in embracing critical Euroskeptic policies.

I examine the explanatory value of these models by concentrating on the Euroskeptic position among the political parties of East Europe, first turning to a general discussion of the role of the European agenda in the party systems. This is followed by sections taking a closer look at the relationship between public opinion and party Euroskepticism, the structure of party systems and Euroskepticism in electoral politics, and the competitive dimensions of party systems and the alignment of Euroskeptic party agendas.

The Europe Question and East European Party Systems

The nature of the party system is a critical element in structuring party alignments on a variety of issues, including accession to the wider Europe. On the one hand, party systems in the nascent democracies of postcommunism are defined by lower levels of institutionalization that exist in established Western democracies, as is evident in higher rates of electoral volatility, persistent high number of competitors, and the fissure and fusion of parties (Bielasiak 2002a; Kreuzer and Pettai 2003). Such conditions produce more open electoral and parliamentary space, establishing an opportunity structure for new political entrepreneurs to enter the competitive arena or for incumbent elites to engage new policy areas, such as the integration question.

On the other hand, such political opportunities may be constrained by broad policy agreement, as in the case of the unusual consensus on European integration in East Europe. Both external and internal factors combined to lower the saliency of the EU question in partisan politics. First, the cultural and economic motivation to "return to Europe" was especially strong during the initial period of the transition, reinforced by the need to adhere to Brussels' conditionality measures. The return ethos and the administrative demand served as a break on political discourse concerning the merits of integration, as political parties interested in governance faced considerable pressure to adhere to Western requirements (Grzymala-Busse and Innes 2003). Second, internal developments reinforced the external pressures. European unification acquired a highly legitimizing value as a clear break with the communist past and as entry into the Western world, and formed a practical policy link between integration and transformation so that the costs of transition were justified by the need to join Europe (Hughes, Sasse, and Gordon 2002, 330–332). For these reasons, unification emerged as a grand project of postcommunism, and the consequent consensus turned the issue into a valence dimension of politics.

As the date of entry to the EU became more immediate, the consensus became more problematic as the evolving integration process revealed problem areas as well as benefits of accession. In particular, the intensity of negotiations associated with closing various chapters of the *acquis* opened up specific policy sectors to the scrutiny of politicians and the public. Growing concerns with highly sensitive issues drove a wedge in the dominant positive assessment (Rohrschneider and Whitefield 2004b). Public opinion began to shift in the late 1990s, and although still predominantly pro-EU, an evident decline in public supports for the integration project began to appear in several EE states (Bielasiak 2002b; European Commission 2001, 2002, 2003; various chapters in this volume). As concerns penetrated the public domain, the issue began to resonate in the political space and afforded party leaders the opportunity to challenge the consensus.

There were two main strategic options for political leaders seeking to advance their cause by means of the Europe question. One was to stay within the dominant paradigm on accession but question the negotiation process and its results, in effect mounting a challenge regarding the competence of incumbent elites to provide the best possible entry deal (Grzymala-Busse and Innes 2003). Questioning integration in this framework did not reject the idea of a unified Europe nor the adjustments necessary to assure fruitful accession. The second option rested on such a rejection, challenging the idea of a united Europe and the necessary policy adjustments. The position went beyond a question of competency in negotiations to a more principled response seeking to safeguard the nationalist interests of the state or protect social groups threatened by entry into the EU.

The primary conceptualizations of Euroskepticism in the candidate states emerge along these two lines of dissent, either as a narrow, technocratic competence issue pursued primarily by mainstream parties or as a principled rejection of Europe by more peripheral actors. This is evident in the distinction between the "soft" and "hard" Euroskepticism in the work of Taggart (1998) and Taggart and Szczerbiak (2004), or the more nuanced typology that combines pro- and anti-European positions with diffuse and specific dimensions in Kopecký and Mudde (2002). This study follows this conceptualization of party positions, concentrating on the political attitudes embracing a Euroskeptic position in contrast to support for integration. The primary goal is to assess the prevalence of party Euroskepticism in conjunction with the development of postcommunist party systems as a dimension of electoral competition. The placement of parties in the Euroskeptic column and their assignment into more specific categories such as party families is based on a variety of academic and expert sources (see References) concerning both the nature of party systems in postcommunism and detailed accounts of the accession issue in EE competitive politics.

Euroskepticism: Public Opinion and Party Representation

A central issue in the manifestation of Euroskepticism concerns the relationship between public opinion and the representation of mass preferences in the party system. The overwhelming initial popular backing for the return to Europe has eroded in the face of negotiation problems. Has the more critical public voice emerged as a significant presence in the arena of party competition? The link between party and public Euroskepticism is especially complex in the confines of emerging party systems (Szczerbiak and Taggart 2001). The weakly institutionalized postcommunist party structures provide openings for entry of political actors seeking to advance new agendas and secure a place in the polity. In such a context, the rise in public Euroskepticism provides entrepreneurial opportunities in politics, albeit subject to contradictory tensions. The valence of EU accession has pushed it outside the prevailing axis of competition, so a dissenting position on the issue is less likely to affect party standings driven by more salient cleavages. Yet, the peripheral nature of the Europe issue may allow established leaders to embrace dissenting positions on integration without undermining their party's core identity, or provide opportunities for new entrepreneurs to reorder the European question to the forefront of electoral competition.

Data on public and party Euroskepticism in the 10 EE candidate states demonstrates no clear patterns regarding the strength of parties, the extent of public opinion, and the linkage between party and public dissent on integration (table A3 in Internet appendix).[1] First, Euroskeptic parties are clearly in evidence in the party systems of East Europe, despite the valence that permeates domestic politics on integration throughout the region. However, there are important national variations in the electoral representation of parties assuming negative positions on the EU, ranging from the absence of Euroskeptic parties in Bulgaria to low electoral presence in Slovenia, Lithuania, and Hungary (4–7 percent), to significant shares of party Euroskepticism in Slovakia, Poland, and the Czech Republic (41–44 percent). Second, public opinion on accession shows considerable national variance as well, both as to opinions on participation in accession referenda and on evaluations of the Union. Interestingly, the countries farthest away from entry into the community, that is, Bulgaria and Romania, have the highest mass approval whereas those on the more rapid track for EU entry are subject to more extensive citizens' disapproval, for example, Czech Republic, Slovenia, Poland and the Baltic Republics (Rohrschneider and Whitefield 2004b; chapters 5, 6, and 9). This pattern supports the claim that closer scrutiny of the negotiation process produces greater concerns among the public. Third, the preference for a no vote and the spontaneous declaration of nonparticipation constitute a significantly greater share of the population than those who evaluate the EU in "bad" terms. The gap supports the argument concerning low saliency of the accession issue among the citizenry, factors evident in the actual accession referenda held in eight East European states in 2003, with considerable abstention rate among voters, from 27.3 percent in Latvia to 54.4 percent in Hungary. Certainly, in view of this evidence, the EU accession does not appear as a first-order political issue whose saliency mobilized citizens to the ballot box.

More specifically, the differential patterns in public and party Euroskepticism and the rates of declared and actual participation presented in table A3 reveal that the relationship between party and public expressions on the EU question is indeterminate. The national trends in the accession states suggest that the parties neither follow the dynamics of popular support nor lead by mobilizing support for their preferred stance on the EU. Systems with low levels of mass skepticism coexist with high levels of party skepticism, for example, Romania, Slovakia, and vice versa, for example, Lithuania, Slovenia. Similarly, there is no correspondence between the level of party Euroskepticism at the last election and negative expressions on the EU through voter disengagement or a negative vote during the 2003 referenda. The resultant disjuncture between the strength of Euroskeptic parties in the competitive space and the public stance on the issue leaves open the question of what drives political parties to engage the Europe dimension, irrespective of the distribution of public opinion (Taggart and Szczerbiak 2004). At the very least, the macroevidence from electoral contestation points to low translation of public dissent on the EU into partisan politics during the time leading up to the accession. Rather, competition within the party systems of EE continues to be defined in a more pronounced way by other cleavages, and the "return to Europe" remains a secondary axis of political contestation. The evidence on the linkage between public preferences and aggregate party support for Euroskeptic positions supports the valence model, which states that the dominant consensus on Europe acts as a break on partisan politics, rather than the mass opinion model that views party politics aligning along public views on Europe.

This propensity of integration as a second-order issue based on valence that is immune to partisan politics is compounded by the nature of party systems in postcommunism. The data here fits well with findings defining the macroevolution of postcommunist party structures, including extensive multipartyism and high electoral volatility that undermine stable partisan politics. This perspective, however, differs with findings at the individual microlevel. Many opinion surveys offer evidence that partisan identification is taking hold: voters identify with specific parties, masses and elites understand the ideological space, and citizens assume congruent preferences with their parties' positions (Whitefield 2002). This micro versus macro discrepancy reflects a different understanding of party system competition, with the former equating it with individual level identification and the latter with systemic stability. However, as is evident on the Europe question, microlevel issue identification does not necessarily translate into partisanship at the ballot box so that while voters express policy preferences, there is no deep attachment to either party or agenda. Instead, political identity tends to be ephemeral during the transition process so that weak parties and weak identities reduce the need to forge links between party positions and mass opinions. In such conditions, political entrepreneurs can assume preferences on criteria other than constituency demands, for example, ideological coherence or power calculations.

Euroskepticism and Party System Structure

Evidence concerning the strength of Euroskeptic political parties and the format of party systems confirms the conclusion that European integration is a "second order" issue in the competitive politics of East Europe (table 2.1). First, there is only a weak relationship between the structure of party systems and the manifestation of Euroskepticism in the electoral process. Second, as we have just seen, there is no linkage between the level of Euroskeptic public opinion and the representation of that view by political parties. Neither the structure of the party system nor the extent of mass opposition to European accession drives political parties to question the merits of the European project or its implementation.

A major proposition on party systems holds that the more open the structure of competition, the more opportunities there are for existing or new political parties to embrace underrepresented issues as policy packages to advance their cause in the electoral contest. The greater visibility of the European question on the political agenda of the EE states at the beginning of the millennium presented the issue as a potential leverage in elections. There is no indication, however, that political actors in the inchoate postcommunist party systems were able to translate such indeterminacy into gains at the ballot box.

An important structural element of party systems is electoral volatility— a measure of settled preferences among voters with higher volatility indicating a more fickle electorate, one that is more open to new policy appeals. Yet, average volatility since the collapse of communism is not a good predictor of voters' support for Euroskeptic positions by embracing parties with an anti-integration agenda. Among the most volatile party systems are the three Baltic States with average volatility since the dissolution of the Soviet Union above 30 percent; two of these, Estonia and Latvia, also reveal the presence of substantial support for parties with a Euroskeptic position, but Lithuania, with the highest volatility (39.3 percent) in the sample, has one of the lowest (7 percent) incidences of anti-European vote at the last election.[2] In contrast, the Czech Republic has one of the most settled party systems as defined by citizens' persistence in adhering to the same choices across elections (13.4 percent average volatility). In this case, however, the extent of support (44 percent) for parties indicating a Euroskeptic preference is the highest throughout East Europe.

The absence of a pattern between the format of party systems and the position on Europe holds when we switch from the demand side of party systems expressed by voter volatility to the supply side expressed by the number of "effective parties" functioning in electoral politics (effective number of electoral parties, ENEP), that is, the extent to which the political space has been seized by few or many political actors (table 2.1). Two distinct hypotheses can be articulated with regard to the ENEP. One is that a crowded political space with many competing players leaves little room for new or existing parties to embrace new policy agendas since these are likely to be already occupied by one of the numerous parties functioning in the system. The alternative view is that the presence of many political entrepreneurs, as is evident in high ENEP, reveals a highly competitive environment that affords considerable opportunities for parties to embrace new policy bundles to advance electoral fortunes. For our purposes, which proposition is more valid is not as important as the fact that the data shows no relationship between the supply side of party systems and the expression of the Euroskeptic position within them. Once again, as in the case of volatility, average national ENEP does not reflect the success of parties associated with negative views on integration. While Bulgaria and Hungary emerge as political systems with a relatively low number of competing parties and low Euroskepticism, the correlation among the other states is much more diffuse. States with the highest ENEP—Poland, Estonia, and Latvia—do show significant penetration into the competitive space by parties associated with dissident views on integration, but at the

Table 2.1 Party systems and percentage of votes and seats of Euroskeptic parties

		Euroskeptic		Party system mean		Last election		
		%V	%S	Vol.	ENEP	ENEP	ENPP	Comp.
Bulgaria	2001	0.0	0.0	25.3	3.6	3.9	2.9	24.5
Czech Rep.	2002	44.0	49.5	13.4	5.1	4.8	3.7	5.7
Estonia	2003	27.0	27.7	31.4	6.7	5.4	4.7	1.2
Hungary	2002	7.4	0.0	25.8	4.9	2.8	2.1	1.0
Latvia	2002	20.2	19.0	36.4	7.1	6.8	5.0	4.9
Lithuania	2000	7.0	0.0	39.3	5.5	5.5	3.3	11.5
Poland	2001	42.2	38.6	27.9	8.2	4.5	3.6	28.3
Romania	2000	19.5	25.6	19.6	5.1	5.2	3.2	17.1
Slovakia	2002	41.1	41.3	21.6	6.2	8.9	6.1	4.4
Slovenia	2000	4.4	4.4	22.0	6.5	5.1	4.7	20.5

ENEP = Effective number of electoral parties; ENPP = Effective number of parliamentary parties; Vol. = Electoral volatility; and Comp. = Competitiveness (difference in vote shares of first and second placed parties).

same time states with lower average ENEP—Slovakia, and the Czech Republic—attract even greater support for Euroskeptic parties.

Another possible approach to the connection between party structure and the Europe question is to concentrate on the format of the current system rather than on the entire period of postcommunism (table 2.1). On this dimension as well, at the latest cycle of elections, there are no clear indications of a relationship between the numbers of electoral political actors (ENEP) and the success of Euroskeptic platforms that meet with voter approval. There is a somewhat better indication of a linkage between the effective number of parties in parliament (ENPP) and Euroskeptism. Here Hungary and Bulgaria emerge as the two cases with the lowest number of relevant parties and low Euroskepticism in the electorate followed by Lithuania and Romania with three plus effective parties and low- to mid-level support for rejectionist parties. Party systems with an ENPP above 3.5 (Poland, Czech Republic, Estonia, Slovenia, Latvia, and Slovakia), however, demonstrate great disparity in the percentage of Euroskeptic party representation. Overall, for East Europe as a whole, the relationship is weak at best.

Another factor influencing party Euroskepticism concerns the degree of competitiveness in the system, measured here as the differential in electoral support between the first and second placed parties during the latest elections (table 2.1). The hypothesis is that in a more contested political environment, leaders have greater incentives to embark along new issues as mobilizing agents to attract public support and gain political office. The evidence on this measure is more persuasive than along the other components of EE party structures, although still not uniform in its effect. Nonetheless, countries with the sharpest contestation, such as Estonia, Slovakia, Latvia, or the Czech Republic, demonstrate among the highest levels of party Euroskepticism (above 20 percent) in the EE party systems. The apparent outlier is Hungary, which had the tightest electoral contest of all the candidate states, but the issue here may well center on the classification of Fidesz-MDF during the 2002 electoral campaign as a Euroskeptic or Eurorealist entity, a matter of some controversy (Bátory 2002a; Kopecký and Mudde 2002; Taggart and Szczerbiak 2004). If, as the last pair of authors has argued, Fidesz-MDF leaders have increasingly turned to a soft Euroskepticism, then its 41 percent vote share would align more systematically the degree of competition with negative expressions on integration in the party structures of East Europe—with tight contestation leading to strategic behavior on the European issue and culminating in significant success at the polls.

Ultimately, most measures on the structure of party systems in East Europe do not correlate with negative expressions on the European issue. The institutionalization model does not explain the presence and scope of skeptic party positions and their ability to gain voter support. Rather, Euroskepticism is a political phenomenon that is distinct from the systemic environment established over the past 15 years of post-communism. At the very least, opportunities seized by political entrepreneurs to express concern with the agenda of integration do not appear to be facilitated by the structure of party systems, either in terms of the number of relevant actors or in terms of changing voter preferences across election cycles, although the degree of competitiveness at the current stage of party system development does bear some impact. One interpretation of the weak impact of systemic properties on party alignments confirms the view that integration has played an essentially second-order role in political contestation so that the valence nature of the issue makes difficult its penetration into politics. However, it is also possible to view weak institutionalization as a potentially enabling condition for the emergence of the EU into domestic politics. In this case, the disequilibria of the East European party systems may make the Europe issue more appealing for partisan purposes, enabling the mobilization of EU opponents and supporters from various parts of the political landscape. This raises the question of whether more concrete properties of parties, as expressed in the competitive and power models, provide more definitive explanations on the impact of party systems on policy positions on European integration.

Euroskepticism and Party Dimensions

The weak association between the extent of public and party Euroskepticism, and between the format of party system and the electoral strength of Euroskeptic parties, leaves open the question of what drives political leaders to assume anti-Union preferences. The extent to which ideology or strategy play a role in defining party positions has emerged as a central debate on the Europe issue with different empirical findings and conclusions. Some studies of member and candidate states find that strategic competitive considerations are primarily responsible for party positioning (Sitter 2002; Szczerbiak and Taggart 2002; Taggart 1998), whereas other findings stress ideology as the main source for parties' stance on EU integration (Kopecký and Mudde 2002; Marks and Wilson 2000; Marks, Wilson, and Ray 2002).

This lack of consensus reflects a focus on different dimensions of party competition as determinants of policy preferences that bears special import for emerging party systems. Ideology speaks to long-standing identities that define policy predisposition so that a structured political environment is a primary influence on the Europe question. Ideological positions are an expression of imbedded societal differences that allow parties to translate cleavages into salient political issues. Yet, within the confines of political systems undergoing extensive transformations in economic, social, cultural, and identity arenas, societal cleavages are likely evolving and uncertain (Bielasiak 2002a; Mainwaring 1998; Mair 1997). True, some surveys of EE publics do find the presence of significant social cleavages that take on identifiable conflict dimensions, but the evidence is at the individual microlevel (Marks and Hooghe 2003; Whitefield 2002). There is still considerable difficulty in rendering these social divisions into salient political identities (Zielinski 2002). The consequence is a weaker institutionalized party system characterized by multiple, evolving social cleavages that surface through the splintering or reconfiguration of political parties and the entry of political entrepreneurs seeking to mobilize new cleavages as currencies of competition (Lewis 2000; Rose and Munro 2003). The resulting inchoate format of party contestation renders more problematic the entrenchment of a left–right competitive spectrum based on stable structural divisions, giving rise to the expression of cohesive demands. In this image, the transitional nature of postcommunism signifies a political space less defined by ideological saliency, enabling more flexible party positioning on policy, including attitudes toward European integration. Rather than ideology, competitive opportunities to win votes or offices emerge as more viable incentives for the articulation of party preferences. In these conditions, strategy, not ideology, is the more likely determinant of positions on the European project.

The empirical evidence on the ideological dimension demonstrates that the location of Euroskeptic parties in East Europe does not align well into prevailing party families. Similarly, although more defined in terms of a left–right axis, parties opposing integration are found on both sides of the ideological divide (table 2.2). Party family and ideology are of course related, but the former reflects a more specified political agenda whereas the latter groups party families into a more defined ideological spectrum. For example, agrarian parties represent the interests of the countryside but can do so from a left or right ideological perspective.

The findings reveal, first, that EE parties embracing a negative attitude toward integration and obtaining voter support at the latest election represent a range of party families that cuts across the ideological spectrum: communist, socialist, agrarian, liberal, Christian, conservative, nationalist, and populist parties are all represented on the skeptic side of the debate. Second, however, the strength of electoral support for parties espousing Euroskeptic views is more structured along party families. Among parties with an anti-European bent, the most successful at the polls are the liberal Centre Party in Estonia and the Civic Democratic Party (ODS) in the Czech Republic, and to a lesser extent the nationalist-populist parties in Slovakia and Romania, followed by agrarian entities in Poland, Latvia, and Lithuania. Evidently liberal parties committed to a market economy but seeking better conditions in the negotiations process provide a policy appeal that resonates with a significant portion of the electorate, as with the 25 percent support attained by ODS in the Czech Republic and Kesk in Estonia. Agrarian parties in contrast are more limited by the sectoral nature of their representation, cannot reach into constituencies outside their primary arena, and obtain therefore 10 percent or less of electoral support. The greatest variation in the extent of voter backing pertains to the nationalist family, although parties in this category are the most numerous among the Euroskeptic camp.

While there is a greater tendency for the expression of Euroskepticism in the nationalist party family, this does not translate in most instances into electoral advances. As noted above, nationalist parties with strong populist appeals have been able to attract a significant share of the vote only in Slovakia and Romania. The nationalist formation in the other EE states either barely managed to cross the threshold for parliamentary representation (the Slovene National party (SNS), the Alliance Fatherland and Freedom (TB/LNNK) in Latvia), or failed to reach that minimum (Republicans in the Czech Republic (RMS), the Independence Party in Estonia (Iseseiv), or the Hungarian Justice and Life Party (MIEP) in Hungary). Thus, while the EE political arena is infused with parties espousing a nationalist ideology that is strongly geared to the defense of sovereignty, few of them are able to convert their ideology into electoral support. On the ideological dimension as well, the integration issue does not form a primary axis of contestation and efforts to bring the issue to a more prominent position in political discourse have not led to electoral success.

For the latest elections in EE, parties on both the right and the left are present in the Euroskeptic camp although there is a clear dominance

Table 2.2 Characteristics of Euroskeptic parties at last elections

	Percent vote	Party family	Ideol. position	System position	Former coalition	Year founded
Czech Rep. (2002)						
Civic Demo. Party (ODS)	24.5	Lib/cons.	R	Opp.	Yes	1991
Comm. Party (KSCM)	18.5	Comm.	L	Opp.	No	1990
Republicans (RMS)	1.0	National.	R	Extra	No	[1990]
Estonia (2003)						
Centre Party (Kesk)	25.4	Lib/populist	R	Opp.	Yes	1991
Christian People's P. (EKRP)	1.1	Ch-D nation	R	Extra	No	1999
Independence P. (Iseseiv)	0.5	National.	R	Extra	No	
Hungary (2002)						
Justice and Life P. (MIEP)	4.4	National.	R	Extra	No	1993
Workers' Party (MP)	2.2	Comm.	L	Extra	No	1990
Independent Smallholders (FGKP)	0.8	Agrarian	R	Extra	Yes	1989
Latvia (2002)						
Green & Farmers Union (ZZS)	9.5	Env/Agr		Govt.	NA	1990/1993
Fatherland and Freedom (TB/LNNK)	5.4	Nat-conser.	R	Govt.	NA	pre-1993
Soc-Demo Workers' P. (LSSP)	4.0	Soc-demo.	L	Extra	No	1989
Soc-Demo Welfare P. (SDLP)	1.3	Socialist	L	Extra	No	pre-2002
Lithuania (2000)						
Lith. Peasants' Party (LVP)	4.1	Agrarian	R	Extra	No	1990
Centre Union (LCS)	2.9	Liberal	R	Extra	Yes	1993

Party	%	Family	L/R	Position	Prev. govt	Founded
Poland (2001)						
Self-Defense (SO)	10.2	Agr-populist	R	Opp.	No	1992
Law and Justice (PiS)	9.5	Conserv.	R	Opp.	No	2001
Polish Peasant Party (PSL)	9.0	Agrarian	L	Govt.*	Yes	1990
League of Polish Families (LPR)	7.9	Christ.conser.	R	Opp.	No	2001
Solidarity Elect Action Right (AWSP)	5.6	Conserv.	R	Extra	(as AWS)	[1996]
Romania (2000)						
Greater Romania Party (PRM)	19.5	Nat-populist	R	Opp.	No	1991
Slovakia (2002)						
Mov. for Demo. Slovakia (HZDS)	19.5	Nat-populist	R	Opp.	Yes	1992
Christ–Democratic Mov. (KDH)	8.3	Christ-demo.	R	Govt.	NA	1990
Communist Party (KSS)	6.3	Comm.	L	Opp.	No	1994
Real Slovak National P. (PSNS)	3.7	National.	R	Extra	No	2001
Slovak National Party (SNS)	3.3	National.	R	Extra	Yes	1990
Slovenia (2000)						
Slovenian National Party (SNS)	4.4	National.	R	Opp.	No	1991

Note: NA: Not applicable.

*The Polish Peasant Party left the governing coalition in March 2003. Abbreviations for Party Families: Agr-populist: Agrarian-populist; Ch-D nation.: Christian-Democratic nationalist; Christ-conser.: Christian-Conservative; Christ-demo.: Christian-democratic; Comm.: Communist; Conserv.: Conservative; Env/Agr.: Environmental/Agrarian; Lib/cons.: Liberal-conservative; Lib/populist: Liberal Populist; National.: Nationalist; Nat-conser.: Nationalist-conservative;

Nat-populist: Nationalist Populist; Soc-demo.: Socialist-democratic.

by political entities on the right side of the spectrum (table 2.2). This is an artifact of the numerous parties with a conservative nationalist agenda in the politics of East Europe, as a counter to the recent historical experience of the communist bloc (Taggart and Szczerbiak 2004), so that the political field defined by the European question is dominated by rightist parties. While nationalist parties are most numerous, the right is also represented by liberal-conservative, agrarian-populist, and Christian advocacy agendas. The Europe issue, then, fits better along the standard left–right placement, although it is clear that dissident voices on accession are expressed through a variety of rightist political agendas—again, with the liberal variant more successful than the other views.

There are significantly fewer parties on the left advocating a Euroskeptic agenda, 6 out of the 26 parties registering voter support at the last elections, although their political agendas are often narrower than their counterparts on the right of the political spectrum. These left parties are mainly unreconstructed, hard-line communist parties that reject the capitalist nature of an integrated Europe and seek to protect the economic interests of the "losers" in the marketization and globalization of the East European economies. In that aspect, their Euroskepticism is in marked contrast to the pro-European stance of the mainstream social democratic parties, most of these reformed ex-communist ruling parties that have adopted a promarket and prointegration agenda. The left Euroskeptic position has not been especially appealing to the East European voters, with the exception of the KSCM in the Czech Republic, a more orthodox former communist party able to tap into popular discontent with economic transformation.

Parties contesting the integration project originate in several party families, are located on both sides of the left–right spectrum, and for most part are unable to attract extensive popular support. As such, ideological placement on the European question is not a significant factor in structuring competitive party politics in the former communist states. The lack of a clear-cut ideological coherence in party positioning in the East confronts some prior studies on the impact of ideology on the Europe issue, which conclude that there is an association on the EU stance and the left–right cleavage, both in the member-states (Marks and Wilson 2000) and the candidate countries (Taggart and Szczerbiak 2004). Rather the evidence here shows a competitive environment that renders European accession more of a "maverick" dimension that cannot be placed in a straightforward left–right axis (Sitter 2002). Perhaps more so than in the Western part of the continent, Europe is a second-order political dimension rather than a cleavage reflecting deep structural divisions in society. Instead, the issue is open to contingent political maneuvering, enabling party leaders from diverse ideological perspectives to assume either Euroenthusiastic or Euroskeptic positions. Indeed, various ideological expressions are compatible with anti-integration advocacy so that in the competitive model, Euroskeptic positions are driven more by opportunistic consideration than ideological commitments.

This last perspective is also compatible with the weak East European party systems articulated in the institutionalization model. Many of the emerging party structures of postcommunism are defined by parties' lacking clear roots in society and strong constituency identifications that can act as breaks on elite entrepreneurial activities, as is usually the case in more defined party systems. Instead, the weaker foundation of political parities may act as an incentive to embark on new policy advocacy to make inroads in the fleeting competitive environment. But given the valence of the accession issue, political leaders in the mainstream are more likely to articulate "competence" challenges to incumbents charged with the implementation of integration, whereas more marginalized elites attempt to penetrate the political space by advocating challenges to the European project in the hope of translating the issue into competitive leverage.

Accordingly, the placement of a party in the ruling structure may serve as a major determinant of issue positioning on the European question, as per the power model of partisanship (Bielasiak 2002a; Taggart and Szczerbiak 2004). A critical element in defining party preferences is the location of party in or out of government. The prevailing view is that parties in government are advocates of the relevant policy, whereas parties in opposition are able to assume a different, even contrasting, policy stance. In East Europe, given the hegemony of the agenda on integration, incumbent parties are identified as supporting entry into the EU whereas the opposition is presumed to be less inclined in that direction, or at least to have greater flexibility in assuming critical positions on accession criteria. This proposition is supported by the data in table 2.2, in conjunction with evidence on current placement in governing coalitions and past participation in such endeavors. On the first of these dimensions, political parties who take part in government and advocate Euroskeptic positions are highly underrepresented in the political systems of East Europe. In instances where parties in government take a critical stance, these are junior partners or members of broad coalitions woven to provide stability in an especially diffuse political system. This is clearly the case of Latvia and Slovakia, whose effective number of political parties during the last elections stands at 6.8 and 8.9, respectively, representing the two most fragmented party systems in the region. In order to overcome the diffusion of the electoral and parliamentary space, governing coalitions in Latvia and Slovakia had to include parties espousing anti-European sentiments. The other case with a Euroskeptic party participating in government is Poland, where the Polish Peasant Party (PSL) took part as a junior partner in the Left coalition formed by the Alliance of Democratic left (SLD) in 2001. The PSL's soft skepticism was associated with the protection of Polish farmers and its attitude on several Europe-related issues led to the disintegration of the governing coalition in March 2003.

Core political parties with a role in governance seldom, if ever, embrace Euroskeptic positions. In the first place, such parties are in effect charged with bringing their countries in compliance with the *acquis* and cannot undermine the prevailing consensus on the "return to Europe." Moreover, parties in power are responsible for the implementation of the reform package that involves unpopular social and economic policies so that the conditionality associated with accession has an instrumental value as justification for the reform (Hughes, Sasse, and Gordon 2002). As a result, mainstream parties in government have difficulty in embracing a negative position on Europe, and even have self-interest in diverting blame for unpopular policies to demands from Brussels. This may also explain why core parties that move from the governing to the opposition side of the aisle become more open in assuming a skeptic position, as for example the ODS in the Czech Republic whose concern with the conditions of accession became more strident after its loss of power in 1997. Other parties on the East European scene, for example, the Estonian Center Party (Kesk), or the Independent Party of Smallholders (FGKP) in Hungary have followed a similar shift as the restraints imposed by governing coalition obligations were lifted, and the parties assumed oppositional roles. The evidence based on party participation in former or current governance warrants the conclusion that parties in power operating within the valence of the Europe issue are constricted in their abilities to articulate concerns with the integration process. Parties in opposition, in contrast, appear to have more incentives to articulate Euroskeptic views as a means of differentiating the political space and making inroads in electoral competition, lending strong support to the model focusing on party positions in or out of power.

The anti-Europe position is most frequently advanced by peripheral parties as is evident in the prevalence of extra parliamentary parties in the Euroskeptic policy space (table 2.2). It is the parties on the margins of the system that have the greatest incentive to advocate the emergence of new issues as a competitive dimension, first of all to differentiate their position from the existing pattern of contestation (Mair 1997; Taggart 1998). For that reason, several Euroskeptic parties are outsider parties, parties operating either on the fringes of normal politics for a prolonged period or as new formations attempting to use anti-European platforms to establish their presence on the political scene. Among the former are parties of the extreme left that remain unreconciled to the transformation program, for example, the Workers' Party in Hungary or the Social Democratic Labor Party (LSSP) in Latvia, whose opposition to Europe is based on a concern with the prevailing liberal-capitalist consensus. Most fringe parties with a Euroskeptic agenda, however, are Rightist parties identified with strong nationalism, for example, the Republican Party in the Czech Republic, MIEP in Hungary, or SNS in Slovakia, whose concern is driven by the protection of sovereignty against the federalist European design. Parties that have mainly antiestablishment, anti–status quo political expressions that are outside mainstream politics are often excluded from potential governing coalitions (Sitter 2002). While these peripheral parties are numerous, they currently generate only minimal popular support, often well below the threshold for entrance into the legislature. Their embrace of a more visible Euroskeptic position, therefore, is part of an effort to use the Europe question as a wedge issue to enhance political standing—although without much success to date.

It is also worthy of note that party Euroskepticism in the accession states is not primarily a phenomenon associated with the emergence of political parties riding the Europe question on a "new politics" agenda, that is, defined by single-issue positioning based on anti-integration. Rather, most political parties in the Euroskeptic camp have a long-term presence in the emerging party systems in the aftermath of communism (table 2.2). Most go back to the dawn of democratic politics in East Europe, tracing their origins to the formative stage of party systems in the region, the 1989–1993 period. In fact, all the accession states with political entities presently associated with anti-integration can trace back such parties to the start-up period of democratization. True, there are a few parties with a strong anti-Europe agenda that have forged on the political scene only in the last few years, such as the Social Democratic Welfare Party in Latvia, the League of Polish Families

(LPR) in Poland, or the Real Slovak National Party (PSNS) in Slovakia but these are not any more numerous or visible at the ballot box than more established parties adopting Euroskeptic position. The overall pattern concerning the pedigree of anti-Europe parties is thus contrary to the expectation that new issue parties are at the forefront of the recent wave of Euroskepticism evident in the accession states. Instead, the Euroskeptic position has been taken up by political organizations already in place in the party system, seeking to use Euroskepticism to enhance their electoral appeal and political fortune. This finding further reinforces the power model of partisanship as longstanding, marginalized political players outside the mainstream system of power attempt to bring the European question into the forefront of the political agenda, seeking to ride the issue to a more secure position in the party system and electoral contestation.

Conclusion

Europe as a political issue has become gradually more visible in public opinion discourse and in the competitive politics of the new East European democracies. But neither of the primary predictive models, centering on mass opinion as a driving force for Euroskepticism or on the structure of the emerging party systems, is a consistent predictor for the success of Euroskeptic political entities in the accession countries. This does not mean, however, that Euroskepticism was absent from the political scene on the eve of accession. All the East European countries except for Bulgaria registered the presence of political parties with an agenda that questioned the value of integration, either on instrumental or on principled grounds. The ability of these Euroskeptic organizations to move beyond electoral contestation to policy input, however, was often circumscribed by low levels of popular support. As table A4 in the Internet appendix makes apparent, there is a discrepancy among accession states with regard to the parties' potential to transform their stance into a significant voice in the policy arena. In most of the countries of East Europe, the import of parties with negative views on integration declines as we move from the electoral to the parliamentary space, and within the latter, in terms of a more meaningful share of political support that can be parleyed into political leverage.

Still there are distinct pathways on the measure of Euroskeptic party significance. In the Czech Republic and Estonia, the parties embracing a negative stance on the issue are able to survive electoral competition and emerge as large parliamentary parties with a potent voice as mobilizing agents or in legislative deliberations. Both these entities, the ODS and Kesk, are the most successful challengers of integration in the region, attaining about 25 percent of the vote at the last election based on instrumental appeals questioning the competence of the accession arrangements. In the other instances of parties attaining a significance threshold of 10 percent electoral support, a soft, instrumental Euroskepticism also prevails (as in Slovakia and Romania) but for the sole exception of Self-Defence in Poland with a more principled rejection of the European project.

In contrast to these states are the cases where political parties are unsuccessful in their attempt to attract voter support and transform their platforms on Europe into political gains in the competitive process, and even less so in the parliamentary forum. Thus, Euroskeptic parties in Hungary and Lithuania are unable to clear the minimum barrier for entry into the legislative chamber, whereas several parties in Latvia, Slovenia, Poland, and Slovakia that meet the minimum requirement for parliamentary representation fall short of a significant 10 percent vote share with better potential for policy impact. Most of these parties have adopted the soft, technical critique of specific polices associated with integration, although there are a few parties embracing a "hard" principled opposition to Europe. The overarching evidence, then, is that Euroskeptic success in the party systems is largely vested in political expressions that question the particular, instrumental provisions of the negotiating process and its consequences, while parties on the fringes of the political spectrum can mount either instrumental or idealistic challenges to the pan-European project.

To reiterate once more the primary finding, the national variance in the "significance" of Euroskeptism on the political scene of the East European states is not a factor of public opinion or the shape of party systems. Skeptic parties do not prevail only in the most volatile and fragmented party structures that are susceptible to raiding by political entrepreneurs willing to test the unstable political waters through the mobilization of new issues as competitive devices. On the contrary, party Euroskepticism is often evident among the more stable party systems in the region. Nor do party families or the left–right ideological spectrum emerge as clear-cut indicators of the parties' abilities to use the political environment to mobilize support for questioning the value of accession. The most convincing evidence for the relevance of Euroskepticism in domestic politics is the power model, as both the tightness of competition and the in-or-out of government placement of parties shape the political incentives and strategic behavior of political entrepreneurs seizing the issue to attain electoral advantage. So far it does not appear that the attempt to translate the Euroskeptic stance to electoral gain has met with success. Throughout the region, "Europe" has remained outside a mainstream discourse reflecting new socioeconomic cleavages or new political fissures with significant bearing on the outcomes of electoral politics, precluding the formation of a new dominant competitive dimension in the politics of East Europe.

For some time, the heretofore prevailing elite and public approval on the "return to Europe" has served to depoliticize the issue as a salient agenda in partisan domestic politics. Yet, with the completion of the integration process, there are growing signs that the Europe question looms larger on the political horizon of the newest members of the European community. The public realization that belonging to Europe entails costs as well as benefits is eroding the former consensus and as such creates incentives for some political parties to echo the public mood of concern and voice more openly Euroskeptic policy preferences. Thus, a more pronounced cleavage on Europe may emerge as a more central element in the competitive politics of the East European states. Clear indications of such political inroads by parties opposing the current shape of European unification are already in evidence in Poland, Estonia, or the Czech Republic. Yet, it is paradoxical that just as the European dimension is becoming more germane and more visible to policy contestation, the party systems of postcommunism are maturing and stabilizing. Under such circumstances, the opportunity structures for political entrepreneurship that have prevailed for most of the past decade are foreclosing and making it more difficult for new issues to alter the political map of East Europe.

Notes

1. The Internet appendix can be found at http://www.indiana.edu/~iupolsci/rrohrsch/PalgraveTables+Figures.pdf
2. It should be noted that there is a possible effect of timing since the election in Lithuania in 2000 antedated the 2002 and 2003 elections in the other Baltic States. If Euroskepticism becomes more evident in proximity to the date of accession, the discrepancy in voter support for the anti-Europe position may be due to the timing of electoral cycles.

CHAPTER 3

Party Ideology and European Integration: An East–West Comparison

Gary Marks, Liesbet Hooghe, Moira Nelson, and Erica Edwards

Introduction

On May 1, 2004, eight former communist societies entered the European Union, with two more anticipating membership by 2007. These are decisive events in the stitching together of Europe after the demise of communism. The prospect and experience of membership in the European Union is simply the most effective means yet devised to disseminate and consolidate the defining ideals of Western civilization—civil rights, markets, and democracy. Enlargement is a geopolitical process extending Western norms, and hence peace and economic growth, to bordering countries. But what are the consequences of enlargement for the European polity? Do East and West view the issues arising from European integration through the same or different eyes?

We ask two questions in this chapter. First, how does party positioning on European issues connect to the basic conflicts that structure domestic politics? How does the ideological profile of a political party in national politics constrain its support for European integration? Second, does European integration map onto domestic competition differently in the East from the West, and if so, how can we make sense of this?

Prior research has shown that, in the West, the structure of domestic competition powerfully constrains attitudes on European integration (Aspinwall 2002; Marks and Steenbergen 2004; Pennings 2002). The orientation of a party to European issues can be predicted fairly accurately if one knows how that party stands on the two dimensions that summarize domestic political competition—an economic left/right dimension and a noneconomic, or new politics, dimension.

Do these findings apply to Central and Eastern Europe? In recent years, several researchers have analyzed the structure of political competition in the accession states of Central and Eastern Europe. We draw on their research and bring to bear an expert dataset covering the EU-15 (minus Luxembourg) and seven accession countries of Central and Eastern Europe (the Czech Republic, Hungary, Latvia, Lithuania, Poland, Slovenia, and Slovakia) plus Bulgaria and Romania.[1] This survey of 238 country experts was conducted in 2002 under the auspices of the UNC-Chapel Hill Center for European Studies; it provides systematic data on party leadership positioning on European integration and 9 EU policies for 98 Western and 73 Eastern parties.

Structure of Party Competition

There are two dimensions that structure competition among political parties in Europe. The first of these is an economic left/right dimension concerned with economic redistribution, welfare, and government regulation of the economy. The left prioritizes economic equality whereas the right prioritizes individual economic freedom. Contestation on this dimension, expressed in democratic class conflict, has predominated in most Western nations in the postwar period (Bartolini and Mair 1990; Lipset and Rokkan 1967) and is diagnosed as the main dimension of party competition in Central and Eastern Europe (Evans and Whitefield 1993; Kitschelt et al. 1999).[2]

A second, noneconomic or cultural, new politics dimension has gained strength since the 1970s in Western Europe (Flanagan 1987; Franklin 1992; Inglehart 1977; Kitschelt 1988). In Lithuania, Poland, Romania, and Slovenia, it is almost as powerful as the economic left/right, and in Hungary it is stronger (Evans and Whitefield 1993; Klingemann 1994; Zielinski 2002). This dimension summarizes several noneconomic issues—ecological, life style, and communal—and is correspondingly more diverse than the left/right dimension. In some countries it is oriented around environmental protection and sustainable growth; in others, it captures conflict about traditional values rooted in a secular/religious divide; in yet others, it is pitched around immigration and defense of the national community. We, therefore, describe the poles of this dimension with composite terms: Green/Alternative/ Libertarian (or gal) and Traditionalist/ Authoritarian/Nationalist (or tan).[3]

These dimensions are best regarded as ways to summarize how actors position themselves on major issues. The structure of political contestation varies in interesting ways across countries and across time. But one can discern a basic generalizable pattern, and it is with this alone that we concern ourselves here.

In the West, there are strong affinities between left and gal and between right and tan. The simple correlation between party positioning on these dimensions, according to the measures reported in appendix I, is −0.64 (see figure 3.1). When we divide the political world according to these dimensions into four quadrants, we find that of 98 political parties across the 14 larger EU countries, only 3 are located squarely in the left–tan quadrant. Liberal parties are drawn to the right–gal quadrant where they are joined by four additional parties, but the remaining 83 parties are located in the left–gal and right–tan quadrants.[4]

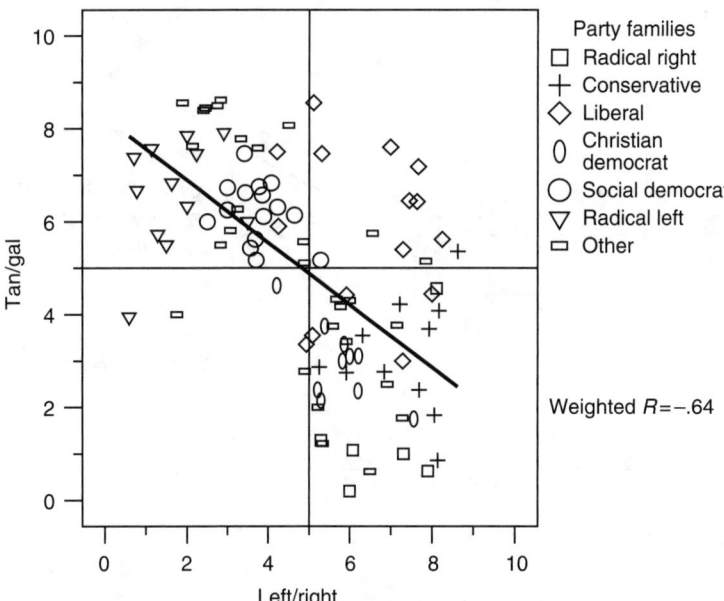

Figure 3.1 Dimensions of party competition in Western Europe. Cases weighted by vote percentage in most recent national election. $N = 98$ parties.

The same dimensions have been diagnosed in Central and Eastern Europe, but placement of parties in this two-dimensional space could hardly be more different (figure 3.2). The left–gal quadrant encompasses just five political parties, and these are located around its southern and eastern edges. Fifty-five of seventy-three parties in the nine countries for which we have data are either left–tan or right–gal. The association between the two dimensions is 0.45. As one would expect given the relative newness of democratic competition in the East, party competition is less structured here. But the structure we do find yields an axis of party competition at a 90° angle to that in the West (Kitschelt 1992, 1995a).[5]

Another way of approaching this is to compare the positions of party families in East and West on these dimensions. We do this in figure A1 in the Internet appendix.[6] Party families are, of course, more established in Western than in Central and Eastern Europe, but following Derksen's categorization of party families,[7] the affiliations of CEEC parties to regional and international party families, and to European-level party groups in the European parliament, we can place all but 6 parties in 10 party families.[8] Party families in the East are not as coherent on the left/right and gal/tan dimensions as those in the West, but the

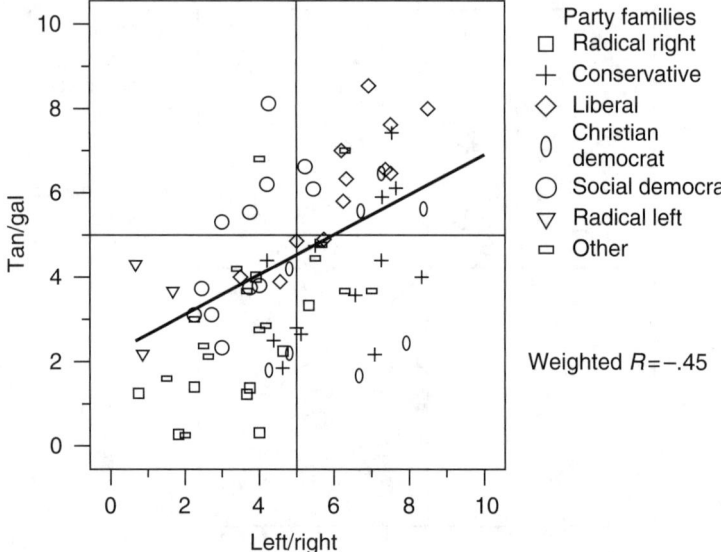

Figure 3.2 Dimensions of party competition in Central and Eastern Europe. Cases weighted by vote percentage in most recent national election. $N = 73$ parties.

difference is not large. The average standard deviation across Eastern party families on the two dimensions is 1.21 on an 11-point scale; for Western party families it is 1.15.

Several party families—social democrats, Christian democrats, conservatives, liberals, and regionalists/ethnic parties—have similar positions in East and West. Responsibility for the sharp, indeed 90°, difference in the axes of party competition can be pinned on large divergences in the positions of the three party families in the left–tan quadrant: the radical Left, agrarian, and radical right (or radical tan) families.[9] The arrows in figure A1 join mean positions of these three families, East and West. The ovals encompass the mean positions of the party families that are similarly located in this two-dimensional space. From this perspective, the source of divergence between East and West appears to be the communist legacy, which serves as an ideological magnet in the extreme lower left corner (Kostelecky 2002; Lane 2002).

Communism in Central and Eastern Europe delivered economic equality to a greater degree than a market economy could or would promise and it sustained authoritarian regimes that suppressed public dissent and alternative life styles. Historically, therefore, radical left economic positions and radical tan cultural and political values went hand in hand in Central and Eastern Europe. For many pensioners, blue-collar workers, unemployed, poorly educated, and rural people, the transition to liberal democratic capitalism was, and is, threatening (Grzymala-Busse and Innes 2003).

Political parties that cater to transition losers by trying to blunt reform emphasize "traditional" values of economic equality and authoritarianism—and are therefore located in the lower left quadrant of figure A1.

Party Positioning on European Integration in Western Europe

The general structuring of party competition allows one to explain party positioning on European integration with some precision. But the predictive power of left/right and gal/tan varies across East and West. We begin with the West, where European integration has been on the political agenda for decades, and where we have a decade-long research program to draw upon.

The Inverted U-Curve

The relationship between left/right position and general support for European integration in the West is most accurately described as an inverted U-curve. Figure 3.3 produces an inverted U-curve by plotting support for European integration on the economic left/right dimension. Centrist parties tend to support European integration; opposition parties on both left and right extremes tend to oppose (Aspinwall 2002; Hix and Lord 1997; Marks, Wilson, and Ray 2002; Taggart 1998).

The European Union is a centrist project. It has been created by mainstream parties—Christian democrats, liberals, social democrats, and conservatives—that have dominated national governments, national parliaments, the European parliament, and the European Commission. Parties on the ideological extremes attack European integration as an extension of their domestic opposition. The radical left views European integration as an elitist capitalist project that isolates decision making from citizens in the interests of powerful corporations. The radical right views European integration as an elitist supranational project that weakens national autonomy and traditional values.

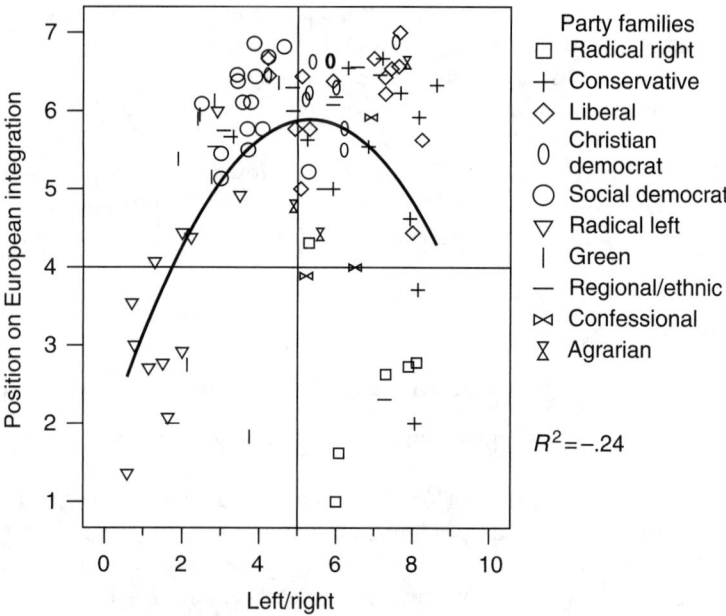

Figure 3.3 Left/right and general position on European integration in Western Europe. N in dataset = 98 parties.

Left/Right

The connections between domestic and European contestation come into sharp view when one disaggregates European integration into its component issues. The left/right dimension constrains party positioning on European issues having to do with the political regulation of the market. According to the regulated capitalism versus market liberalism model (Hall and Soskice 2001; Hooghe and Marks 1999; Pollack 1999; Rhodes and van Apeldoorn 1997), the center–left supports political integration in order to create the capacity to regulate markets, redistribute resources, and sustain partnership among public and private actors. The project of regulated capitalism at the European level was developed under Jacques Delors' decade-long presidency of the European Commission (1985–1994); Delors sought to build an *espace organisé* around social policy, employment policy, and cohesion policy to counterbalance the single market. In the 1990s, regulated capitalism became the overarching project for Europe's center–left parties (Ross 1995). This is an ideological project and it is opposed by those on the right who consider market integration a destination rather than a point of departure for further integration.

The location of Western national political parties on the left/right divide constrains whether they support or oppose EU policies related to regulated capitalism (Hooghe, Marks, and Wilson 2002; Thomassen and Schmitt 1997, 172). Employment policy is a prime example. As table 3.1 shows, the further to the left, the greater is a party's support for a European employment policy ($R = -0.53$).[10] The sign is reversed when one examines political parties' positions on the internal market: Left/right is linearly and positively associated with support for the internal market ($R = 0.34$). This reflects principled opposition to the market project among radical left parties and greater enthusiasm among center–right than among center–left parties.

New Politics

EU issues that engage lifestyle, gender, environment, participatory decision making, and national culture are most closely associated with the new politics dimension. The location of a party on the new politics dimension is strongly correlated with its support for an EU environmental policy ($R = -0.62$), for an EU asylum policy ($R = -0.46$), and

Table 3.1 West versus East: Left/right, Gal/tan, and party position on European integration (correlations)

	West		East	
	Left/right	Gal/tan	Left/right	Gal/tan
European integration	0.04	−0.30	0.52	−0.65
European parliament powers	−0.17	−0.50	0.32	−0.57
Internal market policy	0.34	−0.18	0.64	0.68
Employment policy	−0.53	−0.55	0.12	−0.53
Agricultural policy	0.11	0.29	−0.48	0.30
Cohesion policy	−0.25	−0.18	0.18	−0.30
Environmental policy	−0.59	−0.62	0.11	−0.27
Asylum policy	−0.23	−0.46	0.24	−0.56
Foreign and security policy	0.04	−0.33	0.38	−0.57
Enlargement	−0.11	−0.38	0.59	−0.71

Note: Bivariate correlations. Parties weighted by vote percentage in most recent national election. The number of parties is 98 for the West and 73 for the East.

for strengthening the powers of the European parliament ($R = -0.50$) (see table 3.1).

In some respects, the new politics dimension is more intimately connected to European integration than is the left/right dimension. Those on the tan (Traditional/Authoritarian/Nationalist) side oppose European integration for essentially the same reasons that they oppose immigration: both infuse foreigners into the society and both threaten the national community. The Vlaams Blok's campaign slogan in the 2004 regional and European elections was "less taxes, more Flanders; less crime, more Flanders; less immigration, more Flanders," an update of its "Safe Flanders" in the 2003 Belgian elections. The central plank of the party platform was opposition to immigrant voting rights. In its 2004 European election program, the Vlaams Blok supported "an intergovernmental EU" and was opposed to "European citizenship and a European Constitution as proposed by the European Convention. Only states can decide who their subjects are. The EU is no state and should never become one" (Vlaams Blok 2004).

The defense of national sovereignty lies close to the hearts of those on the tan side of this divide, not because national sovereignty is useful for other ends, but because it is *intrinsically* valued. This distinguishes the radical right from market liberals on the economic right. Market liberals view national sovereignty in terms of its implications for economic exchange. They are opposed to barriers to trade, and they therefore support strong international regimes that can facilitate market integration, even if this eliminates key national competencies, including monetary control.

A party's new politics position is considerably more powerful than left/right in predicting position on integration across issue areas. As table 3.1 displays, gal/tan is a better predictor of a party's position on EU policies than left/right, except for the internal market and for cohesion policy.

Radical Right parties are now by far the most Euroskeptical party family group in the West, including the radical left: their average position on European integration is 2.5 on a 7-point scale, against 3.3 for radical left parties, and 5.6 for all Western parties. Conservative parties that lean to the tan side of the new politics dimension tend to be more Euroskeptical than those that do not. While tan values are a strong indicator of Euroskepticism, gal values are consistent with support for European integration. Support is especially strong for issues that relate directly to core concerns of gal-oriented parties. Thus, green parties are now the most Euroenthusiastic party family in the West for EU environmental policy and for more powers to the European parliament.

Party Positioning on European Integration in Central and Eastern Europe

No Inverted U-Curve

Figure 3.4 plots support for European integration in the East on the economic left/right dimension. In sharp contrast to the West, the relationship is fairly linear, and this result does not change if we substitute gal/tan for left/right.

Party positioning in accession states is highly structured by comparison with the EU-15. The most powerful predictors in the East are the linear variables left/right and gal/tan. If one knows only where a party stands on these two dimensions, one can account for 48 percent of the variance in positioning on European integration across Central and Eastern European parties. The corresponding figure is just 18 percent in the EU-15 minus Luxembourg. Correspondingly, extremism, measured by squaring the distance from the median party on left/right and gal/tan, is less potent in Central and Eastern Europe than in Western Europe. In the West, a model including both extremism measures boosts the fit from 18 to 45 percent, and from 48 to 59 percent in the East.[11]

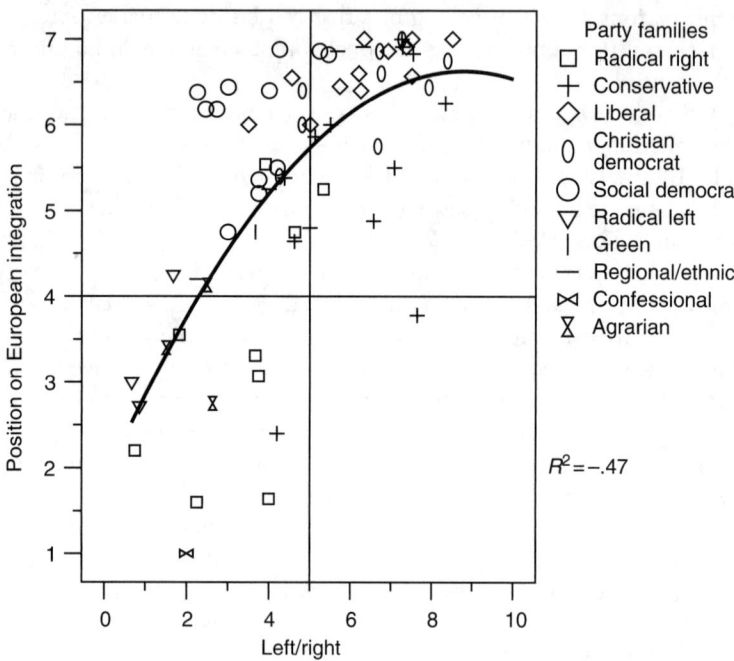

Figure 3.4 Left/right and general position on European integration in Central and Eastern Europe. N in dataset = 73 parties.

In the West, as we have noted, European integration is a centrist project whereas in the East, it is anticommunist. The greater the ideological distance of a party from the bottom left corner of figure 3.2, the more likely it is to support European integration. Two distinct sources of Euroskepticism in the West—hard-line economic opposition and hard-line politico-cultural opposition—coincide in the East.

To summarize, the positioning of political parties on European integration is more structured in the East, and it is structured disproportionately by two linear variables: left/right and gal/tan. The inverted U, a familiar construct in the West, is absent in the East.[12]

Left/Right and Gal/Tan

The dimensions laid out in figure 3.2 powerfully constrain party positioning on European integration in Central and Eastern Europe.

European integration fits quite neatly onto the axis of party competition in figure 3.2. The reasons for this take one to the heart of political conflict in accession countries.

Attitudes to the communist past and economic experience of transition underpin the preponderance of parties in the left–tan and right–gal quadrants. "Transition losers" (Tucker, Pacek, and Berinsky 2002) hark back to an idealized version of their communist past, where "egalitarianism epitomized an important aspect of [their] interests, and support for the authoritarian and paternalistic state was a means to get these interests fulfilled" (Bernik and Malnar 2003, 201; Tverdova and Anderson 2004; see also Meyer 2003). Economic egalitarianism, authoritarianism—and opposition to European integration—go hand in hand. "Transition winners," in contrast, repudiate authoritarianism and egalitarianism—and support European integration—precisely because they seek a clean break with the past. So, for example, the Polish Alliance of the Democratic Left (SLD), founded on the ruins of the discredited Polish communist party, enthusiastically embraces entry into the EU "to demonstrate its repudiation of the past" (Pienkos 2004, 464).

This structure is reinforced by the formal requirements imposed by the European Union on candidate countries. The European Union's Copenhagen criteria require both a market economy and institutional guarantees for transparent democracy and minority protection (Vachudova 2005)—in short, policies associated with the right–gal quadrant of figure 3.2. As Karen Henderson observes, "the EU makes demands of candidate states which coincide with the aims of parties at the pro-market libertarian end of the axis" (Henderson 2001, 10). These EU conditions are resisted by parties in the left–tan quadrant, which defend the recent past, but right–gal parties welcome them because they place their countries back on the path they would have taken were it not for Soviet domination.

Socioeconomic interests appear to underlie this structure. Analyses of voting in the accession referenda confirm that those who voted in favor are disproportionately better educated, professional, and have higher incomes than those who voted against (Pienkos 2004, 469). European integration gains the support of economic winners, who tend to support right–gal parties (Cichowski 2000; Tucker, Pacek, and Berinsky 2002). European integration provokes skepticism among economic losers, and such people tend to support radical left and radical right parties in the left–tan quadrant. In Poland, opponents of European integration support the Peasants Self-Defence party headed by Andrej Lepper, or the Catholic, nationalistic, League of Polish Families, with its close association to the Catholic fundamentalist radio station Marya (Szczerbiak 2001; see also Bátory and Sitter 2004). In Hungary, Euroskepticism has established roots in the radical right as well as the former communist left: the far right Justice and Life Party and the far left Hungarian Workers Party are hard-core Euroskeptic parties (Bátory 2001; Taggart and Szczerbiak 2004). Similarly, in Slovakia, opposition against European integration is pronounced among the radical right (Slovak National Party and the Right Slovak National Party) and the radical left (Slovak Communist Party).[13] All but one of thirteen Euroskeptic parties (i.e., those scoring below four on our 7-point scale for general support of European integration) are located in the left–tan quadrant of figure 3.2. The sole exception is the Czech ODS, the Civic Democratic Party of former prime minister and current President Vaclav Klaus, which is located in the right–gal quadrant, and is moderately Euroskeptical.[14]

The difference between East and West can be summarized in terms of the location of the main axis of party competition and the extent to which orientations to European integration track on to it. In the East, European integration is assimilated within the dominant right–gal, left–tan axis of competition. In the West, general support for European integration is only weakly related to the left–gal, right–tan axis.

In the West, the economic right encompasses neoliberal parties, which support the market-oriented reforms that have been the main thrust of European integration. But there are also radical right parties on the economic right that oppose loss of national sovereignty, even on economic policy. The former parties are defined primarily by their doctrinal market friendliness and the latter parties by their Euroskeptical nationalism. So when it comes to Europe, there is palpable tension between right and tan. Conservative parties are rift between nationalists and neoliberals (Alexandre and Jardin 1997; Baker et al. 1999; Marks and Wilson 2000).

The left in Western Europe is also split on the issue of European integration. Mainstream social democratic parties wish to deepen the European Union to better regulate market outcomes and to anchor gal values in European society. Radical left parties, in contrast, are driven by anticapitalism to principled Euroskepticism.

In Western Europe, European integration highlights tensions in the dominant left–gal/right–tan axis of party competition, and this limits the extent to which political parties can absorb European integration into the existing structure of party competition. By contrast, European integration fits hand in glove with the left–tan/right–gal axis in Central and Eastern Europe, and this explains why positioning on European integration is more structured in the East than in the West.

Issue Bundling

It is one thing for a party to take a position on European integration on the outside, as political parties in the East have done. It is another thing for a party to take a position from the inside, confronted with decisions on whether and how to pursue integration on several fronts, as has been the situation for political parties in the West.

From the outside, European integration is perceived as a bundle, a take-it-or-leave-it proposition on membership. This is what we find in Central and Eastern Europe prior to enlargement. Here, contestation reflects basic differences in worldview—whether a party desires "cosmopolitan opening" or "national closure" (Bátory 2001, 6). European integration is a litmus test for distinguishing among those whose "sense of vision is stuck in the past or looking forward to the future" (Henderson 2001, 16).

Smer, founded in Slovakia in 1999 as a social democratic party embracing a Blairite "third way," defends its proaccession stance in terms of a "European system of values" (Dauderstädt and Joerissen 2004, 12). In its web site, the orthodox communist KSS defends a diametrically opposite view, not because it protests against particular policies, but on the basis of its claim that capitalism has been worse than socialism for Slovakia (Dauderstädt and Joerissen 2004, 13). The same tension characterizes the EU debate in Hungary. "Asked what kind of European Union Hungary hopes for, the EU Integration website (of the Hungarian Socialist party, the MSzP) answers that Hungary wants an efficient, transparent, and open EU" (Dauderstädt and Joerissen 2004, 18). The party explains that "[i]n the view of the Socialists, there is no other way of modernization for Hungary and more broadly Central Europe than joining the process of European integration as soon as possible, voluntarily giving up part of sovereignty and transferring that to the institutions of European integration" (Bátory 2001, 19).

As membership becomes a daily reality, we predict that issue bundling will decrease. Already, we see that despite their general support for European integration, right–gal parties tend not to favor an integrated agricultural policy—a policy designed for a constituency that provides them relatively few votes. The same logic suggests that despite their general Euroskepticism, left parties will tend to respond positively to European employment policy. However, we also predict that party positioning on European integration will continue to be structured by the right–gal versus left–tan divide as long as European integration is perceived as a supranational polity that enhances market capitalism and libertarian values. Each of these characteristics constitutes a sharp break from communism and, as a consequence, points in the same direction across the axis of competition that we identify in Central and Eastern Europe.

Conclusion

The theory of party positioning developed for Western European political parties does, indeed, apply in Central and Eastern Europe. That is to say, the positions that parties take on European integration are coherently and systematically related to the positions they take on the left/right and gal/tan dimensions of contestation that structure domestic politics. But the substantive connection could hardly be more different. In the West, there are two main sources of opposition to European integration: the hard left and hard tan, and these are located at the opposite extremes of an axis of party competition running from left–gal to right–tan. When we track general support for European integration on the axis of party competition, we find an inverted U-curve.

There is a similar logic of opposition in the East. Opposition to European integration also comes from the hard left and the hard tan, but these characteristics are found in the same, not different, parties. The axis of party competition runs from a prointegration right–gal quadrant to an anti-integration left–tan quadrant. Left–tan is a distinctive orientation for parties in three families: the radical left, agrarians, and radical tan. The attraction appears to be rooted in the fact that under communism, economic equality and authoritarianism went together. In Central and Eastern Europe, political parties view European integration as a policy package. European membership signifies a sharp break with the communist past and is correspondingly supported or opposed on that basis.

Central and Eastern Europe and Western Europe share the same causal logic of party positioning in relation to a common set of dimensions summarizing political conflict. However, since the structure of party competition in East and West is so different, this logic leads to contrasting outcomes.

Appendix I: Description of the Variables

Position on European integration	Mean expert score along 7-point scale ranging from strongly opposed to European integration (1) to strongly in favor of European integration (7). Question: "How would you describe the *general position on European integration* that the party's leadership has taken over the course of 2002?"
Left/right position	Mean expert score on 11-point scale ranging from extreme left (0) to extreme right (10). Question: "Political scientists often classify parties in terms of their ideological stance on *economic issues*. Parties to the *right* emphasize a reduced economic role for government. They want privatization, lower taxes, less regulation, reduced government spending, and a leaner welfare state. Parties to the *left* want government to play an active role in the economy. Using these criteria, indicate where parties are located in terms of their *economic ideology*"
Gal/tan position	Mean expert score on 11-point scale ranging from Libertarian/Postmaterialist (0) to Traditional/Authoritarian (10). This score is reversed in the figures. Question: "Parties may also be classified in terms of their views on *democratic freedoms and rights*. 'Libertarian' or 'post-materialist' parties favor expanded personal freedoms, for example, access to abortion, doctor-assisted suicide, same-sex marriages, and greater democratic participation. 'Traditional' or 'authoritarian' parties often reject these ideas; they value order and stability, and believe that the government should be a firm moral authority. Where are parties located in terms of their *ideological views on freedoms and rights?*"
Left/right extremism	Square of the distance of a party from the median left/right position, calculated separately for Eastern and Western parties
Gal/tan extremism	Square of the distance of a party from the median left/right position, calculated separately for Eastern and Western parties

Appendix II: The Expert Surveys

The analysis undertaken in this chapter is based on a dataset gathered under the auspices of the UNC-Chapel Hill Center for European Studies. A survey conducted in 2002 by a team of faculty and graduate students[15] tapped 238 country experts to evaluate the ideological and policy locations of 171 political parties in Bulgaria, the Czech

Republic, Hungary, Latvia, Lithuania, Poland, Romania, Slovakia, Slovenia, and all EU member-states except Luxembourg.

The survey replicates and expands an expert survey of party positioning on European integration conducted in 1999 by the UNC-Center for European Studies, and in 1996 by Leonard Ray at four different time points: 1984, 1988, 1992, and 1996 (Steenbergen and Marks 2006). Both these surveys were limited to EU member-states.

Three sets of questions in the 2002 survey attempt to illuminate policy positions, internal party dissent, as well as dimensions of contestation. First are a set of questions that tap the degree of support across parties for European integration in general and in the following policy areas: EU environmental policy, EU cohesion or regional policy, EU policy toward asylum seekers, EU employment policy, EU agricultural spending, internal market, EU foreign and security policy, expanding the European parliament's power, and EU enlargement. Second are two questions that tap extent of dissent within parties, as well as on type of issues. Third are questions that tap party positions on the basic dimensions of political contestation, including an economic left/right scale and a new politics scale.

Political parties are included in the survey if they fulfill one or more of the following criteria:

1. The party received 3 percent or more of the vote in the general election for the lower chamber in 2002 or the most proximate prior year.
2. The party was represented in the lower chamber of the legislature in 2002.
3. The party was represented in the European parliament in 2002.

The 238 carefully selected experts have recognized expertise on the political parties in a particular country—normally, but not always, their country of citizenship. They completed a detailed questionnaire that can be consulted on http://www.unc.edu/%7Ehooghe/parties.htm.[16] Our estimate of each party's position on each of these questions is the mean of the country experts' evaluations.

The extent to which expert evaluations are reliable can be gauged by examining the mean standard deviations. Table 3.2 presents standard deviations in response to two key questions and suggests that the current survey is within the range of the 1984–1996 Ray data. The Ray data are comparable to the Huber and Inglehart (1995) and Laver and Hunt (1992) data.

Table 3.2 Mean Standard Deviations of Expert Evaluations

	1984	1988	1992	1996	2002
Party position	0.97	0.90	0.82	0.82	0.82
Salience	0.75	0.75	0.69	0.70	0.65

Notes

1. For details on the dataset, see appendix II. To avoid repetition, we use the labels "Central and Eastern Europe," "East," and "accession countries" interchangeably, as we do "Western Europe," "West," and "EU-15."
2. We use the concept "dimension" rather than "cleavage" because we are generalizing about the *positioning* of political actors across a range of issues. Hence, we make no assumption about whether interests are socially rooted or organizationally embedded (Bartolini 2004, 3). The dimensions we diagnose in Western Europe meet conventional criteria for cleavages, whereas this is debated in the East (Elster, Offe, and Preuss 1998, 247–270; Evans and Whitefield 1993; Kitschelt et al. 1999, 262–306; Kostelecky 2002, 90–136; Lawson, Roemmele, and Karasimeonov 1999, 1–17; Zielinski 2002).
3. Gender and color connotations intended. The question with which we measure this, listed in appendix I, is biased toward the libertarian element in gal and the authoritarian element in tan. This imposes a useful conservatism in our analysis because these elements are the most distant from the sovereignty aspects of European integration that, we argue, mobilize gal/tan concerns. Hence, the association we find between support for European integration and gal/tan is *not* an artifact of our inclusion of nationalism as an element in tan.
4. Criteria for party selection are set out in appendix II.
5. A plausible microexplanation for East/West divergence engages citizens' contrasting experiences in their work and private spheres.
6. The Internet appendix can be found at http://www.indiana.edu/~iupolsci/rrohrsch/PalgraveTables+Figures.pdf
7. See "Political Parties: An Introduction," on the Electionworld.org web site: http://www.electionworld.org/party.htm
8. The 10 party families are radical right (or radical tan), conservative, liberal, Christian democratic, social democratic, radical left, green/ecologist, regionalist/ethnic, agrarian, and confessional parties. We follow conventional definitions of party families (Hix and Lord 1997).
9. As figure A1 suggests, the term "radical right" is a misnomer when applied to left-leaning tan parties in Central and Eastern Europe. Perhaps a more appropriate description is "radical tan" parties.
10. In this and following analyses, we weigh party positions by the percentage of votes a party receives in the national election prior to the time point of

the survey. Our results are robust across weighted and nonweighted analysis, and we choose the former because we assume large parties to have a larger impact on the structure of competition.

11. These associations are for political parties weighted by their proportion of the vote in the previous national election. Unweighted associations are stronger and have a similar pattern.

12. It is interesting to note that the two dimensions are far more powerful constraints on party positioning than national location. Anova analysis of general support for European integration using national dummy variables explains 8.6% of variance among parties in the East, and 10.4% in the West. With respect to European integration, one can say that political parties are much more diverse *within* than *among* countries. Similarly, party family is a much better discriminator for party position on European integration than is country. The standard deviation of party positions on European integration tends to be considerably larger within individual countries than within individual party families.

13. The remaining Euroskeptic parties in our survey are the radical tan party of Great Romania, two radical tan Lithuanian parties (Lithuanian Freedom Union and Young Lithuania), the nationalist Slovenian National Party, one agrarian party (Lithuania's Peasant's Party) and the communist party in the Czech Republic.

14. It is worth noting that Klaus's Euroskepticism appears rooted in his neoliberal opposition to particular policies, such as agricultural and cohesion policy, rather than in generalized disapproval of the process itself. This is to say that the ODS unbundles European integration, as do conservative parties in the West.

15. Liesbet Hooghe, Milada Vachudova, Erica Edwards, Moira Nelson, Gary Marks, Marco Steenbergen, and David Scott.

16. Three respondents submitted invalid responses.

PART III
Public Opinion about European Integration

CHAPTER 4

Support based on Values? Attitudes toward the EU in Eleven Postcommunist Societies

Jörg Jacobs and Detlef Pollack

Introduction

The central attraction of the EU to nations in Central, Southeast, and Eastern Europe are the economic prospects associated with EU membership after these countries experienced a period of economic insecurity and social decline. However, although economic integration is a key aspect of linking new accession countries to Western Europe, the integration process among West European member-states also occurred on the basis of shared ideological values. Whereas the economic attraction of accession for postcommunist states may be clear, the accession of new countries raises the question of whether citizens in new EU member-states share the broad value consensus of West European publics.[1]

This chapter takes this observation as its starting point and asks To what extent do value orientations influence citizens' views about the EU net of economic factors? Using a public opinion survey conducted in 11 postcommunist societies, we test the relative explanatory power of economic factors and value orientations in explaining the views of mass publics about the EU.

We first discuss public attitudes toward becoming a member of the EU and construct our dependent variable. In the next step, we introduce measures of political cues and value orientations. The final step will be to determine the relative meaning of value orientations by also considering public perceptions of the economy and citizens' sociodemographic characteristics.

The common denominator of the countries included in our analysis is their communist past. We examine public attitudes about the EU, their determinants in countries that joined the EU in May 2004 (Czech Republic, Estonia, Hungary, Poland, Slovenia, and Slovakia), the current candidate countries (Bulgaria and Romania), the country that hopes to join the EU in the distant future (Albania), one that currently does not want to join (Russia), and a postcommunist country that ceased to exist in 1990 by joining a founding member of the EU (East Germany).

Support for Joining the EU in Central, Southeast, and Eastern Europe

Most comparative studies analyzing support for the EU use data provided by the EU, either the Eurobarometer series for EU member-states or the Central and Eastern Eurobarometer/Candidate Countries Eurobarometer (CEEB/CCEB)[2] for the accession countries (Christin 2003; Cichowski 2000; Jones and van der Bijl 2004; Marks and Hooghe 2003; McLaren 2002; Rohrschneider 2002; Tucker, Pacek, and Berinsky 2002). As Christin states, other surveys concerned with Central and Eastern Europe concentrate either on the political transformation or on the EU, but do not address both fields of research (Christin 2003). The standard question asked in the CEEB is "[i]f [our country] were to join the European Community as a full member in the future, would you feel . . . 1—'strongly in favour,' 2—'somewhat in favour,' 3—'somewhat opposed,' or 4—'strongly opposed?' " As the results show, the optimistic and almost euphoric attitudes held in the early 1990s has given way to a more skeptical view. Already by 1995, after five years of muddling through the political and economic transformation, support for joining the EU had declined in almost all the accession countries. Generally one can say that the support for joining the EU declined parallel to the likelihood of the country becoming a member.

In all the countries that joined in 2004, support for the EU dropped from about 80 percent in 1991/1992 to roughly 50 percent in 2003.[3]

In contrast, in Bulgaria and Romania, where membership is still years off, support remained high in 2003 (table 4.1).

However, the question formulation in the CEEB/CCEB is more likely to measure the short-term mood but not the more general attitude. Therefore, in our surveys, we designed a more refined measurement. In the PCE study,[4] people were asked to answer the following statements concerning their attitudes toward Europe:

1) It would be in the interest of our country to follow the path of the other (West) European countries.
2) Before we join the European Community/Union, our country should develop more self-confidence.
3) [Country] should join the European Union as a full member as soon as possible.
4) [Country] should adapt to the rules of the European Union, even if it costs jobs in the short run, in the long run our country will profit from it.[5]

The four questions address the four dimensions of European politics.

The first indicator addresses Europe as a model for the postcommunist countries. With this item, we wanted to measure whether publics continue to be skeptical about following the path of modernization. The second question is directed at people's sense of national identity.

Table 4.1 Support for joining the EU, 1990–2003 (in percentage)

	1990	1991	1992	1995	1996	1997	2003
East Germany	3	79	81	69	72	66	—
Czech Republic	11[a]	83[a]	85	44	46	49	44
Estonia	—	79	79	45	30	36	38
Hungary	3	82	84	51	47	58	56
Poland	3	79	88	75	82	75	52
Slovakia	[a]	[a]	86	50	47	62	58
Slovenia	—	—	82	—	—	—	50
Bulgaria	3	76	74	51	50	58	73
Romania	3	69	73	—	—	—	81
Albania	—	82	91	—	—	—	—
Russia	—	—	93	56	49	61	—

Note: Figures shown are the answers "strongly" and "somewhat" in favor of EU membership.
[a] Figure for Czechoslovakia.
Source: Central and Eastern Eurobarometer/Candidate Countries Eurobarometer; own calculations.

For the future process of European integration, national pride and self-confidence is likely to strengthen the national position in negotiations about the EU policy with the established member-states. As the British case illustrates, a strong nationalist position might lead citizens to oppose EU policies. The third item addresses the general question of membership, without condition, as long as it happens quickly. The fourth item addresses the price people are prepared to pay for a membership. It asks whether people would accept short-term economic costs if there is reason to believe that the country will profit in the long run from its EU membership.

The answers to these four questions (see table A5 in the Internet appendix)[6] reveal important differences among the accession countries, candidate countries, Albania, Russia, and East Germany. To begin with the general pattern, in all these countries, people are less in favor of the EU if the measure mentions the economic costs of integration. With the exception of Albania, the difference between support for following a Western path (item 1) and adapting to the rules of the EU, even if it costs jobs in the short run (item 4), amounts to as much as up to 20 percent points. This seems to confirm that cost–benefit calculations influence attitudes toward the EU. One notable result is that a majority of East Germans is convinced that it is in Germany's interest to intensify the European cooperation and strengthen European integration. However, only 11.8 percent want to delegate more power to the European Union as quickly as possible, and only one-third is prepared to adapt to European rules if these have negative short-term effects on the labor market. These figures indicate that the prospect of a supranational state in Europe is not very well received.

As for the specific countries, in the two politically most stable and economically most successful countries (the Czech Republic and Slovenia), three-quarters of the respondents want to follow the (West) European path and enter the EU with self-confidence. In these two countries, quick membership is important to only half the respondents. In Estonia, Poland, Romania, and Slovakia, the proportion of support is about the same for all four indicators. In Estonia, the attitudes of the ethnic Estonians and ethnic Russians differ in an important way. A qualified majority of both groups agrees that the country should join the EU with more self-confidence, but the ethnic Estonians agree even more. The speed of joining the EU seems to matter significantly more to the Russian Estonians. These differences might occur due to the societal position of the two ethnic groups within Estonia, where the Russian Estonians are seen as second-class citizens. They might be hoping that joining the EU will help them gain equal opportunities for participating in social and political life and in keeping up their cultural identity (Vetik 1999, 2004, 51).

In Hungary, in turn, we find a unique and significant difference from the two patterns of the other accession and candidate countries: half of the Hungarian respondents agree that the country should join the EU as quickly as possible. But the number of people who think that the country should develop more self-confidence or follow the (West) European path is much smaller. The Hungarian respondents are also the least prepared to follow the rules of the EU when it costs jobs in the short run (see also chapter 7 by Fölsz and Tóka, this volume).

The specific Russian context is demonstrated by their answers to the four questions because it is the country where support for EU membership is by far the lowest. Less than half the respondents said that they want to join the EU as quickly as possible, and only 20 percent would want to follow the (West) European path of development or enter the European market with more self-confidence. Even fewer (10 percent) are prepared to endure the loss of jobs, even if they benefit in the long run. The Albanians, on the other side of the scale, hold extremely positive and almost naïve attitudes toward the EU. This pattern probably results from the very poor performance of the former regime, and the positive effects that NATO intervention had on the country by ending the Kosovo War.[7]

Overall, even though the proportion of people supporting EU membership differs between the countries, the interrelationships among the four items are fairly similar across nations. Since we are interested in the question whether those who are in favor of joining the EU share certain value orientations, we use items 1 and 3 to construct the dependent variable for our further analyses. To agree somewhat or fully to both statements is interpreted as unreserved support and coded as "1." Substantially, the newly constructed indicator shows no differences from the results already discussed above in detail. (See table A6 in the Internet appendix.)

Explaining Attitudes about the EU

In their brief literature review explaining support for the EU in Western Europe, Marks and Hooghe present three groups of explanatory variables found in the literature: first, the calculus of economic costs and benefits, second, the use of political cues as a shorthand guide to complex political issues, and third, "the psychology of group membership and emotional attachment to consider how group identities, and, above all, national identities, bear on support for European integration" (Marks and Hooghe 2003, 1; Tucker, Pacek, and Berinsky 2002). Their results show that national identities play an important role in explaining support for the EU beyond simple economic expectations (Christin 2003, 4–6). We follow their lead and use three groups of variables to model citizens' evaluations of the EU: political cues, ideological values, and utilitarian calculations.

Political Cues

In modern democracies, political parties play an important role in helping ordinary citizens to structure their political world. Due to its increasing complexity, parties serve as a shortcut for processing new information and as a means to form an opinion about remote objects that are not part of everyday life. Since the EU represents such an abstract object of hopes and fears with no immediately visible and noticeable influence, political cues may affect how publics evaluate it.

However, regarding the post-Soviet societies, Miller et al. (2000) question whether the emerging party systems are a fact or a fiction. Some parties were only founded as a platform to promote a single candidature without a large number of party members, and dissolved top–down soon after they served their purpose. As opposed to the post-Soviet societies, one can observe a certain stability of the current party system in most accession countries and East Germany. But one should be cautious as to not interpret this as an indicator of the persistence of these party systems or to assume that the same parties will compete in the foreseeable future or that all have found their position on the political left–right dimension (Miller, Hesli, and Reisinger 1995). To name just two examples, in Hungary, we have seen a major shift of a liberal party toward a more conservative position, and in Bulgaria, the "party of the king" has appeared (Tilkidjiev 2001).

In our survey, we asked respondents an open-ended question about which party they would vote for if there were an election the following Sunday. Since a significant number of the smaller parties will certainly only stand for one election before they vanish or merge, we also asked people about their political, or ideological, camps and used this information as a proxy for their party affiliation. Following the tradition of the Ann Arbor model in voting behavior (Campbell et al. 1960), we assume that the orientation toward a political camp is more important for forming general political attitudes than short-term voting intentions. In the survey, the respondents could categorize themselves as communists, socialists, social democrats, liberals, nationalists, conservatives, christian democrats, or independents.[8] In most of the countries a majority of the respondents claim to be independent. Only in Slovakia and Albania did a majority affiliate with an ideological family. In these two countries we find a polarized dichotomy: socialists on the one side, and Christian democrats in the case of Albania and nationalists in the case of Slovakia on the other side. In East Germany and Bulgaria, a considerable number of respondents chose a camp from the political "right." In the other countries a consolidated "left" political spectrum is not met by a liberal/conservative/ Christian democratic camp.

In eight countries those belonging to the communist camp are not as strongly in favor of joining the EU as supporters of the liberal or conservative camp or the independents. However, the data alone do not yet suffice to confirm the assumption that belonging to a leftist camp automatically coincides with skepticism about the EU. Some of the communist parties reformed themselves and declare their belief in the Western path, others declare their belief in socialism or communism. Obviously there is no common denominator for supporters of the postcommunist parties concerning an EU membership of their country. It seems as if parties from a certain camp follow a national tradition, and as if voting for a communist party is not a symbol of Euroskepticism per se. One explanation might be that in the same way as the communist regimes varied before 1990, so the development of the communist parties also differed within the national party systems since then.[9]

Values and Support for Membership in the EU

If the system change in Central, Southeast, and Eastern Europe was a declaration of belief in the Western political and economic model, we should find a great deal of support for the "Western path." However, there is evidence that a considerable number of the respondents in postcommunist Europe have not chosen the Western model unreservedly. While the indicator about West integration did not ask respondents to explain the specific meaning of Western European principles, the responses reveal a degree of national independence. For instance, in Poland, Slovakia, Romania, and Russia, between 37.4 and 56.3 percent of the respondents would prefer to develop a national path, without learning from the Western principles. However, in all countries but Russia, the majority prefers to combine Western principles with national characteristics or to follow the Western model unreservedly. Russia is again the exceptional case. In Russia, only 10 percent are prepared to follow the Western way and 33.3 percent want to combine Western principles with national characteristics. These data illustrate again how special the Russian view on Europe is when compared with attitudes in other postcommunist countries (see also chapter 11 by Whitefield, this volume). A comparison with the ethnic Russians in Estonia makes it clear that these attitudes might be more a cultural trait than an effect of political institutions. While a majority of the ethnic Russians in Estonia also prefers to follow a national way, the ethnic Estonians want to follow a Western path. However, the pattern of attitudes toward a membership in the EU is similar to that in Russia, Estonia, and other postcommunist countries. Those who favor adopting Western principles also support joining the EU. In contrast, a preference for a national path coincides with less enthusiasm for the EU in all the countries. These descriptive patterns thus suggest that publics have some reservations to adopt fully the Western-based model.

One reason for this may be that the concept of the "West" is a synonym for certain values—a capitalist economy, a social welfare system, and a competitive pluralist polity. If this were the case, then we would expect to find a link between value orientations and support for the EU political system since the EU is usually seen as an expression of these values. Indeed, the bivariate relationships support this hypothesis (data not shown). EU membership is supported if people think that the principles of the market economy are always good, and also if people think the market economy ensures individual benefits. Those who agree with the statement that a market economy allows everyone to make the best of one's opportunities are more in favor of EU membership than those who have a more skeptical view on the market economy. But while most respondents would agree that a market economy affords people freedom of choice and individual benefits, they are not convinced that the principle of a market economy is always good. Only in Albania would a majority of the respondents agree with this statement, whereas the majority in Hungary, Slovakia, and Russia disagrees with it. Even in the Czech Republic, where we usually find a high degree of market support (Večerník and Matějů 1999), one-third of the respondents reject the idea that a market economy is always good.

In part, these patterns reflect the communist legacy. Communist regimes had strongly claimed social equality as an ideal of all their government policy. The ultimate goal of these regimes was to minimize social inequality (of outcome) and to allow governments to determine economic processes. This purpose contradicts the principles of a market economy, where the market forces should be given room to work and the state should only interfere in order to correct outcomes that are unacceptable for a society. Consequently, the more someone favors an active role of the government, the less support there will be for EU membership in all the 10 countries and East Germany (see also chapter 1, this volume).

The bivariate relationships provide initial support for these expectations. Those who are in favor of taking over the Western principles entirely are also particularly in favor of joining the EU; those who object to adopting them are also more prone to oppose the EU. Further, EU membership is supported by individuals who believe that the principles of the market economy are always good and by individuals who think that the market economy ensures individual benefits. In contrast, those with more skeptical views about the market economy are also more critical of the EU. Finally, with a few exceptions, we find that those who agree completely with the democratic principles are also significantly more in favor of joining the EU, and those who prefer socialist principles[10] are significantly less in favor of EU membership. In Estonia, East Germany, Russia, and Slovenia, those preferring socialist principles are not less in favor of joining the EU than those who reject socialist principles or remain fairly neutral about them.

These patterns suggest that the EU appears as an agent of modernization of Western traditions and customs that clash with the preexisting values among postcommunist publics. Due to the system change, the people in Central, Southeast, and Eastern Europe have experienced two antagonistic political regimes—the former socialist regimes, on the one hand, where the communist parties played a central role and controlled the political sphere as well as all social and economic activities; the competitive democratic regimes, on the other hand, where political parties compete to form the government and people are given the political choice. At the same time, welfare benefits were cut down and there was a stronger competition in the labor market.[11]

A third set of predictors focuses on economic factors. Applying rational choice arguments, support for joining the EU should mainly be based on a cost–benefit calculation of the individual situation and the prospect of the country in general. The basis of such a calculation is the specific situation in postcommunist Europe 10 years after the regime change and the ongoing processes of consolidating a competitive democracy and market economy. We noted earlier that the economic situation has the expected effect: people who are better off in terms of income and human capital support EU membership more strongly than people who lack these qualities. Consequently, we include indicators that measure the satisfaction with the way democracy is developing, judge the economic situation of the household and of the country, and the social status of the family as winners or losers of the regime change.

The bivariate evidence initially supports the utilitarian argument. In almost all countries, we find that those who are rather or very satisfied with the political development are more in favor of joining the EU than those who are rather or very dissatisfied. The exceptions to this general pattern are Albania and Slovenia where we find no significant differences between satisfied and dissatisfied citizens. In turn, general economic evaluations influence citizens' degree of support for the EU: in all the 10 countries, people who are fairly or very satisfied with the general economic situation are more likely to be in favor of joining the EU than those who are fairly or very dissatisfied. It is worth noting that the proportion of people who are economically very satisfied is very small. Only 0.5 percent of all respondents in postcommunist Europe consider the general economic situation to be very good and 25.6 percent consider it to be good. This distribution applies roughly to all countries.

Those who assess the economic situation of the household as fairly or very good support EU membership more strongly than those who perceive their economic situation as fairly or very bad. The difference compared with the perception of the general situation is that the economic situation of the household is generally perceived to be much more positive. Even though only 2.5 percent perceive their economic situation as very good, 47.6 percent have a fairly good impression of their economic situation. It is quite typical that we find this discrepancy. Obviously, negative media coverage of the general situation, social pressure, personal pride, or the "real" situation lead people to judge their personal situation to be better than the general state of the country.

Another indicator of "winners and losers of transformation" also hints at the relevance of rational calculations for attitudes toward the EU. People were asked where on the social ladder they would place their families in the 1980s, early 1990s, and the present. It is interesting to note that in the year 2000, only in Albania (64 percent) and the Czech Republic did the majority of the respondents (38 percent) note an improvement in their social status. Despite the functioning welfare system and financial transfers from West to East Germany, even in East Germany only 27 percent believe that their social status had improved. In all other countries, about half of the respondents noticed a decline in their social status through the system change. Importantly, in all countries, people whose social status has improved since the 1980s are more in favor of joining the EU. As it was theoretically assumed, beneficial experiences are positively correlated with attitudes toward the EU. These results initially support an argument that stresses the utilitarian foundations of EU support.

Social Structure and Support for EU Membership

Finally, we include several sociostructural variables that may be related to attitudes toward the EU. These characteristics were selected to show differences along the societal cleavages (religion, socioeconomic) as well as features favorable for gaining a better social status (education), and personal characteristics (age). Since these variables have been discussed extensively in other analyses and received fairly little support, we include them but do not expect them to be significant predictors (Rohrschneider and Whitefield 2004a; Tucker, Pacek, and Berinsky 2002).

The Results

We find a clear and systematic impact of the basic values (table 4.2). To put it succinctly, political values are generally more relevant for attitudes toward the EU than the evaluation of the situation or sociodemographic factors. One might speak of a "rational public" in the sense that general orientations are linked with attitudes toward institutions that represent these orientations. In particular, preferences for democratic principles and the aim to take Western Europe as a role model for economic modernization are predictors for attitudes to EU membership in

Table 4.2 Regression of attitudes toward the EU on social structure, economic situation, political cues, and value orientations

	Albania	Bulgaria	Czech Republic	Estonia[a]	East Germany	Hungary	Poland	Romania	Russia	Slovakia	Slovenia	Aggregate
Age	-.08[b]	-.15	—	—	—	—	—	—	—	—	—	-.07
Atheist	—	—	—	—	—	—	—	—	—	—	—	-.07
Unemployed	—	—	—	—	—	—	—	-.09[c]	—	—	—	—
Income[d]	—	.10	—	—	—	—	—	—	—	—	—	.07
Education	—	—	—	—	—	—	—	—	—	—	—	.06
Social status	—	—	—	—	—	—	—	—	-.07[b]	—	—	.03[b]
Democratic development	—	—	—	—	—	—	—	—	—	—	—	.02[b]
Econ. situation household	—	—	-.10[b]	—	—	—	-.12	—	—	—	—	—
Econ. situation country	-.12	—	—	—	—	—	—	—	—	—	-.08[b]	—
Communists[e]	—	.09[b]	.12	—	.14	—	—	—	—	.07[b]	—	-.06[b]
Bourgeois	—	—	.08[b]	—	.09	—	—	—	.06[b]	—	—	.06[b]
Independent	—	—	—	—	—	—	—	—	—	-.07[b]	—	.07[b]
Government and economy	—	.10[b]	—	—	—	—	—	—	—	—	.07[b]	—
Principles of a market economy are always good	—	—	—	—	—	—	—	—	—	—	—	.04
Market ensures individual benefits	—	—	—	—	.11	.13	.15	.11	.10	.08[c]	—	.11
Western Europe as a model	.11	.20	.12	.14	—	.27	.18	.13	.24	.17	.14	.17
Democratic principle	.19	.15	.16	.10	—	.14	.10[c]	.14	.13	.14	—	.12
Socialist principle	.19	-.08[b]	-.08[b]	—	—	—	—	-.09[c]	.10	—	.08[b]	.05
Nondemocratic regime	.08[b]	—	—	—	—	—	.08[b]	—	—	-.11	.08[b]	—
R^2 (in percentage)	20.0	28.3	23.5	11.3	5.2	17.5	17.8	18.4	15.1	16.8	11.7	17.8
ΔR^2 (value orientation in percentage)	15.0	11.4	12.2	7.3	2.0	12.1	8.7	9.2	11.4	11.3	6.6	9.4

Notes: Coefficients shown are standardized beta with $p < 0.001$. The dashes represent mean coefficients that are not significant at the 0.05 level. ΔR^2 denotes variance.
[a] Analysis for ethnic Estonians shown. For ethnic Russians, the results differ in that democratic principles have no significant influence.
[b] Significant at $p < 0.05$.
[c] Significant at $p < 0.01$.
[d] Income is used as proxy for occupational status.
[e] Social democrats reference category.
Source: PCE data; own calculations.

all countries. The regimes, which emerged after the collapse of the Soviet-style regimes, introduced new political rules, allowed more economic initiative, and expected that people would put up with cuts in social welfare. Those who accept the new principles are distinctly more in favor of their country joining the EU. In all countries, preferences, which in this analysis were classified as value orientations, can explain a substantial degree of variance, even when utilitarian attitudes and sociodemographic factors are controlled for (ΔR^2). We interpret this as evidence that support for joining the EU in Central, Southeast, and Eastern Europe is only weakly based on a utilitarian calculus. Instead, the strongest foundations are the ideological principles that individuals adhere to. It is the model of Western Europe that determines support for the EU to a great deal. Even though the media often emphasize that the bargaining processes and expectations of gain and loss predominate EU debates, the main message in this chapter is that support for the EU is based on more than just a calculation of short-term gains and losses. Similar to findings in Western Europe, people in postcommunist Europe link the EU not only with economic aspirations but also with general political and economic expectations.

In contrast, comparison of neither the sociodemographic characteristics nor the perception of the current situation have the same systematic influence. According to this analysis, the EU is not primarily seen in the light of cost–benefit calculations. It seems there is some calculus beyond the rationale of individual benefits. However, belonging to a political camp does not seem to represent certain viewpoints about the EU. We find that the affiliation with a political camp exerts only a very limited influence on attitudes toward the EU. Obviously the EU is either not contested along the lines of political camps, or the camps are not established as institutions for the formulation of political demands and objectives.

Conclusion

In all the accession countries of Central and Eastern Europe, the majority of citizens voted in referenda in favor of joining the European Union. On the eve of the EU enlargement and the formal ratification of a new EU Constitution, it is still an open question why integration into the European Union is favored by the majority. It is only 14 years ago that these countries became independent of the Soviet empire.

Why would the people voluntarily want to comply with the rules set by the EU? One answer could precisely be the experiences under the Soviet empire, the fear that a renewed form of Russian nationalism might threaten the newly gained self-determination. Obviously the "economic community" forms another argument; the hope that EU membership will lead to an economic boost after a time of insecurity and social decline. In this chapter we have addressed a third reason for joining the EU, namely the sense of community based on value orientations. We have shown that EU membership is particularly supported in postcommunist Europe, if Western Europe is regarded as a model for the national development, and the principles of democracy are valued. It is not only an instrumental understanding of the European Union that leads people to support a membership, but also, even if compared with cost–benefit calculations and political positions, value orientations that have the strongest correlation with attitudes toward the EU. Those who have accepted and those who are in favor of the process of modernization as "Westernization" are also strong supporters of the EU. This principle is the common denominator for pronounced support of the EU in the accession countries, the candidate countries, Albania, Russia, and East Germany. However, since about half of respondents in all countries have certain reservations against the EU, we expect the European integration to be an issue of national debate as a symbol for modernization within the foreseeable future.

Appendix: Documentation of Indicators

Support for EU Membership

What do you think about each of the following statements concerned with the European Dimension of Politics?

1. It would be in the interest of our country to follow the path of other (West) European countries.
2. Before we join the European Community/Union, our country should develop more self-confidence.
3. (Country) should join the European Union as a full member as soon as possible.
4. (Country) should adapt to the rules of the European Union, even if it costs jobs in the short run; in the long run, our country will profit from it.

(5-point scale; EU integration constructed as dichotomous index that combines the answers "agree somewhat" or "agree strongly" of the variables 1 and 3.)

Political Cues

Sometimes you meet people who feel close to a certain party or political camp over a longer period of time. Do you feel close to communists, socialists, social democrats, liberals, nationalists, conservatives, Christian democrats (Albania: democrats), or are you independent (i.e., none of these camps), or do you feel close to another party or political camp (which one)?

Follow the Western Path

There are different directions in which our economy can develop. Would you say that our economy should take Western Europe as a model, or should we try to develop our own way of economic development? Take Western Europe fully as a model; Take Western Europe to a certain extent as a model; Mixed model: Western principles and our specific way; More our own way; Develop our own way.

Market Economy Is Always Good

I will read you some attributes, usually connected with a market economy, as we find it today in our country. E: The principles/ideas of a market economy are always good (5-point scale).

Market Economy Ensures Individual Benefits

1. Now I have some questions about income and equality in (country). B: Allowing businessmen to make good profits is the best way to improve everyone's standard of living.
2. I will read you some attributes, usually connected with a market economy, as we find it today in our country. B: In a market economy everybody has got the freedom of choice and can make the best of his chances.

(5-point scales, index standardized between 0 "no individual benefit" and 1 "benefits.")

Equality of Distribution

Additive index formed from the following variables:

1. Now I have some questions about income and equality in (country). E: The fairest way of distributing wealth and income would be to give everyone equal shares.
2. Now I have some questions about income and equality in (country). G: There should be a mechanism in our country that regulates income in a way that no one earns much more than others.

(5-point scales, index standardized between 0 "no equality" and 1 "equality.")

Nationalization of Economy

Additive index formed from the following variables:

1. To what extent do you think each of the following should be run either by private organizations or companies or by the state? A: Banks.
2. To what extent do you think each of the following should be run either by private organizations or companies or by the state? B: Big companies and factories.

(5-point scales, index standardized between 0 "market economy" and 1 "state-run economy.")

Democracy Good Principle

1. Please tell me for each of the following statements, do you agree strongly, agree somewhat, disagree somewhat, or disagree strongly? A: The idea of democracy is always good.

2. Please tell me for each of the following statements, do you agree strongly, agree somewhat, disagree somewhat, or disagree strongly? B: Democracy is appropriate as the general form of government.

(5-point scales, index standardized between 0 "disagree strongly" and 1 "agree strongly.")

Socialism Good Principle

Additive index formed from the following variables:

1. Please tell me for each of the following statements, do you agree strongly, agree somewhat, disagree somewhat, or disagree strongly? C: I was satisfied with the way socialism worked in (country).
2. Please tell me for each of the following statements, do you agree strongly, agree somewhat, disagree somewhat, or disagree strongly? E: Socialism is appropriate as the general form of government.

(5-point scales, index standardized between 0 "disagree strongly" and 1 "agree strongly.")

Social State of Families Today Compared with the 1980s

Index constructed through subtraction of the following variables:

1. Some people think they belong socially to the top of a society, others believe they have a bottom position. Imagine a seven-rung ladder representing the social position of people in various periods. Where would you locate your family on them, if 7 means the highest and 1 means the lowest position? A: Where would you locate your family in the early 1980s?
2. Some people think they belong socially to the top of a society, others believe they have a bottom position. Imagine a seven-rung ladder representing the social position of people in various periods. Where would you locate your family on them, if 7 means the highest and 1 means the lowest position? C: Where would you locate your family now?

(7-point scales, index standardized between −1 "today lowest position/earlier highest social position," 0 "No change between the 1980s and now," and 1 "today highest social position/earlier lowest social position.")

Economic Situation of the Household

If you judge the present situation, do you think the economic situation of your *household* is very good, fairly good, fairly bad, or very bad?

(5-point scale.)

Economic Situation of the Country

If you judge the present situation, do you think the economic situation of the *country on the whole* is very good, fairly good, fairly bad, or very bad?

(5-point scale.)

Satisfaction with Democracy

On the whole, are you very satisfied, fairly satisfied, not very satisfied, or not at all satisfied with the way democracy is developing in your country?

(4-point scale.)

Notes

1. In Article 2 of the EU Constitution, it is stated that the Union is founded on respect for human dignity, freedom, democracy, equality, rule of law, and human rights. These values are proclaimed to be common in a society distinguished by pluralism, tolerance, justice, solidarity, and nondiscrimination (European Union 2004; Fuchs and Klingemann 2002).
2. For a more detailed description of the surveys, see the German Social Science Infrastructure Service, Central and Eastern Eurobarometer: http://www.gesis.org/en/data_service/eurobarometer/ceeb/
3. Since 1993, the CEEB/CCEB have been policy-driven studies aiming at short-lived up-to-date information. The surveys can neither be used to monitor the transformation processes in Central and Eastern Europe nor can they even be used for extensive basic research. Also, the reasons for

people wanting their country to become a member of the EU cannot be analyzed systematically.
4. The Political Culture in Europe (PCE) project was designed to examine the political culture in Central and Eastern Europe. The survey was conducted in autumn 2000. With random sampling (only in Albania and the Czech Republic were quota-sampling used) 1,000 papi-interviews (Russia, 1500) were carried out. The comparability of the questionnaire was checked through translation-retranslation. Also, a cooperation partner in each country tested the applicability of each question in the national context. The survey addressed political, economic, social attitudes, and religious beliefs. For further details, see EU Project within the fifth Framework Programme, "Democratic Values," Detlef Pollack coordinator: http://www.kulsoz.euv-frankfurt-o.de/EU%20Projekt/EUwelcome.html. We would like to thank the German Research Fund (DFG), the VW Foundation, and the EU (Fifth framework) for generously supporting our research.
5. Each item was answered on a 5-point scale. For East Germany the questions were altered in a way that they would address further European integration, that is, give more power to Brussels.
6. The Internet appendix can be found at http://www.indiana.edu/~iupolsci/rrohrsch/PalgraveTables+Figures.pdf
7. See also chapters 10 and 8 by Loveless and Rohrschneider, and Mungiu-Pippidi, respectively, in this volume for an analysis of how NATO affects EU support.
8. Tables of the following analyses can either be obtained directly from the authors or found on the EU Project within the Fifth Framework Programme web site, in the "Publications" section http://www.kulsoz.euv-frankfurt-o.de/EU%20Projekt/EUwelcome.html
9. Even though we only find the number of the admitting communists among the people to be very high in Russia, we have also taken a look at supporters of the parties which evolved from the communist parties that ruled before 1990. In eight countries we find relevant differences between voters of communist successor parties and other voters. In East Germany, Slovenia and Albania these voters are more in favor of joining the EU. In the Czech Republic, Poland, Bulgaria, Romania, and Russia they are more skeptical.
10. We do not claim that socialist ideals are nondemocratic per se. However, due to the recent past, proponents of socialist principles in postcommunist Europe are less in favor of a competitive, pluralistic political regime. East Germany is the only case where attitudes concerning the principles of democracy and the principles of socialism are positively correlated. In this respect, East Germany is a special case. The financial transfers from West to East Germany and the transfer of the West German system of social welfare helped to soften the negative effects of the system change. In our opinion, this is also one reason why illusions about the ancien régime are much easier to maintain. The so-called Ostalgie (east-algia) can be interpreted as one expression of this illusion (Jacobs 2004; Pollack and Jacobs 2002).

11. Today most people are still able to compare the performance of the current regime with that of the past regime from first-hand experiences. Therefore, following a question developed for the New Democracies Barometer (Haerpfer 2002; Mishler and Rose 1997; Rose, Mishler, and Haerpfer 1998), we have analyzed how preferences for a nondemocratic regime relate to attitudes toward the EU. In eight countries we find that people with a preference for a nondemocratic regime are also less in favor of an EU membership of their country. Only in East Germany, Poland, and Slovenia was the correlation not significant.

CHAPTER 5

The Grass is Always Greener . . . : Mass Attitudes toward the European Union in the Czech and Slovak Republics

Petr Kopecký and Joop van Holsteyn

Introduction

In 1989, it seemed to be the wish of all the people in East Central Europe to "return to Europe". People in the Czech and Slovak Republics were no different at that time. Since then European Union membership has been on top of the foreign policy agenda of all successive governments in both countries. Public opinion showed consistent support for EU membership in the two republics. Between 1994 and 1998, under the third Mečiar government, Slovakia experienced difficulties on its path toward EU membership, as the country was temporarily excluded from the accession negotiations on the basis of alleged shortcomings in its democracy. However, after the change of government in 1998, Slovakia caught up again with the other front-runners of accession, and the country was, together with the Czech Republic and eight other countries, invited to join the EU at the Copenhagen summit of December 2002.

The successful completion of entry negotiations required an incredible effort on the part of the political class in both countries. Some 9,000 pieces of legislation, or the *acquis communautaire*, had to be absorbed. The vast amount of legislation represented by the *acquis* had to be reconciled with the generally low institutional capacity of the Czech and Slovak states to transpose them into their legal systems. This required many bold political measures, such as the introduction of fast-track legislative procedures and the establishment of special EU accession–related executive agencies. At the same time, the public had to be convinced throughout the political process that the exigencies of the enlargement process, such as the price hikes and an increase in value added tax (VAT), would pay off after their countries join the affluent club of European democracies.

The Czech and Slovak Republics officially became members of the European Union on May 1, 2004. The political elites had done their job well. However, given the often-existent disparity in attitudes between the elite and the mass level in matters related to the European Union, some of the key questions remain. What did people think of the EU? Which expectations did they have of the EU? The accession referendums in spring 2003 showed that a majority of the Czech and Slovak voters had supported EU membership. However, considering both the turnouts and the sizes of these majorities, less than half of all eligible voters in both countries had actually voted for EU accession. In other words, majorities in favor of the entry to the EU really were only pluralities.

This chapter analyzes and compares the attitudes toward the EU on the mass level in both countries. The first part focuses on the dynamics in development of attitudes toward the EU, which showed a decline in support over time in both countries, especially in the Czech Republic, on the mass level, Czechs have been consistently more skeptical toward (aspects of) the EU than their Slovak counterparts. The second part of the analysis sharpens this picture by focusing on the referendum results. The third part of the chapter analyzes and tries to explain the cross-national differences. We argue that these variations can largely be explained by the different ways in which the European issue is framed in the domestic political debates by political elites, and by a differing combination of expectations and evaluations on the mass level in the Czech Republic and Slovakia of the EU and the national political and economic situation. Finally, in the concluding section, we relate our findings to the cost mobilization model developed by Rohrschneider and Whitefield in this volume.

The Attitudes of Czech and Slovak Republics

As in most existing EU member-states, the debate concerning EU integration and accession in East Central European (ECE) countries has been conducted mainly at the elite level. Correspondingly, many of the existing studies of Euroskepticism, or of the attitudes toward the EU in general, in the region have focused on the elite level (Bátory 2002a; Kopecký and Mudde 2002; Szczerbiak and Taggart 2001). However, since most of the ECE countries committed themselves to conducting referenda on EU membership, gaining public support always mattered greatly for the accession process. Moreover, the public mood concerning prospective EU membership is an important backdrop to the positions of the ECE political parties (see also below), and it is thus not surprising that mass attitudes toward the EU attracted a fair share of academic attention as well (Cichowski 2000; Gabel 1998a). The aim of this section is neither to repeat these findings nor to provide a comprehensive overview of the Czech and Slovak attitudes. Rather, we simply wish to demonstrate that, from a cross-country comparative perspective, Czech and Slovak's attitudes toward the EU have been quite different—Slovak citizens have been consistently much more Euroenthusiastic than their Czech counterparts.

The first indications in this respect are the differences in the willingness of Czechs and Slovak citizens to vote "yes" in the referendum on accession. Questions regarding a hypothetical EU referendum have been asked consistently over the last 15 years by numerous polling agencies in the candidate countries, and the results represent one of the most widely used measures of public attitudes toward the EU prior to the actual accession referenda. Figure 5.1 provides a cross-national picture for the three-year period before the referenda,[1] which clearly underscores the differences between the Czech and Slovak Republics. It can be seen that support was substantially above average in Romania (almost nine of ten), and in Bulgaria, Turkey, Hungary, and Slovakia (two-thirds to three-quarters). On the other hand, people in Estonia, the Czech Republic, and Latvia appeared less in favor (less than one-half from the entire population would vote for membership). A good first picture concerning the differences between the countries can be given if we calculate the average support for the EU over these three years. Out of the 11 countries where an average can be calculated, the top 3 are Romania (with average support for the EU between 2000 and 2003 of 79.2 percent), Bulgaria (67.9 percent), and Turkey (65.9 percent). Slovakia comes fourth with an average support of 65.5 percent. In contrast, the Czech Republic, with an average support of 50.2 percent, is found in the ninth place; only Latvia and Estonia are placed lower (both with average support below 50 percent).

Average values for the period between 2000 and 2003 can, of course, hide important hikes or drops in the support for the EU. Therefore, possibly the most interesting information is shown by the changes in

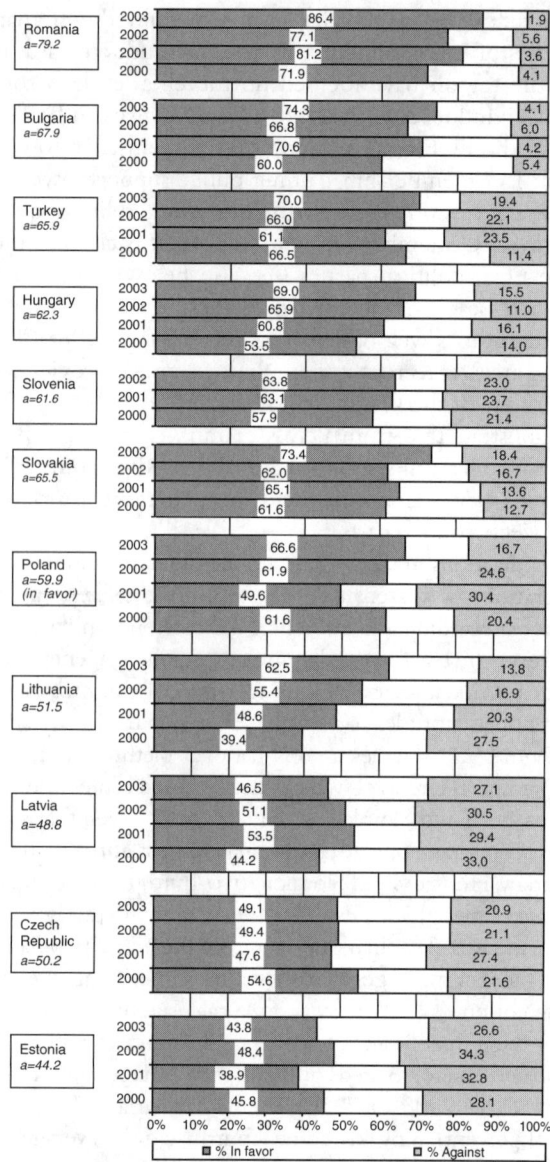

Figure 5.1 Voting in hypothetical referendum on EU accession.
Source: TNS Factum (2003).

support in individual countries. We can see from figure 5.1 that in a majority of the countries, including Slovakia, support for EU membership was higher in 2003 (the year of the referendum) than the year before. In Estonia, Latvia, and the Czech Republic, it was either stable or even lower than in 2002.

The number of opponents to the EU membership is of course as important as the number of supporters. Without any opposition, even a small number of supporters can make the difference. Interestingly, the differences in opinion between the Czech and Slovak Republics come further to the fore when we calculate a ratio of supporters and opponents of EU membership; whereas (in 2003) in Slovakia this ratio was almost 4, in the Czech Republic the value was 2.3.

Moreover, as can be seen from table A7 in the Internet appendix,[2] prior to the referendums, Slovaks were also much more prepared to participate in the plebiscite, whereas the Czechs formed the most reluctant group of voters in comparative ECE perspective.[3] Indeed, in every country the percentage of citizens convinced to participate was higher than 50 percent—only in the Czech Republic was it lower. To be sure, the readiness to participate in the referendum may not necessarily tell the whole story about the support for the EU; it can, for example, also be a sign of opposition against the EU. However, if we combine data from table A7 with those from figure 5.1, this alternative interpretation is rather unlikely; there were more opponents of the EU in the Czech Republic than in Slovakia but, at the same time, also more people without a strong opinion. This suggests that among the Czechs, the European Project was far less alive than among the Slovaks, where not only more people wished to participate in the referendum but also more people were willing to support EU membership.

Another key difference that can be observed relates to the perceptions of the relationship between one's country and the EU. For these purposes, we use data based on slightly different questions. In the Czech Republic, respondents had repeatedly been asked to evaluate current relations between the Czech Republic and the EU. As can be seen from figure A2 in the Internet appendix, the opinions on this matter became more negative as the accession negotiations progressed; less than half of the public evaluated the level of relations as good in general. Moreover, of the group that found these relations good, a large majority was only partly positive. No more than 2 percent of the 2001 respondents thought that the relations were "very good," whereas 39 percent thought that they were "rather good." In addition to these two groups is a large group of 37 percent of the respondents, who thought that the relations were "rather bad" or "very bad." Tellingly, the group that found the relations very bad had increased between 2001 and 1998. Indeed, less than one-fifth of respondents had a negative picture of the relations in 1998, whereas about a half had a positive picture. In 2001, both groups were more or less of the same size.

These figures on the Czech Republic correspond with other surveys. For example, Central European Opinion Research Group (CEORG) polls,[4] comparing the Czech Republic with Hungary and Poland, showed the same picture. These surveys found that those Czechs who thought that it was the EU who benefited from the relations between the EU and the Czech Republic outnumbered those who thought that it was either the Czech Republic benefiting, or both equally. Similarly, other CEORG surveys showed that the Czechs, in comparison with the Poles and Hungarians, were more skeptical when asked about the evaluation of their country's outcome of accession negotiations; almost 40 percent of Czechs thought that it was worse than expected, whereas only about 17 percent of both Poles and Hungarians were of that opinion.[5]

In Slovakia, in contrast, attitudes toward the EU appeared to be much more positive prior to the referendum. While comparable data with the Czech Republic from these polling organizations are unfortunately unavailable, it is very unlikely that Slovak public attitudes would dramatically deviate from the positive picture that was presented above. Indeed, as can be seen, for example, from figure A3 in the Internet appendix, the Slovak public had trusted the EU on quite a consistent basis throughout the entire 1990s (Van de Velde 2003).[6]

Third, on the mass level, Czechs also appear to be more skeptical than Slovaks with respect to the personal expectations related to their country's EU membership. Data in table 5.1 show clearly how different the expectations of benefits and losses are in particular areas of individual life. (Although data for the other candidate countries are available as well, for the sake of brevity, only the data on the Czech Republic and Slovakia are presented here.)[7]

We see that on not a single issue (area of personal and/or family life) are Czechs more positive in their expectations than the Slovaks. This stems from the fact that in the last few years Czechs have started to think more negatively about the possibilities offered to them by the EU. True, Czechs see better opportunities in education and in traveling in 2003, in comparison to 2000 (even though they still remain somewhat somber in comparison to other countries on this point). However, on all the other issues—including important material areas such as the position on the labor market and prices, or psychological aspects such as the feeling of pride in their country—Czechs see on average fewer possibilities for benefits in 2003 than in 2000. Although the data are not

Table 5.1 Expectations of EU opportunities in the Czech Republic and Slovakia

Personal EU opportunities in the field of	Czech Republic	Slovakia
Education		
2000	2.7	2.1
2001	2.6	2.3
2002	2.7	2.1
2003	2.5	2.2
Traveling		
2000	2.2	1.8
2001	2.2	2.0
2002	2.2	1.8
2003	2.2	2.1
Position in the labor market		
2000	3.0	2.5
2001	3.2	2.5
2002	3.2	2.6
2003	3.3	2.4
Environment at your place		
2000	3.1	NA
2001	3.4	3.1
2002	3.1	2.7
2003	3.2	2.6
Standard of living		
2000	3.3	NA
2001	3.5	2.9
2002	3.5	3.2
2003	3.5	2.8
Feeling of pride in country		
2000	3.1	NA
2001	3.3	3.0
2002	3.3	2.8
2003	3.3	2.5
Price level of consumer goods		
2000	3.5	2.9
2001	3.9	3.4
2002	3.8	3.8
2003	3.9	3.4

Note: Average scores; scale from 1 (benefit) to 5 (loss). NA, not available.
Source: TNS Factum (2003).

analyzed on the individual level, they strongly suggest that the decrease in the aggregate support for the EU, together with the feeling that the relations between the EU and the Czech Republic are not getting better, is somehow related to the increasingly skeptical evaluations of the possibilities that the EU might bring to the Czechs in the future.

The 2003 Referenda

The Czech and Slovak governments (i.e., government parties) launched their respective referendum campaigns with opinion polls in their mind. In the Czech Republic, the "yes" campaign, officially run and coordinated by the Foreign Ministry, began in mid-February 2003. Although parts of the campaign were aimed at maximizing turnout, its core focused on addressing fears about the negative impact of accession on citizens' everyday life, which, as could be seen in the previous section, "preoccupied" the minds of Czechs more than their ECE counterparts. The campaign stressed in particular the economic benefits of accession, such as lower unemployment, better quality products, and increased financial subsidies from the EU to the Czech economy and infrastructure. It also tried to convince Czech citizens that their quality of life would improve through better opportunities for travel, study, and business in the enlarged EU (Hanley 2003).

In contrast, the Slovak campaign, run by the Government Office, focused on maximizing turnout (Henderson 2003). All the other messages, like the advantages that membership would bring, were subordinated to the major task of the government, to get the vote out. This was partly caused by different legal requirements concerning the referendum in both countries; though no minimum turnout was required in the Czech Republic, 50 percent participation of all eligible voters was necessary in Slovakia in order for the referendum to be valid. Interestingly, on three of the four previous occasions in which a referendum was held in postcommunist Slovakia, turnout was lower than 50 percent. In addition, opinion polls before the referendum had been showing a comfortable majority in favor of accession. Many politicians therefore feared that voters might prefer to stay home rather than go to the polling stations to vote in a plebiscite of which the result was a fore-gone conclusion.

The contrast in the tone and aim of the two campaigns was also caused by one additional and very important difference between the two countries; the political consensus, or a lack of it, on EU membership. In the ECE context, the Czech Republic has been known not only for its mass level "Euroskepticism," but also for the rather strong "Euroskepticism" on the elite level (Hanley 2002; Kopecký 2004). This showed in the campaign. Although no major political party radically opposed the EU membership, two of the five mainstream parties (the Civic Democratic Party [ODS] and the Communist Party [KSCM]) expressed reservations toward the EU both before and during the campaign. Indeed, the KSCM actually recommended their voters a "moderate no" during the campaign, saying Czech membership of the EU was desirable in a longer term perspective, but untenable under the current enlargement conditions. The ODS recommended their voters a "Yes" vote but stressed that arguments in favor of accession only narrowly outweighed arguments against, and suggesting (in the words of the party's former leader and the current Czech president-Václav Klaus) that the Czech EU membership was "a marriage of convenience rather than a love affair."

The Slovak political scene appeared quite differently. Those parties that resided in the parliament were all openly in favor of the Slovak EU membership. Even Mečiar's Movement for a Democratic Slovakia (HZDS), which previously compromised Slovakia's path to the enlarged Europe, had undergone something of a metamorphosis and became a staunch supporter of the EU. Most importantly, the critique of (certain aspects of) the EU, which had been aired by some Slovak political parties in the past (e.g., by the conservative Christian Democratic Movement [KDH]) was entirely muted in favor of achieving a strategically important "yes" result prior to the referendum. Indeed, even the hard-line Slovak Communist Party (KSS), which made it to the parliament in 2002 for the first time in the postcommunist period and frequently manifested its distaste for the EU, recommended its voters to support EU membership. Therefore, unlike in the Czech Republic, where the EU membership and thus the referendum itself were at least partly contested, the Slovak plebiscite was a decidedly uncontested event. It is therefore also far less surprising that the key aim of their countries' respective official promembership campaigns differed so markedly, especially given that the Slovaks, for example, already knew the results of referenda in neighboring Hungary.

Indeed, it was precisely Hungary that was haunting the "yes" campaigners—as was the case in most countries where a referendum was to be conducted after the Hungarian results became known. As can be seen in table A8 in the Internet appendix, a convincing majority in favor of the accession was secured in Hungary, as predicted by opinion polls. However, turnout fell below the 50 percent mark. If the same had happened in a similarly uncontested referendum in Slovakia, the political elite would have faced an invalid vote, and thus an argument about how to go ahead with the EU accession without valid popular agreement. The situation was the same in Poland where the "no" vote's best chance to win the referendum was actually to stay at home.

In the end, Slovak politicians succeeded in getting both the turnout and the result (see table A8). The almost 94 percent of "yes" votes was the highest endorsement of EU accession from all the 10 candidate countries. The votes cast represented 52 percent of the eligible voters, just enough to proclaim the referendum valid. In contrast to Slovakia, Czech voters proved somewhat more reluctant to endorse the accession, though both the almost 77 percent of "yes" votes and over 55 percent turnout were better than predicted by most opinion polls. Indeed, Czech turnout was only slightly lower than in the general elections in 2002 (58 percent), whereas in Slovakia the 52 percent turnout was much lower than the 70 percent achieved at the parliamentary elections that preceded the referendum by six months. Perhaps uncomfortably for the many pro-European politicians, however, in neither of the two countries did more than half of the eligible voters actually support the EU accession; it was 41.7 percent of the eligible voters in the Czech Republic and 48.2 percent of the eligible voters in Slovakia who voted "yes."

Cross-Country Variations: Toward an Explanation

Czech and Slovak public attitudes toward the EU before the referendum differ in many ways: in contrast to the Slovaks, the Czechs were far less willing to endorse EU membership; they had (slightly) more negative perceptions of the relationship of their country with the EU; and they expected less from EU membership. The actual behavior of voters during the accession referendum went somewhat against these attitudes, in that a comfortable majority endorsed the EU in both countries with a turnout that was even slightly higher in the Czech Republic than in Slovakia. Even so, the Slovaks proved themselves again as far more enthusiastic supporters of the EU.

These findings run contrary to the expectations in some respects. For example, one could argue that citizens in a newly independent nation-state like Slovakia will be far more reluctant to almost immediately give up part of their sovereignty to a supranational body and will therefore be more negative about the EU membership than the citizens of an already established or secure nation-state like, arguably, the Czech Republic. Some authors argue, for example, that deep cultural differences exist between the two populations, with "civic" as opposed to "traditionalists" cultures prevailing in the Czech Republic and Slovakia, respectively, implying that Slovaks are more nationalistic than the Czechs (Carpenter 1997). Similarly, given that Slovaks were far more reluctant to endorse the radical economic reforms in the former Czechoslovakia (often cited as one of the reasons for the split of the federal state), and given that the EU is a project that also further ensures liberalization and extension of economic markets, Slovaks might be expected to be more skeptical than the Czechs toward the EU membership. However, this is not the case.

To be sure, one aspect of mass attitudes toward the EU appears to be rather similar in both countries: the sociodemographic variation in EU support (prior to the referendum). Thus, the young, the students, and the economically better off (entrepreneurs and professionals) were more or less consistently more in favor of their country's accession than older people (pensioners), manual workers, or farmers. In Slovakia, this sociodemographic variation also obtained a distinct geographical pattern, in that voters in three regions of central Slovakia were more or less consistently less in favor of accession than, for example, the voters in the region of Bratislava (Henderson 2001; Van de Velde 2003).

Similarly, and in relation to the above, EU attitudes are correlated with party choice. Broadly speaking, in both countries, the supporters of leftwing parties were less willing to endorse EU membership when compared with the supporters of right-wing parties. Indeed, if one looks at the data on the voting intentions of supporters of different parties, a more or less consistent picture emerges in both countries. In Slovakia, the supporters of HZDS (of former prime minister Mečiar), that is also the less educated, more rural, retired, and manual workers, were less enthusiastic about the EU than the supporters of the Slovak Democratic Coalition (SDK) and later the Slovak Democratic and Christian Union (SDKU), that is, the city dwellers, the young or middle aged, the economically active, and those from the region of the capital Bratislava. In a similar vein, supporters of KSČM and, partly, Czech Social Democratic Party (ČSSD) in the Czech Republic were among the "Euroskeptics," whereas supporters of the ODS, Christian Democratic Union-Czech People's Party (KDU-ČSL), and Freedom Union (US) were, in a majority, in favor of EU membership. Indeed, the ODS has, in this context, always been an oddity; although the party supporters have always been the most enthusiastic supporters of EU membership, the party elite and the party itself have been known as one of the most Euroskeptic formations in ECE (Kopecký 2004; Kopecký and Mudde 2002).

Therefore, it appears that the attitudes of the Czech and Slovak citizens to the EU can largely be explained with the same kind of independent sociodemographic variables. The broader question, therefore, is why such a broadly similar social demography of EU support was translated into stronger (Slovakia) or weaker (Czech Republic) EU support prior to the referendum? At this stage, it is important to note that, from a theoretical and empirical point of view, the attitudes (values) of citizens are probably much more interesting than their actual behavior during the referendum. For the strategic importance of the referendum, together with the campaign that stressed "inevitability" of EU membership even among the opponents and strong critics of the EU, meant that people might have been willing to say "yes" even though their actual attitudes were far from positive. In that sense, the results of the referenda, however important and interesting they may be (in comparative perspective), may offer us little clue as to what the ECE publics actually think about the EU.

What can therefore explain the stronger support for the EU in Slovakia before the referendum? Two things might go some way in explaining these differences. First, as indicated above, there was a very strong elite consensus on EU membership in Slovakia during the referendum campaign. This consensus can largely explain the overwhelming yes vote in Slovakia, since the opposition to the EU membership was, certainly in contrast to the Czech Republic, virtually nonexistent. Most importantly, the consensus about EU membership did not appear in Slovakia just prior to the referendum campaign, but in fact had already emerged in the late 1990s, after the formation of the first Dzurinda government (1998). It was then that the race to catch up with the other front-runners of EU enlargement in ECE began in earnest. It was also then that some more Euroskeptic parties, like the Association of Slovak Workers (ZRS) and (later) the Slovak National Party (SNS), fell into oblivion, whereas others, most notably the HZDS, openly declared their pro-European orientation. In the context of ECE, where partisan loyalties are comparatively weak, it may of course be doubted whether citizens' attitudes to such a distant thing like the EU can be fully conditioned by their party sympathies. However, the strong consensus at the elite level that emerged in Slovakia on EU membership had at least not opened up wide avenues for the formation of alternative attitudes. This stands in contrast to the Czech Republic, where both EU membership and the EU itself were long presented, by at least two major parties, as problematic choices.

Second, the Slovaks had strong feelings about the EU membership as a potential way of improving their own living circumstances. As such, this is not a decisive factor; there were high expectations in other candidate countries as well, although we showed (see e.g., table 5.1) that people in Slovakia expected more benefits from entry to the EU than people in the Czech Republic did. More likely, it is the combination of expectations of the benefits of EU membership and the (negative) evaluation of the national political and economic situation that interact and may very well explain the stronger support in Slovakia. A negative evaluation of the national situation combined with positive expectations of EU membership may have led to support for the EU in Slovakia, whereas in the Czech Republic a more positive evaluation of the national situation and institutions interacts with less positive expectations of the benefits the EU and resulted in less support for entry to the EU. Interestingly, while the economic situation, real (unemployment) or perceived, have deteriorated after the Dzurinda government came to power in 1998, the Czechs experienced their major economic (but also political) dip in the late 1990s, with both the economic situation and political circumstances improving in the run up to the referendum. This makes the relatively low, and in some respects even decreasing level of, support for the EU understandable.

This interpretation is supported by some data from the Eurobarometer that were collected in September–October 2002 in the candidate countries of the EU (European Commission 2002). From an economic perspective, the impression from the other data sources we already presented is confirmed. In Slovakia, 70 percent of the people believed that being a member of the European Union would help the national economy. In the Czech Republic, where the economic situation was not as bad as in Slovakia, only 48 percent believed this to be the case. But it is the combination of economic and political factors that do the trick, and it can be shown that in Slovakia, the image of the national political situation is rather bleak when compared with the image of the EU. In Slovakia, for instance, only 24 percent said that they tended to trust their national government, compared with 35 percent in the Czech Republic. That people in Slovakia were not only critical toward the government of that moment but also in general more skeptical about the way democracy functioned is clear from responses to a question about how satisfied or unsatisfied they were with the way democracy was working. No less than 77 percent said that they were not very satisfied or not satisfied at all and only 19 percent said that they were fairly or very satisfied. In the Czech Republic, responses to this question were much more balanced; 49 percent were not very or not at all satisfied and 42 percent were fairly or very satisfied.

In Slovakia, the rather high level of discontent and distrust on the national level is combined with relatively high trust in the European Union; the EU ranked third among a list of 10 listed institutions in Slovakia and 62 percent said that they tended to trust the European

Union; in the Czech Republic, in contrast, the EU ranked fifth and 51 percent trusted the EU. That people in Slovakia had rather high hopes of the EU—we think at least partly because it was seen as a savior of the country—is also clear from the top-of-mind reactions people gave in response to the question "Taking everything into consideration, what will the European Union have brought in ten years' time for the European citizens?" In Slovakia, 57 percent of the reactions were positive and only 21 percent negative; in the Czech Republic, with less need for a European savior, 38 percent of the reactions were positive and 33 percent negative. That the relatively high level of support for the EU in Slovakia may have originated from the comparison of the evaluation of the national and European possibilities for political and economic development can also be derived from the fact that in Slovakia, a majority of 57 percent wanted a more important role of the EU in their daily life in the near future, compared with the minority of 38 percent in the Czech Republic.

Finally, if we compare trust in the European Commission, the institution that comes closest to the government at the national level, we see that in Slovakia 36 percent tended to trust the Commission and this is substantially more than the 24 percent who trusted their own government (see above), whereas in the Czech Republic trust in the European Commission is with 28 percent under the level of trust in the national government (35 percent). This all helps explain why in Slovakia the number of people who thought their country may benefit from the accession to the EU outnumbered the people who do not think so by a ratio of four to one; in the Czech Republic this ratio was only two to one.

Conclusion

The main focus of this chapter has been the variation of attitudes between the Czech and Slovak publics toward the EU before the referendum that sealed EU entry for these two postcommunist countries. Perhaps not surprisingly, we have found that mass attitudes toward the EU in these two countries differ. However, contrary to what one might expect, we found and documented that it was the Czechs rather than Slovaks who appear to be far less enthusiastic supporters of the EU. In contrast to Slovaks, Czechs were far less willing to endorse EU membership prior to the referendum. They had (slightly) more negative perceptions of the relationship of their country with the EU. And they expected less from EU membership. We argued that it is the combination of expectations of the benefits of EU membership and the evaluation of the national political and economic situation that interact and explain this variation in attitudes toward the EU. Indeed, our empirical analysis provides considerable support for the thesis that a negative evaluation of the national situation combined with positive expectations of EU membership may have led to support for the EU in Slovakia, whereas in the Czech Republic, a more positive evaluation of the national situation and institutions interacts with less positive expectations of the benefits of the EU and resulted in less support for entry to the EU.

The data presented in this chapter also lend some support for the cost mobilization model as presented by Rohrschneider and Whitefield in this volume. Although the cost mobilization model is primarily developed to probe into the position of political parties on the issues of European integration, the corresponding hypotheses concerning the effects of integration's proximity on the stances and salience of integration issues are general enough to be applied to the mass attitudes as well. Indeed, though not specifically tested in this chapter, we found considerable support for the hypothesis that broad ideals of integration were more strongly supported in the Czech and Slovak Republics prior to the referendum than the integration instruments. This may partly relate to the fact that, as Rohrschneider and Whitefield argue, the integration instruments (i.e., introduction of the Euro currency) are likely to produce winners and losers and thus give rise to greater polarization in attitudes. It may also reflect the shallowness of attitudes toward the EU in general, in that most citizens simply do not know (or do not want to know) enough about the specific aspects of EU integration. Interestingly, however, we found little support for the hypothesis that with the greater proximity to accession, support for general ideals of integration is likely to be lower. The case in point here is Slovakia where general support for the EU accession had actually increased rather than decreased prior to the referendum. In our opinion, this again shows that attitudes toward the realities of international political and economic integration are highly conditioned by domestic considerations (particularly, in our analysis, perceptions of national political and economic well-being) and the (lack of) party polarization on the same issues.

Notes

The first version of this chapter was presented at the conference on "Public Opinion about the EU in East-Central Europe," Indiana University, Bloomington, April 2–3, 2004. We would like to thank participants of this conference, in particular Edeltraud Roller, for their helpful comments. Additional thanks go to Jan Herzmann and Olga Gyárfášová for their help with the data, and to Cas Mudde for his comments.

1. The question was: If you would take part in the referendum on [local country's] EU membership, would you vote for or against? The answer categories were for, against, or don't know. Note that in Slovenia and Hungary, the survey was conducted after the referendum was held in that country. This is why in Slovenia it did not contain the question on referendum voting in 2003; in Hungary, the question about voting in a possible new referendum was asked.
2. The Internet appendix can be found at http://www.indiana.edu/~iupolsci/rrohrsch/PalgraveTables+Figures.pdf
3. The question was: This year a referendum on [local country's] EU accession will be held. Will you personally take part in this referendum? Answers: definitely yes, probably yes, probably not, definitely not, don't know.
4. For further details, see the Central European Opinion Research Group website http://www.ceorg-europe.org.
5. See the Central European Opinion Research Group, January 2003: http://www.ceorg-europe.org/research/2003_01.html.
6. See also the third section of this chapter in which we use some Eurobarometer data for the EU candidate countries from fall 2002.
7. The question was: Do you think, in the following areas, you personally and/or your relatives are likely to benefit or lose out if [local country] becomes a member of the EU? The indexes were constructed as a weighted average of a 5-point scale, $1 =$ definitely benefit, $2 =$ rather benefit, $3 =$ don't know, $4 =$ rather lose out, $5 =$ definitely lose out. In table 5.1, only average scores are presented.

CHAPTER 6

Knocking on Europe's Door: Public Opinion on the EU Accession Referendum in Poland

Krzysztof Jasiewicz

Introduction

On December 13, 2002, the 15 states then composing the European Union made a historic decision to expand the Union by including 10 new members, mostly postcommunist countries of East–Central Europe, among them Poland. This decision was ratified by the legislatures of the current member-states and, in a referendum on June 7 and 8, 2003, by the people of Poland. It took effect on May 1, 2004.

Ever since the demise of the Soviet bloc, Poland's membership in the European Union has enjoyed wide support among the Polish public. In the mid-1990s, when polling institutions began to register opinions on this issue, as many as 80 percent of Poles opted in favor of Poland joining the EU, whereas the percentage of opponents recorded was in single digits (see table 6.1). This overwhelming enthusiasm receded somewhat toward the end of the decade, when the idea of "return to Europe" (as the membership in the EU was often labeled by the media and perceived by the public) began its journey from the sphere of collective dreams to the realm of political reality. Still, between May 1999 and June 2002, it stabilized at the level slightly below of 60 percent, though the fraction of Euroskeptics never exceeded the level of 30 percent of the entire adult population.

Table 6.1 Support for Poland's accession to the EU, 1994–2002 (in percentage)

Year	1994	1995	1996	1997	1998	1999	2000	2001	2002
Month	June	May	May	Apr	May	May	May	June	June
In favor	77	72	80	72	66	55	59	54	55
Against	6	9	7	11	19	26	25	29	27
Undecided	17	19	13	18	15	19	19	17	18

Source: Compiled by the author from CBOS research reports.

Among Polish political elites throughout the 1990s, all major parties, from the postcommunist Alliance of Democratic Left (SLD) on the left, to the centrist Freedom Union (UW), to the Electoral Action Solidarity (AWS) on the right, shared a virtual consensus in favor of a quick accession to the European and Atlantic structures. Poland achieved a major goal in this respect in March 1999, when it was accepted as a member of NATO. In the Polish parliament, only one faction, the seven-deputies-strong Catholic organization—Polish Alliance—voted against the ratification of the Washington Treaty. In the October 2000 presidential election, candidates critical of Poland's EU membership did not fare well, collecting together no more than 10 percent of the vote. Yet, in the September 2001 parliamentary election, Euroskeptical forces recorded significant gains. The League of Polish Families (LPR—a grassroots Catholic coalition stemming from the former Polish Alliance), which made its anti-EU stand the focal point of its campaign, won 8 percent of the vote and 38 seats in the Sejm. The Self-Defence (SRP), which emerged in the early 1990s as a radical organization of Polish farmers, won 10 percent of the vote and 53 seats by voicing strong objections to policies of all post-1989 governments and questioning the conditions of Poland's entry to the EU. Several other parties, such as the Polish Peasant Party (PSL), the Labor Union (UP), and a new post-Solidarity organization, Law and Justice (PiS), expressed only conditional support for the integration with the EU. Only two parties, the SLD and the Civic Platform (PD) (another new post-Solidarity organization in opposition to the current government), which between them garnered 265 of the 460 seats in the Sejm, might be considered unequivocally pro-EU. The popularity of Euroskeptical parties was reconfirmed in the October 2002 municipal elections, as well as in the June 2004 election to the European Parliament (for results see below). From an unquestionable objective of Polish foreign policy, Poland's membership in the EU, as well as its specific conditions, has become an object of political debate.

Political Cleavages in Poland: Economic Interests or Values?

The controversy over the nation's future place in Europe reflects fundamental cleavages in Polish politics.[1] As soon as the first free elections were conducted in Poland and elsewhere in East–Central Europe, scholars began to speculate about the prospects for the development of pluralist democracy and competitive party systems across the region. Some authors expected that the party competition space in the early stages of transition to market economy would be defined by two cross-cutting cleavages, between market versus distributive and libertarian/cosmopolitan versus authoritarian/particularist political strategies (Kitschelt 1992, 1995b). Others anticipated that the actual patterns of party competition might be country specific, involving at least three dimensions: socioeconomic, ethnic (in multiethnic states), and valence (like the issue of nation-building in break-away states) (Evans and Whitefield 1993). For Poland, Evans and Whitefield predicted that socioeconomic cleavages should become the main basis for party competition (in the absence of sizeable ethnic minorities or the break-away factor), with specific issue dimensions defined by redistributive, authoritarian, anti-West attitudes vying with promarket, liberal, cosmopolitan ones. Also, native analysts have put the emphasis on multidimensional character of party competition and have pointed out the virtual impossibility of distributing Polish parties and their constituencies along a single continuum (Gebethner 1992; Grabowska 1991; Jasiewicz 1993; Wesołowski 2000; Wiatr 2000).

Despite the many differences among them, all the cited authors seem to agree that party competition and voter identification in post-1989 Poland have been defined by two cross-cutting cleavages. The first, of a socioeconomic nature, represents the discord between supporters of neoliberal free market/free enterprise policies and those in favor of state interventionism in the economy and welfare state-type social policy. The other, labeled in various ways by different authors, reflects a conflict of ideological or even axiological nature. On the most general level, it can be understood as strife between universalistic and particularistic visions of social and political order. In terms of specific attitudes, it manifests itself chiefly as a conflict between confessional and secular approach to politics and policies and is closely related to the contrasting assessments of Poland's communist past and opposing stands on the issue of de-communization. Unlike in Western Europe, in the language of Polish politics, this ideological cleavage, not the socioeconomic one, is defined as the left–right dimension.

The salience of these two cleavages, as well as their cross-cutting configuration in the political spectrum, has been well documented in empirical studies (Jasiewicz 1993; Kitschelt et al. 1999; Markowski and Toka 1993; Żukowski 1994). Yet, conventional wisdom has attributed the swings of electoral mood among the Polish voters almost exclusively to the hardships of economic reforms and the longing for the social safety net of the bygone communist era. This point of view is based on the presumption that societies undergoing a rapid social and economic change bifurcate into the winners and the losers, the haves and the have-nots, causing massive feelings of relative deprivation, which in turn generates political populism. The hardships of transition feed retroactive sentiments—longings for the times of full employment and a reliable, if merely minimal, social safety net. Such attitudes have supposedly accounted for the remarkable comeback of former communists to political prominence across Eastern Europe.

This reasoning hardly defies the common sense and seems at least reasonable. In the literature of the subject, it is probably best expressed by Petr Mateju, Blanka Rehakova, and Geoffrey Evans in their contribution to the volume *The End of Class Politics? Class Voting in Comparative Context*, edited by Evans (1999). They point to four processes that reinforce class interests (and, by implication, class, that is economically based, voting) in postcommunist societies undergoing the transition to market economy:

1. The emergence of class of proprietors and entrepreneurs.
2. The increase in class-consciousness of workers, deprived of the special position given to them by communist ideology and threatened by rationalization of industrial production and employment.
3. Growing economic inequality.
4. The strengthening of materialist (as opposed to postmaterialist) values due to a rapid transition from the economy of shortage to the economy of abundance.

In the authors' view, this analysis applies not only to the Czech Republic but also to other postcommunist polities in Central Europe, including Poland. The authors recognize the initial role of ideological or identity factors, but predict that the outlined processes "create conditions for the strengthening of class-based voting behaviour and the crystallization of the 'traditional' left–right political spectrum" (Mateju,

Rehakova, and Evans 1999, 235). For the Czech Republic, they find strong empirical evidence to support these predictions.

For Poland, a similar point of view has often been expressed by the analysts of elections and voting behavior, both domestic and foreign (Bell 1997; Chan 1995; Gibson and Cielecka 1995; Wnuk-Lipiński 1993). Yet, in many cases, the conclusion that economic or class voting dominates in Poland has been drawn from analytical models based solely on economic variables, without the introduction of any noneconomic (cultural, ideological, or even demographic) controlling variables. Other authors who do include social and cultural variables in their analyses, present, in effect, more balanced descriptions of the complex network of economic, cultural, and ideological considerations behind individual voting preferences (Kitschelt et al. 1999; Powers and Cox 1997; Tworzecki 1996; Szczerbiak 1999; Wade, Lavelle, and Groth 1995). Even Éva Fodor, Eric Hanley, and Iván Szelényi who expect the emergence of class-based voting in Poland and Hungary, point out that in the early elections (before 1995), religiosity, not class, was the best predictor of party preferences (Fodor, Hanley, and Szelényi 1997). Other authors who focus their analyses exclusively on economic voting and completely disregard the role of cultural factors (Duch 2001) agree that for Poland in the 1990s there was no evidence of economic voting. Among scholars based in Poland, Mirosława Grabowska and Tadeusz Szawiel have pointed to the role of ideological (and specifically religious) factors as determinants of voting behavior (Grabowska 1993, 1997; Grabowska and Szawiel 2001; Szawiel 1999).

All in all, it is fair to say that voters' support for either of the two major political camps, the postcommunist SLD and the post-Solidarity AWS (and their respective candidates in presidential races), was, throughout the 1990s, unrelated to voters' policy preferences regarding economic and social issues (unemployment, taxes, privatization, etc.). Instead, it was determined by voters' values or their general political and ideological identity, of which the best available indicator was one's religiosity. Economic considerations seemed to play some role only in the case of support for less popular parties, such as the Polish Peasant Party (PSL) or the Freedom Union (UW).

Yet, as Poland entered a period of economic disturbances in late 1990s (high unemployment, slowdown in economic growth, crisis of public finances, etc.), it is possible that the relative importance of economic versus value factors could have changed. Considerations stemming from economic and social policy failures could have overridden those general political identities as motivations of voting behavior. This tendency, almost completely absent in all elections of the 1990s and hardly visible during the 2000 presidential race (which could have been due to the very nature of presidential elections in a system where the president is in fact not accountable for the state of the economy), surfaced as a significant factor during the September 2001 general election (Jasiewicz 2003b). Its major manifestation was evident in the support given to the Self-Defence by members of Poland's emergent underclass (or those who perceive themselves as the losers in the economic and political transition). There are also other parties that may be associated with specific classes or quasi-classes: the Polish Peasant Party represents farmers (although it should be noted that it lost electoral support in rural areas to both SLD/UP and Self-Defence), the Civic Platform speaks for the emergent middle class (or urban professionals, to be more precise), whereas the Freedom Union, despite its elimination from the Sejm, has not ceased to be the voice of Polish traditional intelligentsia. Still, support for the most powerful, at the time of the 2001 election, actor on Polish political scene, the postcommunist SLD, has been better defined in identity (religiosity) terms than in socioeconomic ones. The same has been true about several post-Solidarity parties: the Electoral Action Solidarity of the Right, Law and Justice, League of Polish Families, and, to a lesser extent, the Civic Platform.

The empirical evidence suggests further certain asymmetry in the intensity with which values determine political behavior on either side of this ideological (or axiological) cleavage. On the one side, there is a well-defined traditional system of values combining Polish nationalism with a strong attachment to Catholic dogmas and a condemnation of communism as a virtual negation of these values. The other side is defined more by rejection of this nationalistic-Catholic syndrome than by any positive factors.

Fundamentalist Catholicism and ethnic nationalism generate rejection of the EU as allegedly based on "materialism," secularism, and "cosmopolitanism," which, once Poland becomes a member, would destroy her national identity and the religiosity of Polish people. Such ideas have been strongly articulated on the waves of Radio Maryja, a nationwide radio network, which reaches out to as many as 4 million regular listeners and enjoys a virtual monopoly on Catholic broadcast in Poland. From the mid-1990s onward, it has become the focal point of anti-European resistance. It has been joined in its campaign by daily newspapers such as *Nasz Dziennik* and *Nasza Polska*. All these media outlets have already proven their political efficiency, as in 2001 they were instrumental in securing seats for the League of Polish Families in the Sejm.

Since Euroskepticism is closely associated in the political elite with a strong attachment to the Catholic faith, one might expect that on the mass public opinion level, religiosity will also be a good of predictor of pro- and anti-European attitudes. Yet, analyses of public opinion polls conducted in the late 1990s and early 2000s suggest that the variance in these attitudes stems rather from structural factors (Jasiewicz 2003a; Jasiewicz 2004; Kolarska-Bobinska 2001; Kosela et al. 2002). Pro-European attitudes have been positively correlated with social status (education, occupation, income) and place of residence, and negatively with age; Euroenthusiasts have dominated almost completely among well-educated young urban professionals, but remained a minority among poorly educated, older peasants. While there has been a positive correlation between religiosity and Euroskepticism, it has never been as strong as correlations with structural factors. It is fair to say that among Euroskeptics, one finds mostly people who perceive themselves as losers in the transition away from communism and who feel vulnerable to the challenges that Poland's entry to the Union might pose for them, their families, and their communities. These groups appear to make up the core constituency of the Self-Defence, which in the 2001 (parliamentary), 2002 (municipal), and 2004 (European parliament, EP) elections was able to attract a following not only among the rural but also among the urban population. Furthermore, political leaders and experts, Polish as well as European, have also pointed out structural issues, and specifically the agricultural sector, as the source of anti-EU attitudes (Karpowicz, Osiecka, and Kojder 2002; Kolarska-Bobinska, Rosner, and Wilkin 2001).

The ideological opponents of Poland's entry to EU, therefore, use arguments of both an axiological and a pragmatic nature. They have focused in particular on the potential for unfair competition between Polish and European producers and merchants, not only in the agricultural sector but also in manufacturing and services. The public at large has demonstrated at least some receptiveness to the ideological Euroskepticism, in particular to the arguments based on economic (purchase of land by foreigners) and political (national sovereignty) nationalism. Furthermore, the anti-EU media (Radio Maryja) enjoy, because of their Catholic identity, relatively easy access to the milieus in which economically and socially motivated Euroskepticism is the strongest. These are, in particular, not only farmers, but also other dwellers of rural areas, and certain pockets of dissatisfied urban population.

Additional complexity to the political situation on the eve of the referendum could have been added by the very dynamics of the negotiations between the Polish government and the EU. The mainstream media, in the months preceding the referendum, tended to focus, for obvious reasons, on the more controversial aspects of the deal made by Polish and European negotiators in Copenhagen. Yet, public opinion polls indicate that the public was, in general, satisfied with the outcome of negotiations. Where there was no satisfaction, it was replaced by indifference rather than outrage. According to a CBOS poll, only 17 percent adult Poles followed the negotiations with great interest, and another 40 percent with some interest, whereas 41 percent admitted no interest at all (CBOS Public Opinion Research Center 2003). The same poll reveals that positive opinions about both the substance of the accession treaty and the actions of Polish negotiators (in particular their commitment to represent vital national interests) significantly increased once the negotiations were completed. The Euroenthusiasm of Polish populace, which first declined (from its peak in the mid-1990s), and then (in the period 1999–2002) stabilized, seemed to regain momentum in the months immediately preceding the referendum. Among all eligible voters, the fraction of those determined to vote "yes" increased from 55 percent in June 2002 to 63 percent in January 2003 (first poll after the Copenhagen summit), declined slightly in late winter and early spring and rebounded to 67 percent on the eve of the referendum (see table A9 in the Internet appendix).[2] The numbers of those intending to vote "no" dwindled from 27 percent (June 2002) to 18 percent (June 2003), with the fraction of undecided remaining stable at 15–18 percent.

The June 2003 EU Accession Referendum

Though opinion polls consistently indicated that supporters of EU accession decidedly outnumbered opponents, the referendum was never considered a mere formality. Controversy (political and/or legal) might arise if the turnout fell below 50 percent of eligible voters. Such a turn of events seemed quite likely in the light of notoriously low levels of voters' participation in referenda and elections. Hence, the government, the pro-EU opposition, and the Euroenthusiastic independents conducted a campaign focusing on securing an adequate turnout in the referendum. On the other hand, accession opponents seemed caught off guard and torn between calling for a boycott of the referendum or calling on people to vote "no." The first option became practically moot, at least for those motivated by religious factors, after June 1, when the Roman Catholic Episcopate of Poland issued a pastoral letter urging believers to participate in the referendum (without, however, any suggestions on how to vote).

The voting took place on June 7 and 8, 2003, in the usual orderly fashion. The officially recorded turnout in the referendum was 58.85 percent of eligible voters, of whom 77.45 percent cast a "yes" and 22.55 percent a "no" vote.

The official data[3] reveal one interesting phenomenon. In the northern and western provinces of Poland, both the turnout and the support for the EU accession were, on the average, higher than in the central, eastern, and southern provinces. This relationship goes against conventional wisdom and expectations based on previous studies. Each of the eight northern and western provinces is, in its entirety or at least in substantial part, composed of land awarded to Poland from Germany after World War II. Previous studies indicate that people who do not want citizens of the EU countries to be able to purchase land in Poland tend to be significantly more Euroskeptical than those who have no such objections (Jasiewicz 2003a, 2004). Furthermore, anti-EU media spread the image of Germans coming back to East Prussia, Pomerania, or Silesia to claim (or simply to buy back) "their" land. For this reason, the Accession Treaty included different transition periods for purchase of land by foreigners. In the north and west, it has been set for seven years, whereas elsewhere in the country for only three.

Regardless of how realistic expectations were of any massive German grab for Polish land, people living in the formerly German territories should have been more concerned about such a possibility and hence more motivated to vote "no" in the referendum. Yet, in reality, the opposite happened. Neither the economic benefits of border trade with Germany (applicable only to counties within a one-hour drive to the border) nor other economic factors can fully account for this phenomenon. This issue will be revisited below.

The issue of Poland's place in the EU is certain to play a most significant role in Polish politics for the years to come. The elections to the European parliament (which took place on June 13, 2004) turned out to be a major test before the parliamentary and presidential elections, both due before the end of 2005. In the EP election, with the turnout at a mere 20.9 percent, the PO emerged as a clear winner (24.1 percent of votes), followed by the LPR (15.9 percent), PiS (12.7 percent), Self-Defence (10.8 percent), the SLD/UP coalition (9.4 percent), UW (7.3 percent), PSL (6.3 percent), and the new Polish Social Democracy (5.3 percent). The outcome of the June 2004 vote (a more detailed analysis of which exceeds the scope of this chapter) and post-referendum opinion polls in 2004 indicate, in addition to the rapid decline in popularity of the ruling SLD/UP coalition, not only the growth of the moderate, strongly pro-EU center (Civic Platform and the Freedom Union), but also the consolidation of the Euroskeptic right (LPR) and left (Self-Defence). Furthermore, the absence of an heir apparent to President Kwaśniewski increases the likelihood of a forthcoming major realignment in Polish politics, in which the EU-related policy issues may play a critical role.

This chapter explores both ideological and structural sources of pro- and anti-European attitudes in Poland. In addition, it places the vote in the referendum in the broader context of voting behavior in Poland by utilizing variables compatible with the Polish General Election Studies (PGSW).

Outline of Analyses

Structural and cultural (ideological) phenomena are often interrelated. Religiosity (at least in its behavioral component) is associated (not only in Poland) with an older age, lower education, residence in rural areas, and gender (women tend to be more religious than men). Public opinion poll reports usually present only bivariate relationships between the views on Poland's entry to the EU and various demographic, social, economic, and ideological variables. However, it is possible—indeed, quite likely—that some observed relationships are, in fact, spurious. People may object to a pro-EU policy not because they are devout Catholics and reject the allegedly overly secularized Europe, but because they live in the countryside and work on a farm and feel threatened by the competition from French or Austrian farmers, or because they feel too old and poorly prepared to cope with the forthcoming changes. The reverse relationship is also conceivable: the old, poorly educated peasants may oppose the EU because of their deep religiosity and a genuine rejection of the libertarian and materialist West.

To find out the real character of these relationships, one must perform multivariate analyses. In addition to variables reflecting demographic and sociooccupational status of respondents (sex, age, education, place of residence, occupation, employment status and sector, income, etc.), and those describing their ideological (religiosity, self-placement on the left–right continuum) and political (party allegiance, voting patterns) preferences, one should also utilize variables reflecting people's views and opinions (in particular those assessing the performance of political institutions and the economy). Structural factors, such as one's social status and individual or group social mobility, seldom have a direct and immediate effect on one's policy preferences. In relation to the postcommunist Poland, it has been observed, for instance, that it is easier to predict one's voting behavior on the basis of a person's *subjective* assessment of the regime change than on the basis of any *objective* individual factors, such as occupation, income, or the actual level of deprivation (Jasiewicz 2003a, 2004; Powers and Cox 1997). One can, therefore, expect that stances on the issue of Poland in the EU may be influenced by the individual's evaluation of the current political and economic situation on the national level, in his own household, and his expectations for the future. Furthermore, attitudes toward the EU may be affected by an assessment of the entire process of the transition away from communism and with a citizen's level of satisfaction with his or her position in the new political, economic, and social order. This assessment is often reflected in individual's attitudes toward political elites, various elements of the democratic political process, and even democracy as such. In the Polish context, the strong showing of Euroskeptic parties (LPR and Self-Defence) in the 2001 parliamentary and 2002 local elections can be interpreted as an antiestablishment or even antisystem vote. To explore these phenomena, variables measuring attitudes toward democracy need also be incorporated.

To address these issues, we use a dataset combining the outcome of two public opinion polls conducted by the CBOS polling center on representative samples of Polish adult population shortly before and shortly after the June 7–8, 2003 referendum.[4] Both polls included a standard set of background variables routinely used by the CBOS, as well as a series of standard questions measuring citizens' assessment of political and economic situation in the country. In addition, in the pre-referendum poll respondents were prompted to disclose their intentions regarding the referendum (whether they intended to vote and how), whereas in the postreferendum poll they were asked about their actual behavior (whether they did vote and how). These variables were treated as mutual equivalents in the merged file and appropriately recoded.[5] When controlled by the time of the survey execution (before or after referendum), these new variables displayed differences below the level of statistical significance. They are used in this chapter as dependent variables and tested against the background of three groups of independent variables: (1) sociodemographic (or structural) ones (sex, age, place of residence, province, education, occupation, sector of employment, and income per capita in the household), (2) variables reflecting respondents' religiosity (participation in religious services), ideology (self-identification on the left–right dimension), and political preferences (party allegiance at the time of the survey and voting behavior in the 2001 general election), and (3) attitudinal variables describing respondents' assessments of economic and political developments in the country. We begin by presenting a brief summary of bivariate relationships between the independent and dependent variables to conclude with an examination of several multivariate models explaining voting behavior in the EU accession referendum.

Summary of Secondary Analyses

Respondents' sex had virtually no impact on their behavior in the referendum. Surprisingly, there is also no relationship between age and the way the respondents voted. However, the oldest respondents were significantly less likely to participate in the referendum than all other age groups.

All the other reported relationships between the demographic variables and voting behavior are significant, at least at the $p \leq .05$ level and, in most cases, at the $p \leq .001$ level. Interestingly, relationships based on ordinal variables (such as education, place of residence, and income) are all nonlinear. In all cases, there is a single category at one end of the scale that significantly deviates from all others: *less than primary* for education, *village* for place of residence, and the highest quartile for income. Similarly, two nominal variables (occupation and sector of employment) both have a single category that emerges as a spectacular outlier—farmers. There are no single outliers in the case of the provinces, and the survey data are congruent with the official referendum results presented above. In the western and northern provinces (i.e., the lands awarded to Poland from Germany at the Potsdam Conference after World War II), the percentage of those voting in favor of Poland's accession to the EU was significantly higher than in the rest of the country.

The nature of these outliers is consistent with expectations based on previous research. The outliers are correlates of a lower socioeconomic status (lower education levels, living in the rural areas, working on a farm). There is only one outlier recorded at the higher end of the socioeconomic continuum: Poles with the highest income differ significantly from the three other income quartiles. To a lesser extent, the same is true of respondents whose occupation has been classified as *professionals and medium- to top-level managers* (or *salariat I*). There is obviously a far-reaching overlap between this category and the top earners: 53 percent of professionals and managers are in the top quartile of income.

The effect of religiosity on voting behavior in the referendum is similar in its nonlinearity to effects of demographic variables such as age, education, or place of residence. One category, those who attend religious services more than once a week, stands out in terms of the frequency of the negative vote (although it is still only 30 percent). This same group also records the lowest turnout, much lower than those going to church once a week but comparable to the turnout among those seldom attending religious services.

The relationship between political ideology and voting behavior is linear, running from the highest support for the EU accession among the left to the lowest among the right. The "centrists" most often reported that they did not—or would not—vote. These results are also reflected—albeit with some corollaries —in the patterns of relationship between support for political parties and the choices made in the referendum. Both indicators of party affiliation—the party vote in the 2001 general election (as reported almost two years later) and the declaration of current party preference—generate almost identical results. Supporters of the fundamentalist Catholic (and self-depicted rightist) League of Polish Families are the most Euroskeptic and this is the only party constituency giving the EU a collective "no" (by a three-to-two margin).

Supporters of Self-Defence are more skeptical than others, but among them a three-to-two margin favors the "yes" vote, with the turnout lower than among followers of any other party. (While the socioeconomic program of Self-Defence places it on the extreme left, the self-identification of its followers mirrors the distribution of leftists, centrists, and rightists in the entire sample.)

Constituencies of all other parties voiced strong support in the referendum for Poland's integration with Europe, ranging from over 70 percent among the followers of the Polish Peasant Party to over 90 percent among supporters of the SLD, PO, and the Freedom Union. The lack of discrepancy between the two party affiliation variables in their impact on the EU accession vote is probably in part due to the deficiencies of human memory (people tend to "forget" that in the past they did vote for a party other than their current first choice), but is still worth noting in the context of the rapidly changing party loyalties on the Polish political scene.

With regard to the performance variables, the overall picture emerging from the analysis is one of a society deeply dissatisfied with its current situation. Its expectations for the coming year are rather pessimistic, although moderately better than the view of the present (as if the present was so bad that it could not get any worse). Furthermore, there is a clear linear association between both the assessment of the current situation and the expectations for the future, and the patterns of behavior in the referendum; the better the assessment and the higher the expectations, the higher the turnout and the more affirmative the votes cast.

Finally, variables dealing with support for democracy and satisfaction with democracy in Poland turn out to be good predictors for voting behavior in the referendum, although in somewhat nuanced ways. The more general "support for democracy" seems to be more strongly associated with the turnout in elections (i.e., those supporting democracy as the best form of government are more likely to vote than those willing to accept other regimes and, in particular, those claiming that the issue is irrelevant for people like them), whereas the more specific "satisfaction with democracy in Poland" is strongly associated with the vote (yes or no) the respondent actually cast in the referendum.

To sum up all bivariate analyses: there are some significant relationships between particular variables (such as education, income, place of residence, or occupation) describing the respondent's socioeconomic status and their voting behavior in the EU referendum. For most of these variables, there was a single category (such as no primary education, farmer, residence in a village, etc.) that stood out as an outlier. For the variables reflecting the individual's worldview (such as religiosity, ideology, or party preference) and opinions on the developments in the country (current, past, and expected in the future), there is a relatively strong—and predictable—impact on the patterns of behavior in the referendum.

Multivariate Analyses

In order to properly assess the role of particular variables in determining the behavior in the EU accession referendum, one must perform multivariate analyses that allow us to examine the impact of a single variable controlling for the effect of all other variables in the model. From among appropriate methods of such analysis, we selected here binary logistic regression. It allows us to determine, for binary variables such as *did vote versus didn't vote* or *voted yes versus voted no*, how belonging to a given category (such as being male as opposed to being female or being a farmer as opposed to being a worker, a manger or an unemployed) changes the likelihood of a given type of behavior (how much more likely or unlikely it is to vote "yes" rather than "no" if one belongs to a given category as opposed to another). As dependent variables for this operation, we selected vote in the EU referendum (yes or no) and being in June 2003 a nonvoter (a binary variable created by recoding the original *behavior in the EU referendum* variable). For the sake of better clarity of tables, we also recoded several independent variables into binary ones.[6] By design, these new variables capture either the outlier categories of the original variables or extreme categories for ordinal variables that showed linear relationships with voting behavior in the referendum. The only exception is the variable reflecting unemployment, which was added due to the many speculations in the Polish press on the possible role of the rising unemployment in generating anti-EU resentments. Further, the variable measuring the political orientation (left–center–right) was included in analyses in its original form. Also, since both variables showing party identification, vote in 2001 and party preference in 2003, have very similar effects on both dependent variables, only the latter was included. Finally, the variable sex was included as well, despite its lack of discriminating power revealed in secondary analyses, to follow the industry standards and routines.

We present here the outcome of eight (of several tested) models of binary logistic regression. We created four explanatory models and applied each of them to each of the two dependent variables. The first model is composed exclusively of demographic and structural variables; in the second religiosity has been added; the third includes variables reflecting one's attitudes toward political, social, and economic reality in Poland; and the final model includes party preferences.

In interpretation of binary logistic analysis, we focus at the relative predictive strength of particular independent variables (Mertler and Vannatta 2001), measured by the odds ratios indicated by the Exp (B) statistic.

We begin with the analysis of the turnout in the referendum, measured here by the nonvoter variable (see table 6.2). In the first model, composed of structural variables, odds ratios are statistically significant (at the .05 level) for education, age, income, and unemployment, but not for place of residence, region of residence, status of being a farmer, or sex. The second model adds religiosity as a statistically significant independent variable. The addition of attitudinal (performance) variables in the third model changes the composition of statistically significant odds ratios: unemployment and religiosity are

Table 6.2 Determinants of participation in the EU referendum (likelihood ratios for nonvoting)

Model	Variables in the equation	Exp (B)	Variables not in the equation
1	Education=primary	2.129	Sex, place of residence,
	Income=high	.450	farmer, province
	Age=over 70	1.627	
	Unemployment	1.413	
2	Education=primary	2.138	Sex, place of residence
	Income=high	.452	farmer, province
	Age=over 70	1.578	
	Unemployment	1.424	
	Religiosity=high	1.404	
3	Political ideology=right	.903	Sex, unemployment,
	Political ideology=center	1.596	religiosity, farmer, place
	Education=primary	1.779	of residence, satisfaction
	Income=high	.584	with democracy,
	Support for democracy=high	.559	religiosity province
	Assessment of the current situation=negative	1.492	
	Expectations for the future=pessimistic	1.342	
	Age=over 70	1.458	
4	Education=primary	1.804	Sex, unemployment,
	Income=high	.571	religiosity, farmer, place
	Political ideology=right	1.612	of residence, satisfaction
	Political ideology=center	.964	with democracy,
	Support for democracy=high	.563	religiosity, province, SRP
	Assessment of the current situation=negative	1.375	03
	LPR 03	.324	
	Expectations for the future=pessimistic	1.375	
	Age=over 70	1.479	

removed from the model, leaving education, income, and age, with the addition of political orientation, assessment of the current situation, expectations for the future, and views on democracy. Finally, the addition of the party identification variable adds to the list variables with statistically significant odds ratios the preference for the League of Polish Families (more likely than supporters of any other party to be nonvoters). All in all, the odds ratios are fairly small in all models and the predictive value of the models presented here is rather limited. Still, these models show that absenteeism from the referendum could have been motivated by either structural factors (low education, low income, older age) or by ideological ones (critical assessment of the current situation, pessimistic outlook for the future, weak commitment to democracy, and political association with the right, in particular with the LPR), or, most likely, by a combination of both types. There is no evidence, however, of any mass-scale ideologically motivated boycott of the referendum.

An application of the identical four-step analysis of the actual vote in the EU referendum (with the focus on explaining the vote rejecting the accession) brought about more discriminating results (see table 6.3). The structural variables composing the first model generated statistically significant (.05 level) odds ratios for being a farmer, being over 70 years old, living in a village (positive correlation with the no vote), as well as having income in the upper quartile and living in one of northern or western provinces (negative correlation with the no vote). Religiosity, added in the second model, made it to the equation (positive correlation with the vote against) and led to the removal of age from the equation, leaving variables farmer, village, income, and residence in north-western provinces. Yet, the third model, which also includes attitudinal variables, changed the composition of statistically significant predictors, removing income, leaving in farmer, village, religiosity, and residence in north-western provinces, and adding, with relatively high odds ratios, political orientation, pessimistic outlook, negative assessment of current situation, low satisfaction with democracy (all positively correlating with the no vote), and strong support for democracy (negative correlation). Finally, the inclusion of party identification variables in the fourth model led to the following changes: The variable farmer was removed from the list of statistically significant odds ratios, leaving as the only structural variables the different reflections of one's place of residence: the rural versus urban dimension (village) and the geographic location (northern and western provinces versus the rest of the country). Religiosity was also removed, but the attitudinal variables stayed in the model, with odds ratios similar to those in the third model. Yet, the odds ratios for the added variables (party identification with the LPR and SRP) by far exceeded anything recorded previously: knowing that a person is a Self-Defence sympathizer increases one's chances to guess how this person voted in the referendum fourfold; for the League of Polish Families supporters, this number jumps to almost 15 times.

All in all, although structural variables are not irrelevant in determining the vote against Poland's accession to the EU, such a decision is

Table 6.3 Determinants of vote choice in the EU referendum (likelihood ratios for vote "no")

Model	Variables in the equation	Exp (B)	Variables not in the equation
1	Place of residence = village	1.914	Sex, unemployment, education
	Income = high	.461	
	Province = northwest	.640	
	Farmer	2.149	
	Age = over 70	1.643	
2	Place of residence = village	1.906	Sex, unemployment, education age
	Religiosity = high	2.432	
	Income = high	.494	
	Province = northwest	.636	
	Farmer	2.119	
3	Political ideology = right	3.178	Sex, age, unemployment, income, education
	Political ideology = center	2.160	
	Place of residence = village	2.642	
	Expectations for the future = pessimist	2.508	
	Satisfaction with democracy = low	2.470	
	Assessment of the current situation = negative	2.053	
	Farmer	2.774	
	Support for democracy = high	.497	
	Province = northwest	.651	
	Religiosity = high	1.924	
4	LPR 03	14.713	Sex, age, unemployment, income, education farmer, religiosity
	Place of residence = village	2.810	
	Expectations for the future = pessimist	2.546	
	SRP 03	3.883	
	Political ideology = right	2.713	
	Political ideology = center	2.015	
	Satisfaction with democracy = low	2.276	
	Assessment of the current situation = negative	2.098	
	Province = northwest	.625	
	Support for democracy = high	.501	

much more strongly associated with one's political orientation and attitudes toward various facets of the state of affairs in the country.

Conclusion

At the beginning of this chapter, we presented two different—although complementary—hypotheses about the causes of Euroskepticism in Poland. One linked anti-EU resentments with structural factors generating "competitive disadvantage" among individuals and groups; the other pointed out the motivational role of ideological factors—beliefs that Poland's membership would harm her national and religious (Catholic) identity. Both hypotheses found some—even if only limited—confirmation in the analysis above, which suggests at least the possibility of a significant shift in patterns of voting behavior in Poland away from a vote based mainly on one's cultural identity (values) toward a vote based more on economic interests.

A full explanation of why for over a decade after the establishment of pluralist democracy in Poland people tend to be guided in their voting preferences both by their worldview (for which religiosity was used as an indicator) and by their economic interests (or class) seems impossible with the use of survey data only. A lack of correlation between Poles' positions in social stratification and their political preferences has been evident for decades, if not centuries, back. Norman Davies, the British historian, used the term "two nations" to describe this phenomenon (Davies 1989, 45). The concept may be strong but it also seems justified. In the times of partitions (from the late eighteenth to the early twentieth century), some noblemen rebelled and were sent to prison, exile, or gallows, whereas others launched bureaucratic, military, or political carriers in Prussian, Austrian, or German structures. (Sometimes, an individual would do both in his lifetime. Romuald Traugutt, a colonel in Russian army, led an unsuccessful anti-Russian uprising in 1863–1864.) Some Polish peasants in those days would denounce noble insurgents to the occupiers; others would volunteer to serve in rebel forces. Similarly, in communist Poland, some intellectuals, workers, and peasants would join the party and remain faithful to it till the bitter end, whereas other intellectuals, workers, and peasants would risk their professional careers and the well-being of their families by joining underground organizations, producing and distributing *samizdat*, or simply refusing to sign an oath of loyalty to the regime. These choices were not only moral, but also political in their nature. Many of the nineteenth- or twentieth-century "collaborators" claimed, often not without merit, that their actions brought the nation greater benefits (for instance, economic development) than the lofty, but doomed from the beginning, deeds of the "rebels" (Jasiewicz 1988).

Polish politics (and, specifically, patterns of voting behavior) of the 1990s seem to have carried this "two nations" pattern into a democratic Poland. The choice of whom to vote was defined much more by the past (pre-1989) credentials of political actors and past experiences of the voters than by present policy issues. The former were well defined and easily understood; the latter were foggy and poorly articulated.

Grabowska and Szawiel compare Poland of the 1990s with Ireland of the 1920s: as the attitudes toward the Anglo-Irish Treaty split Irish society and polity across class lines in half, so the Solidarity versus communists conflict defined Polish politics without much relevance to the current social and economic policy issues (Grabowska and Szawiel 2001). Hence, the relative importance of cultural issues: one's position on the question of abortion was in the 1990 a very good predictor of voting behavior whereas positions on the questions of unemployment, tax policy, privatization, or crime prevention were not.

It is interesting and perhaps paradoxical, therefore, that structural variables (individual's positions in the multidimensional social stratification) emerge as a significant factor—almost as significant as religiosity—in determining voting behavior in the EU accession referendum. As indicated at the beginning of this chapter, since Euroskepticism among the political elite was often articulated in cultural or ideological terms (European secularism versus Polish Catholicism), one could hardly expect that economic or social issues would emerge at the time of the referendum with a strength rivaling that of religiosity. If they did emerge anyway, it might be simply due to the flow of time (let us remember that they first appeared with some significance at the time of the 2001 general election, two years before the referendum). This may confirm the expectations of authors such as Evans, Whitefield, or Szelényi: economic inequalities are growing, the new classes are emerging and fledging, their class (or group) consciousness is solidifying. The old identities still count but people seem more than previously inclined to vote by their pocketbooks.

Yet the very topic of this referendum may be relevant as well. The flow of the time means, above all, the accumulation of personal experiences. The analyses presented here demonstrate that an anti-EU stance is associated not so much with structural factors or religiosity per se, but rather with a perception of "the things going in the wrong direction" for the country and/or the respondent, and of having gone so over the course of the years past since the 1989 regime change. Being an actual loser in the process of transition (we may define such a "loser" as a person whose standards of living declined after 1989 in real or even only relative terms) increases chances of this person objecting to the EU accession. Yet much more important here is one's subjective perception of being a loser. Those who feel that the reforms—political as much as economic—launched after the collapse of the communist system did not bring any improvement in their personal lives and/or for the country (or even brought about a setback) tend to be more skeptical about the EU itself and about Poland becoming a member. They perceive—correctly, it seems—the nation's membership in this rather exclusive club as a logical consequence and completion of the post-1989 changes. Rejecting the changes, they reject the EU; being anxious about the future, they shy away from the unknown and the unexplored that awaits them behind Europe's door.

Appendix

Dependent Variables

In the prereferendum poll, respondents were prompted to disclose their intentions regarding the referendum (whether they intended to vote and how), while in the postreferendum poll, they were asked about their actual behavior (whether they did vote and how). These variables were treated as mutual equivalents in the merged file and recoded to two new variables:

1. behavior in the referendum (with three attributes: did not vote, voted yes, voted no)
2. vote in the referendum (with two attributes, voted yes and voted no and the nonvoters recoded as missing data).

Independent Variables

Since for most of nominal and ordinal variables used in bivariate analyses there was a single category that stood out as an outlier, those variables were recoded into binary ones, creating the following new variables (for each the code "1" means that a given respondent belongs to a given category, the code "0" that he/she does not belong there):

1. age=over 70 (age = 70 and older)
2. place of residence=village (respondent's place of residence in a village, as opposed to a town or a city)
3. education=primary (education = primary or less than primary)
4. farmer (occupation = farmer)
5. unemployment (occupation = unemployed)
6. income=high (income in the highest quartile)

7. religiosity=high (participation in religious services more often than once a week)
8. LPR03 (party preference in 2003 = LPR)
9. SRP03 (party preference in 2003 = Self-Defence).

Another new variable, province=northwest, reflects residence in one of the eight north-western provinces that include, at least in part, territories transferred to Poland from Germany after World War II.

The variable measuring political orientation (left–center–right) was included in analyses in its original form, with left being treated as the residual category.

In the dataset used in these analyses, there are several variables (most of them questions asked routinely by the CBOS in its monthly polls of political issues) that reflect people's opinions on the situation in the country and the expectations for the next year. The entire questionnaire opens with the question, "Generally speaking, is the situation in our country going in the right or the wrong direction?" followed by a question measuring general expectations for the year to come, and a series of questions regarding current political situation, current economic situation, current situation on the job market, current situation in the respondent's workplace, and then expectations for the next year in political life, the economy, the job market, and the respondent's workplace. Further down in the questionnaire, respondents were asked to assess the current standard of living of their family and their expectations for the next year in this respect. Finally, a similar set of two questions, this time aimed specifically at the assessment of material conditions in the respondent's household and their expected dynamics with a year's span, is included among the background questions. With the exception of the first question, all others use a 5-point Likert scale format (either very good—good—neither good nor bad—bad—very bad, or much better—better—no change—worse—much worse). Responses to these questions were converted into two composite variables, one measuring the assessment of the current situation and the other the expectations for the future. This conversion was accomplished by a simple operation of addition of appropriately recoded responses to single questions, and then grouping of the results of this operation into five categories (extremely positive—positive—neutral—negative—extremely negative). In effect, two new variables were created:

1. assessment of the current situation=negative (the lowest quartile in the assessment of current situation)
2. expectations for the future=pessimist (the lowest quartile of the outlook for the next year).

Finally, in the postreferendum poll only, there were two questions reflecting the general assessment of democracy and the way it has been functioning in Poland. Such indicators correlate highly with the evaluation of the entire process of reforms. They were converted to binary variables in the following way:

1. support for democracy=high (respondents, who in the relevant question chose "democracy is preferable to any other regime," as opposed to "in some cases an undemocratic regime is preferable" or "for people like me it is all the same")
2. satisfaction with democracy=low (response definitely not satisfied on a 4-point Likert scale).

All frequency tables, bivariate analyses (as cross-tabulations and/or graphs), and full tables of binary logistic regression are available at request from the author.

Notes

An abbreviated version of this chapter appears in *Problems of Post-Communism* 51(5): 34–44.

1. The following paragraphs recapitulate the discussion of political cleavages in postcommunist Poland presented by this author in other publications (Jasiewicz 1999, 2002, 2003b).
2. The Internet appendix can be found at http://www.indiana.edu/~iupolsci/rrohrsch/PalgraveTables+Figures.pdf
3. The official data are available at the State Electoral Commission of Poland Web site: http://referendum.pkw.gov.pl/sww/kraj/indexA.html
4. The prereferendum poll was executed from May 29 to June 1, 2003, on a sample of 1260 individuals. I was able to secure access to this data set through the Institute for Political Studies of the Polish Academy of Sciences. The post-referendum survey took place from July 4 to July 7, 2003, on a sample of 952 individuals. I was able to purchase this data set from the CBOS thanks to a grant awarded to me by the National Council for Eurasian and East European Research. The total number of cases in the merged file is 2212 (1260 + 952).
5. For details see appendix in this chapter.
6. For details see appendix in this chapter.

CHAPTER 7

Determinants of Support for EU-Membership in Hungary

Attila Fölsz and Gábor Tóka

Introduction

This chapter examines public support for the EU in Hungary between 1991 and 2003. Our argument is that support for EU membership is likely to have multiple roots given the complexity of the EU and citizens' limited information about it. Chief among them are individuals' preference for characteristics associated with the Union and its individual member-states to trust in political leaders pursuing integration. We further postulate that popular opinions about complex and multifaceted attitude objects like the European Union are strongly assisted by information shortcuts provided by media coverage, partisanship, ideology, and retrospective as well as prospective performance evaluations.

This chapter develops these themes. We start our exposition with general hypotheses along these lines. Then, where possible, we confront some aspects of these propositions with the available data about levels of EU support over time.

Possible Sources of Support

Clearly, the EU is a remote, complex, and rather abstract phenomenon. Hence, as Rohrschneider and Whitefield suggest in the introduction, popular opinion about it may be strongly shaped by the cues and endorsements issued by political parties as well as the media coverage of the accession process and EU affairs in general (hypothesis 1). Of particular noteworthiness is the fact that all major Hungarian political parties, despite otherwise deep ideological conflicts dividing them partly along nationalist versus cosmopolitan lines, supported their country's EU membership throughout the entire period from 1990 to 2003. We would expect that this elite consensus continued to mobilize popular support for EU membership.

Yet other bases of evaluation are also readily available for citizens: after all, EU membership has been associated in the public mind with a wide variety of—more or less likely—consequences that many would come across in their everyday life (see table A10 in the Internet appendix).[1] On the eve of Hungary's referendum on EU membership, some even expected that population decline would stop after accession. A larger proportion thought that social spending would be curtailed and there would be more horror and porn movies around; an apparent plurality thought that regional inequalities would increase, that people would pay less attention to each other, and that national assets would come to be owned by foreigners. An absolute majority apparently expected the accession to bring about greater social inequalities and higher prices alongside such attractive things as higher living standards, better infrastructure, a greater international prestige and influence for Hungary and its culture, more study and work opportunities abroad, as well as a greater choice of consumer goods and medication (see table A10).

Surely many expectations concerned things that can in almost no way be directly influenced by EU membership—for example, health services, Internet access, social expenditure, or the number of suicides and alcoholics. Clearly, the Hungarian public was not particularly knowledgeable about the actual reach of community jurisdiction inside the EU. But they had a powerful—although in some respects misleading—cue that handily substituted knowledge of details about the EU. By and large, table A10 suggests that most Hungarians expected that EU membership would bring their country closer to the stereotypical image that they had about West European countries. Note that this was not merely an instance of wishful thinking, since—apparently because of the same cue—many Hungarians expected the appearance of greater inequalities, more crime, more porn, and more drug addicts from EU membership. These features were, of course, part of the conventional, communist era negative stereotypes of the West, and were rather unlikely to be further promoted by EU membership in a country as far from the stereotypical image of communist country—poor and puritan, with the virtual absence of drugs, porn, and inequalities—as Hungary already was by 2003.

Hence the public expectations revealed in table A10 clearly witness the strong reliance on stereotypical images of the West in judging the consequences of EU membership. We are tempted to believe that this may be crucial for understanding popular attitudes. The myriads of vivid, credible, and widely available impressions suggesting to Hungarians that the West and North European countries have a better performing economic system, public administration, political democracy, legal system (and so forth) than their own country make it easily understandable why European integration seemed, by and large, desirable to them.

At the same time, table A10 also suggests that at least some Hungarians recognized that EU accession was not to promote all the features associated with Western Europe equally, that is, that the EU has more to do with the promotion of market economy (cf. consumer choice, foreign ownership, income inequalities, and living standards) than with generous social benefits. Hence, public opinion on the EU may have had a rather distinct ideological—or, to put it less pompously, policy—basis too, even though most prior analyses focus on instrumental factors (Cichowski 2000; Tverdova and Anderson 2004). For instance, a recent study of public opinion about integration and foreign ownership found that ideological norms are the strongest predictor of integration in 13 postcommunist nations (Rohrschneider and Whitefield 2004a). Along these lines, we expect that opposition to a market economy may have led to disagreement with European integration, and promarket attitudes are expected to be associated with stronger support for accession (hypothesis 2).

Converse's theory of attitude formation submits, however, that most citizens are unlikely to have policy preferences on rather complex and technical issues like European integration (Converse 1964). At least some people will develop political allegiances on the basis of perceived group benefits instead. For instance, even if people are indifferent or ignorant about the EU, they expect people like them to be affected by it, which may impact their attitudes toward that framework. Indeed, the Hungarian public, too, developed views about likely group differences in benefiting from EU accession (see table A11 in the Internet appendix). By and large, young people, residents of urban areas, more highly qualified occupational groups, politicians, and big business were rather unequivocally expected to benefit, whereas a plurality assumed that small entrepreneurs, the elderly, and people working in agriculture would be unfavorably affected. Consequently, we can expect that support for EU membership varied across social groups in proportion of the expected group benefits (hypothesis 3).

It is apparent in tables A10 and A11 that some expected direct economic and other benefits, whereas others foresaw painful losses from their country's EU membership, irrespective of the implications of accession for the political, social, and economic structures, policies, and processes. To a degree, the expectations regarding outcomes may themselves have been based on beliefs about the merits of the integrated market plus the policies and spending commitments of the EU. But they may also have been affected by backward-looking, performance-based considerations (Gabel 1998b), like experiences cumulated over the entire postcommunist transition process and its impact upon the country and the personal lives of the people. After all, EU accession was often presented as the instrument of much the same thing—that is, economic and cultural opening, building a market-based economy, consolidation of democracy, establishing the rule of law—as the postcommunist transformation as a whole. In Hungary in particular, all post-1989 governments considered it a key item on their agenda, and something thoroughly consistent with the general direction of their policies anyway. Hence we could expect that generalized evaluations of postcommunist conditions and the way the country was heading also impacted the assessment of EU membership (hypothesis 4).

However, it is probably insufficiently appreciated in the literature on support for European integration in Eastern Europe that strikingly different relationships can emerge between the evaluation of the postcommunist transition and the EU accession processes among different countries, individuals, and indeed within the calculating mind of the very same individual too. Some may consider the two transformations as closely related developments, and their opinion about the EU should then be positively impacted by their views about the postcommunist transition in general. Or, quite to the contrary, negative opinions about how things are going in their country may make them regard the EU as a savior from the present misery and mismanagement. We suspect that the first type of inference became increasingly dominant as the impact of the EU on the status quo became more obvious—that is, with the progress of the given country's accession process. Similarly, the emergence and consolidation of EU compatible economic and political institutions in candidate countries and the comprehensive integration of their national economy in the European market must have left less and less room for perceiving the EU as a possible savior from domestic troubles, and give more and more reason to judge the merits of EU membership on the basis of how things develop in the given candidate country. In other words, the direction of the relationship between the evaluations of the domestic political and economic status quo and its immediate prospects on the one hand, and opinions about the EU on the other, may well have changed from negative—or nonexistent—to positive over time (hypothesis 5).

We cannot offer here truly compelling tests of these propositions, since the available historical data are full of discontinuities and were, at any rate, obviously not collected specifically to test our hypotheses. What we can do, however, is to test several key implications of this argument to individual level survey data and to discuss their potential for explaining the shifts that occurred in public support for EU membership in Hungary over time.

Level of Support for EU Membership

Attitudinal support for the European Union and EU membership was always rather high among Hungarians (see table 7.1). Furthermore, the opponents were not only massively outnumbered, but also far less likely to participate in politics than supporters. In the March 2003 poll cited in table 7.1, for instance, opponents were two-and-a-half times more numerous than supporters among those who said that they would surely not vote in the April 12, 2003 referendum on EU membership, but were outnumbered five-and-a-half times among those who were sure that they would vote (data not shown). Taking this into account, it came hardly as a surprise when a month later in the referendum, a whopping 83.7 percent voted yes, on a lackluster turnout of 45.6 percent.

Both the high level of support and the apparent demobilization of opponents are consistent with hypothesis 1, stressing the importance of elite cues. Among the political parties, the administrative, business, and media elite, only some relatively isolated forces—in the early 1990s just the rather small, extra-parliamentary orthodox communist party—offered any overt opposition to accession (Bátory 2001, 2002b). In the referendum campaign itself, only extreme nationalist organizations called for a no vote—and they did so in a poorly coordinated way and with little opportunity to have their voice heard through the mainstream media. The massive dominance of pro accession views in

Table 7.1 Support for Hungary's EU-accession over time

Date	Question wording	Supporters in percentage of valid responses
October 1991	A	96
November 1992	A	95
May 1994	B	89
November 1995	C	81
April 1996	D	82
November 1996	C	75
November 1997	C	86
May 1998	B	83
April 1999	D	89
April 2001	D	83
March 2003	D	79

Note: Table entries are the total number of respondents in favor of accession in percentage of valid responses. On question wording, see the appendix.
Source: Central and Eastern European Barometers No. 2, 3, 6, 7, and 8; May 1994 and May 1998 CEU-Medián postelection surveys; April 1996, April 1999, April 2001, and March 2003 monthly omnibus surveys of the Medián Public Opinion and Market Research Institute. All samples are clustered random samples of the adult population. The data are weighted so as to correct for the impact of nonsampling error on the demographic composition of the sample.

elite discourse may explain the size of the yes-camp in the public at large, as well as the demobilization of the opponents.

However, it could also be the case that elite discourse simply reflected the state of the same real-word events and processes that directly influenced public opinion, too. In this alternative account, the 1996–1999 jump in support, which is so visible in table 7.1, could be explained, for instance, by the changing credibility of the accession process. After all, the much-awaited accession talks were finally started in December 1998, but then progressed slower than expected in Hungary—which could explain the next low tide of support that started in 1999. Alternatively, in line with hypothesis 4 about the impact of performance evaluations on support for EU membership, the 1996–1999 jump in the latter may have reflected the strong economic growth and sharp improvement in the mass public's performance evaluations that started in early 1997 and continued for several years afterward. Thus, further empirical tests of hypothesis 1 are necessary. In order to do so below, we review elite discourse on EU membership in Hungary, and then consider longitudinal survey data regarding its possible impact on mass opinion.

Elite Cues Regarding Accession

In the absence of systematically collected time series data on Hungarian political discourse about accession, we need to rely here on conventional accounts of its overtime development.[2] These accounts stress that in the whole period since the beginning of the postcommunist transformation process, and particularly in its early years, Hungary played a pioneering role in establishing ever-closer ties between Central and Eastern Europe and the EC/EU. As the EC/EU gradually deepened its relations with the region as a whole, higher levels of cooperation were first offered always to a narrower group in which Hungary and Poland were always included, and only then extended to other postcommunist countries as well. Similarly, during the accession negotiations, when the most controversial chapters were on the agenda, the Union often settled the dispute first with Hungary, and the agreed solution then served as a pattern for agreements on the same chapter with other candidate countries.

The Hungarian political elite was always very self-conscious of the country's leadership role on the long road from the collapse of communism to accession, and constantly urged the EU to consider all candidates individually according to their own merits and preparedness. This position received sporadic support from EU leaders as well. As a result, in Hungarian domestic politics accession was regarded as a reaffirmation that Hungary was more advanced than most other former communist countries in creating a functioning modern economic system, somehow more European, more democratic, and so forth. Consequently, opposing integration almost had an unpatriotic air to it.

Although many experts warned that ultimately the EU may have no other choice but to postpone accession till a larger number of East European countries can enter the Union simultaneously, the official Hungarian position—for tactical reasons or otherwise—was always stuck to the illusion of the possibility of fast accession for the most qualified candidates. Thus, it emphasized that each applicant country should advance in the accession process with the appropriate speed; fast-moving countries should not be made to wait for the laggards.

As the accession process unfolded much slower than expected, and the EU did not differentiate too much among the candidates, the Hungarian elite became more and more frustrated and partly critical toward the EU. The unequal treatment of new members on issues like agricultural subsidies or labor mobility just aggravated this. By 2004, when accession finally became a reality, it was judged anything but a success story as far as the timing and the terms of accession were concerned. This was echoed—and maybe to a small extent even anticipated—by the changing tone of media coverage of accession negotiations and the EU in general.

Already from the mid-1990s, when enlargement seemed to be delayed further and further, justifying the most pessimist expectations, the Hungarian media occasionally questioned the basic commitment of the EU concerning enlargement. Once the accession talks started, the media usually presented them as a zero-sum bargaining between two counterparts with opposite interests. Media commentaries lamented about the prospects of a second-class membership, blaming present members for short-sightedness and lack of generosity. The political and media elite was almost unanimously critical of the final financial package about the amount of subsidies for the first three years. In the meantime, the Hungarian media provided significant publicity to unfounded rumors, like those about the possible ban of poppy seed cakes—a traditional Hungarian delicacy—within the EU.

The media coverage obviously concentrated mostly on the conflict-ridden issues, hence striking a more skeptical tone than the politicians themselves. But independent commentaries also turned increasingly critical toward the EU, occasionally questioning the merits of accession per se. From 2000 on, the EU was increasingly portrayed as an overgrown, undemocratic, and overtly bureaucratized institution with non-transparent procedures and constant bickering about the distribution of costs and benefits among the members, in which new members and small countries start with a handicap. Accession became more often presented not so much a good thing in itself, but something that is necessary because staying out would be even worse, bringing about isolation and increasing backwardness for the country. To be sure, most expert analyses remained firmly optimistic about the overall impact of accession, but the dissenting voices became increasingly louder as the accession date approached (Ellison 2004b).

Though it is certainly plausible that elite discourse on EU accession in Hungary contributed to both the generally high level and the gradual erosion of public support over time, there are serious obstacles to ...ing this proposition empirically. The first is the possible colinearity between elite discourse and the real-world events influencing how favorable the likely terms of accession for Hungary seemed to be for both expert observers and the lay public. The second is the absence of any hard data on the development of elite discourse over time. Therefore, in testing hypothesis 1, we consider only the impact of party political discourse on mass opinion. The advantage of this research strategy is that the differences between the rhetoric of different parties regarding the EU, as well as the major turning points in interparty differences, are relatively easy to identify. Thus, by comparing the development of support for EU membership among the supporters of the various parties, we can gauge whether the cues provided by trusted elites may have impacted popular opinion. As a background to this comparison, the following gives an overview of interparty differences regarding support for accession.

In Hungary there has always been a consensus among the main political actors that "joining Europe has no alternative." According to the domestic political jargon, there used to be a "national consensus" on foreign policy in general and over EU accession in particular. At the beginning of the 1990s, only the orthodox communist Workers' Party argued against EU accession, on an anticapitalist ground. This party, however, never gained parliamentary representation and was largely ignored in the public discourse. The major preoccupation of the chief successor of the ancien régime, that is, the reformed Socialist Party (MSZP) was to prove its prodemocratic and pro-Western credentials. Hence it could not stop outbidding in Euroenthusiasm the five major nonsocialists parties that then dominated the political scene. Among the non-socialist parties, the moderately nationalist right—represented by the Hungarian Democratic Forum (MDF), the Christian Democratic People's Party (KDNP), and the Independent Smallholders' Party (FKGP), that is, the government parties of the 1990–1994 period—was initially as supportive of EU integration as the market liberal Federation of Young Democrats (FIDESZ) and the Alliance of Free Democrats (SzDSz).

When the radically nationalist Party of Hungarian Justice and Life (MIÉP) emerged in 1993–1994, it was the first on the right to articulate EU criticism. When in 1994–1998 a socialist–liberal coalition was in power, Euroskeptical remarks slowly gained currency in the discourse of the center–right too. This received particularly widespread attention because it demonstrated the more general ideological shift from a liberal party to a conservative formation that took place in FIDESZ-Hungarian Civic Party (MPP) (Tóka 2004).[3]

The bulk of the negotiations about EU accession took place between 1998 and 2002, while Fidesz-MPP—in coalition with smaller center–right formations—was the major governing party. This factor probably slowed down the articulation of ideological divides regarding Europe among the major parties of the left and the right. Nonetheless, by the time of the 2003 referendum, when a socialist–liberal coalition was in power again, the public perceived fairly sizeable differences between the positions

Table 7.2 Positions attributed to the four parliamentary parties regarding EU membership, March 2003

How characteristic do you think it is for . . . [PARTY] that it supports EU membership?	Fidesz-MPP	MDF	MSzP	SzDSz
Not at all supportive	7	2	0	0
A little bit supportive	19	13	2	3
More or less supportive	49	60	19	37
Very supportive	25	26	79	60

Note: Poll by the Medián Public Opinion and Market Research Institute with an $N = 1,200$ clustered random route sample of the adult population, interviewed on March 6–10, 2003. The data are weighted so as to correct for the impact of nonsampling error on the demographic composition of the sample.
Source: Table entries are column percentages that sum up to 100 percent except for rounding errors.

of the four parliamentary parties regarding EU accession.[4] Table 7.2 documents this sizeable gap between the distinctly Euroenthusiastic positions attributed to the socialist MSZP and the liberal SzDSz on the one hand, and the less sanguine but still definitely pro-European stance attributed to the center–right Fidesz-MPP and MDF on the other.

Bozóki and Karácsony (2003) argued that the ebb and flow of party politics can also explain most of a 10 percent drop in support for EU membership in the latter half of 2002—note that this decline is obscured in table 7.1 by the impact of a reversal of short-term changes in early 2003. However, their evidence is not entirely convincing even with respect to the latter half of 2002, as they found nearly as much decline in EU support among the supporters of the left-liberal government parties as among the supporters of Fidesz-MPP, which indeed shifted to a more Euroskeptic tone at the time.

Testing the Elite Cues Hypothesis against the Alternatives

It remains an open question whether real-world developments regarding the terms of accession impacted public opinion more or less directly or through the cues provided by party elites. We try to answer this question through a series of logistic regression analyses of the dependence of EU support (a variable dichotomized to yes–no alternatives) on various cues in 10 different survey datasets collected between 1991 and 2003 (for technical details on these surveys and question wording, see the appendix at the end of this chapter). If elite cues played an important role (as hypothesis 1 predicts), then, at least in the first half of the 1990s, supporters of the major left-, liberal, and right-wing had to be more supportive of EU accession than other citizens. This last referent group consisted partly of the supporters of the less visible parties, but mainly of that roughly 40 percent of all survey respondents in Hungary in the 1990s who had no party preference at all. Over time, the positive effect of left and liberal party allegiance must have remained steady or even increased, whereas center–right party allegiance had to receive an increasingly ambiguous role, probably failing to exercise any positive effect on EU support at the mass level by 2002. Similarly, we would expect that supporters of the extreme parties—that is, the communist Hungarian Workers' Party (MMP) and, after its emergence, the radical nationalist MIÉP—were less likely than others to support accession throughout the whole period. Consequently, we include three dummy variables among the independent variables in our regression analyses: CENTER–RIGHT PARTY PREFERENCE, LEFT OR LIBERAL PARTY PREFERENCE, and EXTREMIST PARTY PREFERENCE.

Even if the above expectations about the statistical effects of these variables are confirmed, it is still possible that elite cues were not important for attitude formation—maybe it was merely that most parties attracted supporters who shared their views in the first place. However, if the above expectations are not confirmed by the data, then it will be hard to believe that party elites had any hold over the swings of public opinion about EU membership.

Hypothesis 2 holds that support for accession had a policy basis. A critical test for this hypothesis is whether attitudes toward the market economy predict EU support. Since the creation of a common market is a—and for some the—fundamental objective of European integration, we would expect that supporters of free market policies were more likely to endorse EU nmembership than opponents of such policies. We would also expect that this effect became stronger over time as citizens—presumably—became more knowledgeable about the meaning of EU accession. Note that in the analysis of the 10 surveys we had to rely on 3 different indicators of promarket attitudes; therefore, the interpretation of changes in the impact of our POLICY OPINION variable will require some attention to these changes in measurement over time. Though these changes limit our ability to examine changes over time, we are still able to determine the relative predictive power of policy opinions within each survey.

Hypothesis 3 posits that expectations about group benefits impact public opinion about EU membership. As table A11 showed, young people, more highly qualified occupational groups, politicians, and big business were rather unequivocally expected to benefit, whereas a plurality assumed that small entrepreneurs, the elderly, and people working in agriculture would be unfavorably affected by accession. Because of the negligible size of some of these groups in the citizen population and limits of data availability, we incorporate in our analyses just five dummy variables referring to the possible impact of expected group benefits. Two of these identify the 18–35 years old cohort and the pensioner-aged among the respondents, respectively; two distinguish between groups in terms of educational qualifications; and a third identifies the tiny group of people living from agriculture.

Hypothesis 4 holds that citizens, seeing EU membership as a logical continuation of postcommunist regime transformation, judge its likely benefits on the basis of how they evaluate the performance of the current regime. Hypothesis 5 submitted, however, that at least at the beginning of the 1990s, EU membership could also be seen by many as a possible savior from current troubles and mismanagement by the national government and political elite. These hypotheses will be tested through a look at the effects of the PERFORMANCE 1 and PERFORMANCE 2 variables in our regression analyses. Each of these two variables is based on a single questionnaire item about generalized evaluations of regime performance, which appeared with identical phrasing in a sufficiently large number of surveys.

Findings

Table 7.3 displays the results of our multivariate analysis regarding the possible dependence of support for accession on the various cues discussed above. All observed effects of policy opinions and performance evaluations are in the expected—given the coding of the variables, positive—direction, and quite a few of them are statistically significant. Hence both hypotheses 3 and 4 receive support from the empirical analysis. In contrast, while table 7.3 does not rule out the possibility of some increase over time in the impact of performance evaluations, it fails to give any explicit support to hypothesis 5. In fact, the finding that evaluations of regime performance had a positive effect on EU support already in 1991–1992 directly contradicts this hypothesis, and hence we reject it.

We notice, however, an upward trend over time in the impact of POLICY OPINION on EU support. Though this increase is statistically not significant, it may deserve some attention as a sign of some learning effects taking place over time. At first sight the seemingly large effects of POLICY OPINION in some of the later datasets may seem to be due to the rather powerful and sophisticated measures of promarket opinions employed in those surveys. However, POLICY OPINION tends to have a larger and more consistently significant effect than performance evaluations even in the Eurobarometer surveys (see the 1991, 1992, November 1995, November 1996, and November 1997 data), where the former was measured through a similarly simple dichotomous item as the one that the PERFORMANCE 1 variable is based on. Similarly, the apparent increase over time in the effect of POLICY OPINION cannot be blamed entirely on improved measurement. The 1994 and 1998 surveys relied on the same measures, yet they show an increase over time—albeit a statistically insignificant one. Exactly the same is the case when we make a comparison across the Eurobarometer datasets only, or across the April 1996, April 2001, or March 2003 datasets.

As table 7.3 shows, party preferences and sociodemographic characteristics rarely registered statistically significant direct effects on support for EU membership in surveys taken over the 1991–2003 period, and even when they did, the effect was not always in the expected direction. Although the young and the highly educated almost always showed above average EU enthusiasm (data on bivariate relationships not shown), the direct effects of age and education tend to be insignificant in our model. Therefore, we conclude that group benefits/losses occurring to relatively large groups—like the young, the old, the poorly or highly educated—were unlikely to influence support for EU membership in the egoistic way presumed by hypothesis 3.[5] The expected losses of the agricultural sector were probably more likely to have such an influence, since, despite the very low number of relevant respondents in the samples, working in agriculture had the expected negative direct effects on EU support for most of the time, and these negative effects were statistically significant in the 1992 and 2001 datasets. However, the evidence is somewhat inconclusive on this point, since the observed effect is positive in three out of the nine datasets.

There is only slightly more support in the findings regarding the impact of cues provided by party elites. As explained above, the test regarding this hypothesis is rather tenuous, since the impact of EU attitudes on party support could also generate the same findings as those anticipated by hypothesis 1. Yet, even such seemingly supportive findings are few and far between, which raises doubts about the validity of

Table 7.3 Dependence of support for EU membership in 10 different surveys on available cues: Sociodemographic group membership, policy and performance evaluations, and party preference

	Nov. 1991	Nov. 1992	May 1994	Nov. 1995	April 1996	Nov. 1996	Nov. 1997	May 1998	April 2001	March 2003
Socio economic characteristics										
18–35 years old	.28	−.02	**.58**	.10	−.12	**.66**	**−.54**	.31	.46	.25
60+ years old	−.44	**−1.05**	−.25	**1.17**	**−.52**	.11	.36	−.18	−.28	.03
Education high	−.13	−.28	−.19	.15	−.38	.19	**2.02**	−.05	−.33	.41
Education low	.98	−.01	−.28	**−.88**	−.17	.42	−.45	−.11	−.09	−.25
Agriculture	—	**−3.56**	.10	−.42	−.78	−.08	6.96	−.54	**−1.13**	.12
Attitudes										
Policy opinion	**1.34**	.48	**1.35**	**1.00**	**4.50**	**1.50**	**1.78**	**1.89**	**5.77**	**4.86**
Performance 1	.59	.41	—	.08	**.89**	.40	.04	—	**.83**	**.94**
Performance 2	.79	.43	.51	**1.86**	—	**1.55**	.40	**1.20**	—	—
Party preference										
Center right	−.56	.92	.13	.09	−.02	−.06	−.47	.21	.36	.22
Liberal & left	.05	−.23	.15	.03	−.04	.50	**.90**	**.67**	.02	**.58**
Extremists	**−2.24**	—	−.60	**−1.46**	**−1.39**	−.36	**−1.61**	−.50	**−.84**	−.23
Model fit and unweighted number of cases in the analysis										
Nagelkerke R^2	.12	.08	.06	.21	.24	.20	.23	.13	.34	.36
Number of cases	843	757	1775	590	967	639	717	1332	1062	1042

Note: Table entries are logistic regression coefficients and the number of cases and model fit for each equation. Constants are not shown. Coefficients significant at the $p < .05$ level are printed in bold.

Source: Central and Eastern European Barometers No. 2, 3, 6, 7, and 8; May 1994 and May 1998 CEU-Medián postelection surveys; April 1996, April 2001, and March 2003 monthly omnibus surveys of the Medián Public Opinion and Market Research Institute. All samples are clustered random samples of the adult population. The data are weighted so as to correct for the impact of nonsampling error on the demographic composition of the sample.

hypothesis 1—as well as about a possible impact of EU support on party preferences.

To begin with, allegiance to an extremist party does show the expected negative direct effect in all the surveys. Although the effect fails to reach conventional significance levels in half the datasets, this could be blamed on the relatively small number of extreme party supporters in the datasets. Given the centrality of an anti-Western, anti-market, and—in the case of MIÉP—radical nationalist stance for the identity of these parties, however, it is quite possible that the causation goes from attitudes toward the EU to party allegiance, rather than the other way round.[6]

Similarly, it is consistent with hypothesis 1 that center–left or liberal party preference shows the expected significant positive effects for most of the time. Yet, if opinion leadership by parties sways public opinion, then it is a bit hard to understand why it took so many years until this effect became, from late 1996 on, consistent in direction from one survey to the other, and statistically significant in strength. Yet, the most serious blow to hypothesis 1 is the consistently insignificant effect of CENTER RIGHT PARTY PREFERENCE on EU support. This cannot be blamed on an unfortunate combination of small sample size with an objectively small—albeit real—causal effect because the sign of the effect shows trendless fluctuation between positive and negative values over time, whereas the parties concerned gradually shifted from a distinctively pro-EU position to a less enthusiastic but still clearly pro-EU stance.[7] Yet, their supporters seemed no more pro-EU than nonaligned citizens—not even in the early 1990s, under the conservative government that signed the Europa Agreement.

Conclusion

We argued above that the Hungarian public judged the possible impact of EU membership largely through the inference that accession will make their country more like a Western European country. Deviations from this rule occurred only where widely available information suggested otherwise, as it probably was the case with respect to the greater emphasis on market integration than developing a common social policy within the EU, or with respect to the low probability that the agricultural producers of new and old member-states may receive the same subsidies.

If so, then the extensive, repeatedly reinforced experiences of the Hungarian public about East–West differences can easily explain the rather high level of support for membership. The ready and extensive availability of beliefs about these differences may also explain why, as our analysis suggested, the public made relatively little use of elite guidance to develop firmly held attitudes on the matter. It is less clear why, as our analysis suggests, expectations about group-specific benefits failed to shape support. It may be that the link between possible benefits and losses, on the one hand, and group membership, on the other, was not seen particularly tight except in the case of fairly small groups like agricultural producers. But it may also be the case that public evaluations of EU membership followed a sociotropic, rather than egocentric logic, which would not be surprising in light of most previous findings regarding the economic determinants of political support (Norpoth 1996).

At the same time, we should think that popular beliefs about East–West differences remained probably fairly stable over the 1991–2003 period. Thus, even if we had data about its variation over time, it would probably not take us very far in explaining the dynamics of public opinion in Hungary. Temporal variation in support for policies associated with the EU, or evaluations of the performance of the current regime—which was, supposedly, taking steps to bring the country closer to the West—may give a better explanation for the sizeable drop of support between 1991 and 1996, and the partial recovery of support afterward (see table 7.1). Indeed, in the 1991–1997 Eurobarometer time series, we find that support for the free market economy declined till 1995, and remained steady from then on, whereas performance evaluations kept turning ever more negative until November 1996, only to become more positive afterward (data not shown). Regarding the 1997–2003 period, our data reveal little parallel between trends in EU support with temporal changes either in performance evaluations or in policy opinions. As our discussion of elite discourse already suggested, the ups and downs of support for accession in this period may be explained by other real-world cues, like information about the progress of the accession negotiations.

Given the limits of the available survey, we cannot go any further than these rather tentative propositions regarding the factors that moved the dynamics of support over time at the aggregate level. However, our individual level analysis of the same data certainly suggest that direct personal evaluation of real-world cues—about East–West differences, regime performance, and policies believed to be promoted by the

EU—were most probably more important determinants of public opinion than the endorsement of membership by the political elite.

Appendix I

The Wording of Questions Used for Table 7.1 and as the Dependent Variables in the Regression Analyses Reported in Table 7.3

A: "If Hungary were to join the European Community in the future, would you feel strongly in favor, somewhat in favor, somewhat opposed, or strongly opposed?" The responses were recoded as 1 = strongly or somewhat in favor, 0 = strongly or somewhat opposed.
B: "Which of the following statements support your own views: (1) Hungary should join the European Union as soon as possible; (2) Hungary should stay out of the European Union?" The responses were recoded as 1 = join, 0 = stay out.
C: "If there were to be a referendum tomorrow on the question of Hungary's membership of the European Union, would you personally vote for or against membership?" The responses were recoded as 1 = for, 0 = against.
D: "If there were a referendum next weekend about whether Hungary should join the European Union, would you vote in favor of entering the EU or against entering the EU?" The responses were recoded as 1 = in favor, 0 = against.

Appendix II

Independent Variables and Their Coding in the Regression Analyses Reported in Table 7.3

18–35 YEARS OLD: All respondents aged 18–35 were coded 1, and everyone else 0.
60+ YEARS OLD: All respondents aged 60 and above were coded 1, and everyone else 0.

EDUCATION HIGH: All respondents with a completed university level education were coded 1, and everyone else 0.

EDUCATION LOW: All respondents with maximum elementary education were coded 1, and everyone else 0.

AGRICULTURE: All respondents currently employed in agriculture—including farmers—were coded 1, and everyone else 0.

POLICY OPINION: This variable measured promarket attitudes and was scaled between 1 (maximal support for market) and 0 (minimal support market).

In the 1991, 1992, 1995, November 1996, and 1997 (i.e., Central and Eastern Eurobarometer) datasets, the respective question was worded as "Do you personally feel that the creation of a free market economy, that is one largely free from state control, is right or wrong?" The responses were recoded for the present analysis as 0 = wrong, 1 = right, 0.5 = do not know, no answer.

In the May 1994 and May 1998 datasets, a multiple-item scale was constructed by summing responses to the following questions: "Nowadays, there is a lot of talk about the fact that foreign companies and citizens buy up Hungarian companies. What do you think would be the right thing, that (A) foreigners should be excluded from buying up Hungarian companies; (B) foreigners would only be able to buy up unprofitable companies; or (C) foreigners would be able to buy up any Hungarian company if they offer the highest price?" (Responses to this item were recoded as A = 0, B or C = 1, no answer or do not know = 0.5.) "Do you agree or disagree that the government should provide work for those who want to work?" (Responses to this item were recoded as 0 = completely agree, 0.33 = rather agree, 0.5 = do not know or no answer, 0.66 = rather disagree, 1 = completely disagree.) "Do you agree or disagree that privatization will help a lot to solve the country's economic problems?" (Responses to this item were recoded as 1 = completely agree, 0.66 = rather agree, 0.5 = do not know or no answer, 0.33 = rather disagree, 0 = completely disagree.) Responses to these items were summed up and divided by three.

In the April 1996, April 2001, and March 2003 datasets, a multiple-item scale was constructed by summing up responses to the following questions (with all responses recoded as 1 = completely support, 0.66 = rather support, 0.5 = do not know or no answer, 0.33 = rather oppose, 0 = completely oppose) and dividing the sum by five: "Would you support or oppose it: (A) if the Hungarian forint would cease to exist in a few years time and a common European currency were introduced in Hungary instead? (B) If any citizen of the member-states of the European Union could freely to take up employment in Hungary? (C) If any citizen of the member-states of the European Union could freely buy real estate and agricultural land in Hungary? (D) If Hungarian companies had to compete on the Hungarian market with high-quality West European products? (E) If Hungarian companies had to comply with strict EU norms regarding food products, which even set a maximum fat content for meat products?"

PERFORMANCE 1: This variable is based on a single item: "In general, do you feel things in Hungary are going in the right or in the wrong direction?" The responses were recoded for the present analysis as 0 = wrong direction, 1 = right direction, 0.5 = do not know, no answer.

PERFORMANCE 2: This variable is based on a single item: "On the whole, are you very satisfied, fairly satisfied, not very satisfied, or not at all satisfied with the way democracy is developing in Hungary?" The responses were recoded for the present analysis as 0 = not at all satisfied, 0.33 = not very satisfied, 0.66 = fairly satisfied, 1 = very satisfied, 0.5 = do not know, no answer.

CENTER-RIGHT PARTY PREFERENCE: The item is based on responses to a question about "Which party would you vote for if there were elections to Parliament next weekend?" Responses mentioning MDF, KDNP, FKGP, and—from 1995 on—Fidesz-MPP were coded as 1, and all other responses as 0.

LEFT OR LIBERAL PARTY PREFERENCE: The item is based on responses to a question about "Which party would you vote for if there were elections to Parliament next weekend?" Responses mentioning Hungarian Socialist Party (MSzP), SZDSZ, and—before 1995—FIDESZ were coded as 1, and all other responses as 0.

EXTREMIST PARTY PREFERENCE: The item is based on responses to a question about "Which party would you vote for if there were elections to Parliament next weekend?" Responses mentioning the MMP or MIÉP were coded as 1, and all other responses as 0.

Notes

1. The Internet appendix can be found at http://www.indiana.edu/~iupolsci/rrohrsch/PalgraveTables+Figures.pdf
2. Some accounts focus on the presentation of the EU and the accession process in the Hungarian media (Hegedüs 2001, 2003; Sükösd 2003; Szilágyi-Gál 2003; Terestyéni 2001), whereas others concern the development of

Hungarian elite and expert opinion over time (Ellison 2004a), or the evolution of party positions on integration (Bátory 2001, 2002b; Bozóki and Karácsony 2003; Kopecký and Mudde 2002; Szczerbiak and Taggart 2001, 2002).

3. Recent works on party-based Euroskepticism in accession countries present controversial findings. Bátory (2001, 2002b) and Szczerbiak and Taggart (2001) label Fidesz, the major center–right party after 1997, as a "national-interest soft Eurosceptic" party, whereas Kopecký and Mudde (2002) label the party "Euro-enthusiast." Indeed, the record of Fidesz-MPP allows such conflicting judgments. It never does anything spectacular that might question its commitment to the EU, but it likes to send ambiguous messages that are not straightforward enough to alienate pro-EU centrist voters, but at the same time hard enough to attract nationalist anti-EU voters. This strategy of the party may be responsible for the significant fall in public support for EU membership in the latter half of 2002, when partisan sentiments went high.

4. The 2003 survey data available to us about party positions only covers these four parties because the far-left MMP never gained parliamentary representation, whereas the far-right MIÉP lost all its seats in 2002.

5. Some may counter that expected group benefits may have influenced support indirectly, through policy and performance evaluations, or in an altruistic way, that is, by old people supporting accession because they thought it will benefit the young. With the data at hand, we cannot test this last possibility. Regarding the possible indirect effects, it is true that when support for accession is regressed merely on the five sociodemographic variables, low education and young age record statistically significant effects of the expected direction—that is, negative for the first and positive for the second—in a little more than half the surveys in question (data not shown). However, the wording of the questions on performance evaluations and policy opinions makes it unlikely that responses to these items were influenced by the expected group benefits of EU accession—especially when they failed to have such a direct effect on support for EU membership itself. Rather, we think that most of the observed indirect effects of education and age on EU support via other attitudes were due to the fact that policy opinions and performance evaluations differed by age and education for reasons unrelated to the expected group benefits of EU accession.

6. The fact that the impact of the EXTREMIST PARTY PREFERENCE variable seems to have declined over time (see table 7.3) also contradicts the notion that the anti-EU discourse of these parties could have instilled like-minded attitudes among their supporters.

7. A careful observer may notice that the effect in question was usually—albeit not always—positive under right-wing governments (i.e., from 1990 till May 1994, and then again from spring 1998 to spring 2002), and negative under the left-liberal governments in 1994–1998 and after summer 2002.

CHAPTER 8

East of Vienna, South of the Drina: Explaining the Constituencies for Europe in Southeastern Europe

Alina Mungiu-Pippidi

Introduction

The links between Southeastern Europe and Western Europe have always been ambiguous. The old border on the River Drina between the Western Roman Empire and the Eastern one was somehow kept alive throughout history; the later frontier between the Ottoman and the Habsburg empires fell about there as well; today, the lucky part of former Yugoslavia fully accepted by Europe lies North and West, while to the South and East the periphery starts. Samuel Huntington (1991) placed there the dividing line between the European civilization and the rest, that is, between Western Christian denomination and the Balkan Orthodox and Muslim. Greek guides may well claim to tourists that Europe's birthplace falls on their island; Balkan inhabitants have always known that Europe starts only west of Vienna. Indeed in old times, travelers from the region going north and west in Europe knew that their journey led "inside."

However, peripheral Southeastern Europe does have a specific European identity, drawing on a twofold tradition: as the heir of the Byzantine Orthodox Church, a tradition it shares to some extent with Russia, and as a postcommunist region, a more recent heritage it shares with Central East Europe.

This chapter discusses the roots of the Balkans' attraction to Europe with a focus on Romania and Bulgaria, the most advanced EU accession countries, drawing on both distant and recent history, comparing them with the rest of the Balkans as well as to Central Europe. The data used for public opinion models comes from a regional survey in Southeastern Europe organized by the Fifth Framework EU program and from the well-known World Values Survey. Recent Eurobarometer data are also quoted.

The Balkans from Periphery of Europe to EU Accession

Regions are often conventional constructs, made to fit scholars or diplomats' needs. According to different criteria, one can build different sets of regions. If we judge by the clusters of public opinion observed by Ronald Inglehart, the postcommunist world—European or non-European—makes roughly just one region (Inglehart 1997). But according to its treatment by the European Union, postcommunist Europe divides into three. The first group is made of the eight new EU members; the second group is made of Russia and most of the successor states of the Soviet Union, whose future is seen as clearly distinct from Europe; and the third group consists of countries that for various reasons missed the first group but cannot, due to their geographical location, belong to the second. This is the gray zone known as "the Balkans" or Southeastern Europe. In 1945, this region included only five countries: Romania, Bulgaria, Yugoslavia, Albania, and Greece (sometimes Turkey was added), with a fair mixture of denominations: Orthodox, Catholic, and Muslim with few protestants. Nowadays, there are 10—the additional being Croatia, Bosnia, and Macedonia, whereas Montenegro and Kosovo are waiting in the wings.

But many dispute their placement in the Balkans. Romania has long claimed to be misplaced as the Balkan Mountains are not even close to its territory and its language is Latin-based. Croatia and Slovenia have also done their best to escape the mark of the region by emphasizing their Habsburg past and their Catholicism. Greece only sees something positive to the label "Balkan," and Bulgaria endures it with stoicism (her national air carrier, Balkan Air, went bankrupt in recent years). In studies of nineteenth- and twentieth-century nationalism and nation-building, the custom has indeed spread to use the term "Balkan" as a negative, albeit poorly defined, attribute, in relation to ethnic diversity, mass violence, and intricate wars. The legitimacy of such definitions has recently come under attack as they clearly reflected less geographical or socio-economic realities and more cultural stereotypes (Todorova 1997; Wolff 1994), but they are still prevailing in journalism and best-selling travel books.

What remains uncertain is whether, East to Trieste or South to the Dniestr, there was ever, or still is, a community of some coherence. As Stevan K. Pavlowitch put it, are the Balkans more than just "a unity imposed by history" (Pavlowitch 1999)? With Slovenia already in the European Union, Romania negotiating—alongside Bulgaria—to join in 2007 and Croatia preparing to start negotiations for its own entry, the region is shrinking fast.

There is, however, a common historical background to Southeastern Europe that is strong enough to justify the ranging of Croatia, Bulgaria, and Romania alongside the rest of the Balkans. This part of postcommunist Europe has been under Ottoman domination. It not only shares a common culture, being mostly Christian Orthodox, but it has also experienced Ottoman religious autonomy and the peaceful existence of numerous denominations. They have shared the common experience of mismatch between ethnicity and statehood. These countries were also considerably poorer than Central European countries and remain so. The percentage of the population depending on agriculture was historically another element of likeness. The World Bank classifies them presently as "lower-middle-income economies," together with Maghreb countries, Central America, China, Russia, and Turkey—but not Central Europe. That means a 2001 GNI per capita[1] at $1,710 USD for Romania and $1,560 for Bulgaria, compared to Slovakia's $3,700, Russian Federation's $1,760, and Yugoslavia's—what is left of it—$940.

In short, countries of the region belong to the same cluster of rural underdeveloped societies. Politically, in modern times they were all monarchies, more or less constitutional, endowed with dynasties of Western origin as yet another sign of Western interventionism (otherwise they would not have even been granted independent statehood at the Berlin Congress in 1878). And their Ottoman and Byzantine legacies are undoubtedly common. The Ottoman Empire not only granted religious autonomy to the Balkan peoples, but it also adopted many of the Byzantine political practices making them its own. This meant that Balkan societies were left behind on two accounts. On the one hand, they followed passively the Ottomans in their stagnation and decline, being both politically and economically subordinated; on the other hand, their church remained suspended to the late Byzantine Empire.

The legacies with a lasting impact for the present Balkans include a pattern of small rural holdings, weak cities and scarce elites on the social side, unchallenged power of the autocratic state over society and church on the political side, and on top of this the successful manipulation of demography in order to preserve ethnic heterogeneity and rivalry. The Ottoman demographic intervention, consisting in displacements of whole populations and playing one group against another, prevented that process of ethnic homogenization that took place in most of Western Europe.

This history strongly grounded in the geopolitics of Southeastern Europe influenced in brutal and subtle ways the current path of Balkan peoples. Therefore, the temptation becomes when explaining individual countries' performance in the region to settle for the *bon mot* of Emil Cioran: "Nous sommes mal placés!" ("We are badly placed") and stress their placement as the key explanation. And indeed local elites indulge frequently in blaming geopolitics for the present state of their societies. Historical facts, such as the resistance of local princes to the Ottoman advance in Europe are turned into full explanatory and justifying myths: the Balkans are backward when compared with Western Europe because they defended Western Europe at the cost of their own Europeanness. Only exceptionally is the opposite argument found, that the Byzantine tradition is *not* European, and its legacy of autocracy and synthesis of powers in the person of the monarch is completely different from the Western story of competition among various powers (Iorga 1929; Todorova 1996).

The perceived pattern of "abandonment by the West" continued after a few decades of independence in the first half of the twentieth century. Regional geopolitics were played out again, more strongly for Romania and Bulgaria, which unlike Yugoslavia or Albania, turned communist solely due to Soviet occupation. From the *antemuralis Christianitatis* to the "betrayal" of Yalta, which still haunts public opinion in Belgrade, Sofia, and Bucharest, the story of Southeastern Europe as told by its inhabitants is one of nostalgia for the brief time when the Balkans were nearly European—between the two world wars—and of longing for a return that they fear will take many years and may never happen. The "return to Europe" of the Central European first group of eight countries, accomplished by 2004, was itself fought over until the last moment and owes quite a debt to the tragic fate of postcommunist Yugoslavia. For a region so predisposed to recognize only gloom and doom as the Balkans, the happy end is far from being already scripted and many ambiguities remain to this day associated with their European status.

However, recent history seems kinder to the Balkans. The invitation of Romania and Bulgaria in 1999 to join the European Union by 2007, extended to Croatia in 2004, and the negotiation and concluding of a range of Stability and Association Pacts (SAP) with countries of the Western Balkans suggests that geographical gloom and doom may be left behind. It may still take some years, but they are literally at the doorstep of Europe, having achieved a status quite unimaginable five years ago. The EU perspective is emerging as "the *Archimedean point* of the entire process of stabilisation and development" for the battered Balkans, providing both the peoples in the region and the international community with a real prospect for a breakthrough that would lead the region away from the divisions and the conflicts of the past and toward Europe (Van Meurs and Yannis 2002). The attraction of Europe is as strong in the Southeast as in Central Europe and the words of Adam Michnik equally apply to the postcommunist Balkans:

> For us, Europeans from behind the Iron Curtain, the idea of Europe was simply a rejection of the Communist project. It symbolized freedom instead of servitude, creativity instead of obedience and fear, colorfulness and pluralism instead of greyness and uniformity, human rights instead of the principle that people are property of the state, open borders and legality instead of barbed wire, the Berlin Wall, and preventive censorship. (Michnik 2001)

As in Central Europe, the first vote against communist parties in free elections signified also and mostly "a return to Europe." The prospect of joining the European Union has, from the very beginning, been the engine of democratization and transformation that has taken place in the region. A "Return to Europe" was what citizens voted for in the first free elections (O'Connor and Kearns 2002). After the fall of Slobodan Milosevic, no significant political leader in the region now dares to be openly anti-European. Former nationalists converted overnight under the pressure of popular enthusiasm for European accession and lure of European funds. Though millions of Balkan inhabitants cross daily the Western border legally or illegally to work in the European Union, technocrats, experts, and selected politicians in Western as well as Southeastern Europe struggle to bring Europe to the battered Balkans. There is no alternative project, neither on the table nor in the social imagination.

A return to Europe, but to what kind of Europe? Ordinary people have some grasp of the current EU due to inexpensive cable TV and the temporary labor migration that exploded in Romania and Bulgaria in recent years. And the European parliament socializes politicians via exchange programs. But intellectuals are the ones left behind. They are slow to understand that Europe is now the EU. In fact they accept the idea only in part, as it was not the Europe they dreamed of "returning to" during the communist years. Michnik spoke on behalf of intellectuals in the whole region when asking, "Is the new, united Europe born from the spirit of philosophy or the spirit of economics? From Aristotle and Plato, or Schroeder (or better Kohl) and Van den Broek? If the new Europe is to be uniquely the product of economy and Brussels' bureaucracy, will its labyrinths created at the beginning of the new century put into practice Kafka's labyrinths from the beginnings of the last century?" (Van Meurs and Yannis, 2002). What gave the EU its strong initial attraction, the identification with Europe, was later revealed as an important source of misunderstanding and reciprocal disillusionment (Rupnik 2003).

The French-speaking elitist Europe that N. Titulescu, G. Seferis, or Ivo Andric so successfully made their own between the two world wars is gone. It subsists only in the memory of Southeast Europeans. A tour from Tirana to Bucharest to meet editors of cultural magazines and research institutes can still be done by speaking French only. But contemporary Europe is less attractive for intellectuals. Although struggling to demonstrate that Aristotle was himself Balkan, in order to turn shame into fame, Balkan intellectuals know little of the present European project and the little they know, they mostly do not like. Too much talk of market and institutions and too little of spiritual affairs, they deem. Paris has persisted as *the* cultural capital in both Sofia and Bucharest, despite the investment of the Wissenschaft Kolleg from Berlin in local advanced studies institutes. Vienna, London, and Berlin come second to Paris, while the youngest and the most pragmatic skip Europe altogether by crossing the ocean. Though ordinary Bulgarians and Romanians have learned the ways of Schengen work permits and three months visa-free stays, cultural life in both Sofia and Bucharest seems at times to be placed in the European cultural 1960s and 1970s, if not earlier. The return to Europe means the freedom to translate from Jung or Spengler, from Lacan and Heidegger, not from the obscure Robert Schuman or Jean Monnet.

Political elites have quite a different stance. Though fully unaware of cultural affairs and truly committed to Europe as a development dream, most of them remain fairly ignorant in European affairs. A television report excoriated Romanian MPs after the European Commission's highly publicized Progress Report on Romania and Bulgaria in 2003 revealed how few of them were able to name the organization that produced such reports or even place it in Brussels. Party position papers on European accession produced by individual parties in Romania and Bulgaria remain the exception rather than the norm. The discourse on Europe remains fairly general and nonspecific. The few technocrats who have some knowledge about Europe are all involved in negotiations on both sides, either the domestic government or the local EU delegations that represent the European Commission. Most of the local expertise, which is both quantitatively and qualitatively limited, is mobilized by EU-funded agencies like the European Institutes. The purpose of such agencies is to inform policy by producing impact accession studies, but actually the few good studies that are occasionally produced originate from independent think-tanks. By and large, enlargement for Romania and Bulgaria progresses similarly to the whole postcommunist wave, based more on the experience of previous accessions rather than the in-depth assessment of what EU integration would actually mean for these countries and economies. The stage of the negotiations is very present in the media and the overwhelming majority of the mainstream and tabloid press is in favor of EU integration.

Hypothesis on the Drive toward Europe

Where does attraction to Europe come from? There are quite a few distinct theoretical traditions explaining the drive to unify the European continent. The answer differs considerably when publics, cultural, or political elites are considered. Cultural elites seem attracted by the myth of a common European cultural identity; political elites see in Europe the ultimate safeguard of their national interests (Milward 1992), which, in the case of Eastern Europe, mostly refers to historical threats such as Russian expansion. However, as in the recent exceptional history of Eastern Europe, quite a few intellectuals became heads of state, so the two drives merge to some point. In the words of an intellectual who become prime minister of Slovakia,

> Today, in our talk about the European Union we stress European directives, talk about regulations, prepare a far-reaching institutional reform. But if our project is to be strong, it would have to rely on something different than just these aspects, however

important they are. European Union of the future is not a matter of regulations, it is a matter of our creativity. Europe will still be defined by its vision.[2]

As for the publics, they seem more divided than elites on the issue. However, East European publics are considerably less divided than West European ones. Despite the doubts shed by the low turnout in the 2004 European elections in new member-states, the wave of proaccession referenda in the region as well as the regular polls show that the spirit of "return to Europe" still prevails. Romania and Bulgaria, as well as Turkey, top the hierarchies of confidence in Europe, the desire to join Europe, and the belief that Europe is good for them (see table A12 in the Internet appendix).[3] In 2003, as trust in the European Union regressed slightly in the new entrant countries (-2), in Bulgaria and Romania it increased again (with 6 and 7, respectively). The two countries are already above the average at both confidence in EU and support for EU integration.

Explanations of public support for EU originate in studies of West European publics (see Rohrschneider and Whitefield, introduction to this volume). When discussing East European publics, the preliminary question to be addressed prior to the country by country analysis is to what extent there are the same general factors driving EU support in the East compared with the West. The trauma of Western Europe by the time unification as conceived by the founding fathers was continental war due to conflicts between France and Germany. The trauma of Eastern Europe in the same period and up until present times is to have its borders and regime decided by outsiders, conspicuously by Russia. Western Europe enriched gradually and developed a "social" model of the market economy as it went along with unification; Eastern Europe was subjected to savage redistribution, destruction of property rights and the class of owners until regaining its freedom in 1989. In other words, there are good reasons to look for differences in why East and West Europeans endorse Europe, as well as in their expectations of it; the general attraction of Europe is likely to be grounded in the specific and quite different recent *histories* of the East and West. Beyond this historical and geographical specificity, one can reasonably expect that some factors that cause an individual to be in favor of Europe play similarly in the two halves of the continent.

A review of the literature allows a synthesis of a few broad categories of determinants of an individual's attitude toward Europe. They can then be operationalized into variables to be tested in a model.

For the East European public, the Balkans included, a survey of these probable causes of pro-European attitudes returns the following determinants.

Recent Historical Trauma and Need for Security

The aftermath of World War II led to an unprecedented domination of the region by the Soviet Union, which led to the installation of communist regimes. The only exception was Greece. Central European countries, as well as Bulgaria and Romania, were forced into the Warsaw Pact and were coerced through the cold war to be in the camp of their oppressor, the Soviet Union, and against the free West. As Michnik and the other dissidents often observed, it was this forced allegiance to the anti-Western camp that instilled in the broader publics of the region the desire to belong to the West, with which Europe was equated. A special survey in the Balkans on this topic finds this reality to have endured thus far (Krastev 2004).

From this perspective, integration with Europe would then simply be the last chapter of the East European anticommunist revolution, as the "return" to Europe has been its first symbolic page. By joining the European Union, the only political club offered to them, East Europeans seek to fulfill the same ideal as with joining NATO: becoming a part of the West forever, secure and untouchable by any new geopolitical hazards of the East. This means that we should find a powerful association between variables measuring anticommunism (such as center–right or right-wing ideology) and, more generally, pro-Western support and the pro-European attitudes. This reason, so primed by thinkers of the region, before and after the "split" into a new and an old Europe during the Iraqi crisis, should be no trivial explanation, but the key determinant of the drive to join European Union. Its paradox consists in its mixed character, both idealistic and instrumental. The "ideology" hypothesis was also tested in the West in a different context (interpreted as class partisanship) and Inglehart, Rabier, and Reif discovered Eurobarometer evidence that left partisans support European integration less than right partisans (Inglehart, Rabier, and Reif 1997). This is what we would expect in Eastern Europe, as anticommunists are also the most prodemocratic and pro-Western in all the regional surveys. As to the general security hypothesis, we would simply expect the same people who are in favor of the EU to be also in favor of the United States, or any Western (so more than just European) club, such as NATO.

Figures for the Balkans show a marked difference between Romania and Bulgaria, on one side, with a pattern perfectly similar to Central Europe and former Yugoslavia (see figure 8.1). The former display a great correlation between support for the EU and support for NATO, and support is high. In former Yugoslavia, we find somewhat more support for the EU than for NATO, identified with bombing Serbia and Montenegro, and siding with Albanians in the resolution of the Macedonian crisis. However, the two remain firmly correlated, supporting the idea that "West" and "Europe" are barely distinguishable concepts for the great public.

Personal Expected Benefit

That the drive toward Europe is primarily motivated by economic expectations has long been hypothesized as the so-called utilitarianism hypothesis (Anderson 1998; Anderson and Reichert 1996; Gabel and Palmer 1995; Inglehart 1970). It argues that citizens of an integrated Europe support the integration project to the extent that they benefit from it, as benefits are quite different for various social categories. It predicted, therefore, that support for Europe is associated with higher education and more sophisticated occupational skills. Europe is also

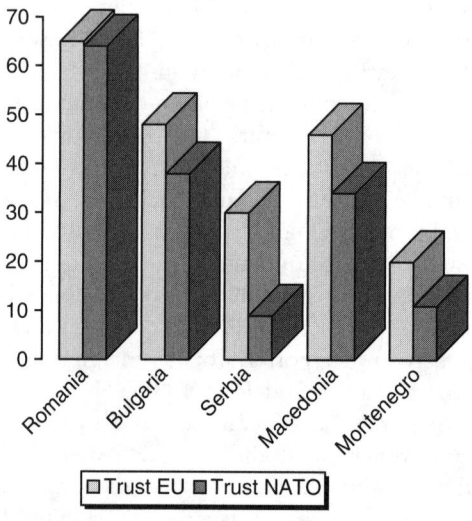

Figure 8.1 NATO and EU confidence compared (in percentage).

presented in the media as economically advantageous, with an economy stronger and more competitive than national ones. Most models include more than just one variable measuring this factor, from individual skills to evaluations of national economy, household economy, and perceived economic threats. Reviewing the evidence in 2000, again for West European publics, Gabel found the most substantial support for utilitarianism against every other hypothesis (Gabel 1998b).

In an Eastern context, a lot can be said on behalf of this hypothesis. Part of the attraction of the West, visible mostly in the divided Berlin during the cold war, was clearly material. The so-called demonstration effect that led to the desertion of communism even by its most staunch supporters refers to this materialist component: as the joke went during communism, a person on welfare in West Germany was making more money than the richest worker of Eastern Europe. The European funds for agriculture and regional development were fought over fiercely during negotiations, especially by Poles, and thus became intensely publicized in all accession countries. Other EU benefits, such as the freedom to travel or work in the European Union for East Europeans, who make in their own countries below a third of the income of West Europeans, are fairly obvious. More than the hard-to-grasp benefits of belonging or not to Euroland, East Europeans have simpler, clearer EU benefits to expect. And indeed Romania, Turkey, and Bulgaria have the highest economic expectations from the accession countries and the new members, excepting Hungary (European Commission 2003; Gral-Iteo 2002).

When it comes to operationalizing these variables, we encounter some problems. Education, at the individual level, may be indirect proof that an individual expects to do better in united Europe, but it is direct proof that somebody has better knowledge of Europe, a necessary precondition of trust in general (mentioned in the literature as the "cognitive mobilization" hypothesis) (Inglehart 1990). We would then expect EU supporters to be better educated on both accounts, and it is rather difficult to distinguish among them. On a similar line, we expect individuals who are better traveled to Europe to be more in favor of EU, but how can we tell if this occurs due to their superior knowledge of Europe or to their superior networking in Europe, which may lead to expect personal advantages (such as finding a temporary or permanent job) over those who are not networked? Personal satisfaction with household economy remains a clear indicator, but in an East European context, there is still less income differentiation, even so many years after communism, compared to Western

Europe. We reasonably expect urbanites, regardless of whether they are blue-collar, or white-collar laborers having transferable skills, to fare better in united Europe than peasants, so we should find more support for Europe in urban areas. East Europeans are attracted by Western values and by Western security at the same time, and they judge the latter to be the consequence of the former. The sacrifice endured during transition in order to mold these societies after the Western model—the European one in the second half of the transition—shows the same mixture of realism and idealism. Some differentiation can perhaps be made on the basis of Inglehart's work, which found in studies on the Western publics that the drive toward Europe is fed by postmaterialism (Inglehart 1990). Here again we find important differences between West and East, as the majority of East Europeans, in fact of all postcommunist citizens, are strongly materialistic according to the World Values Survey. The macroeconomic reform consisted of inflation stabilization and generation of growth, precisely the items used to measure materialism, presented as key objectives of reform.

National Identity and Nationalism

Nationalism and national identity are often quoted as being in opposition to the drive toward reunification of Europe. While there is some evidence at the national level, such as right-wing nationalistic parties being as a rule Euroskeptic, at the individual level, the evidence is mixed at best. Social psychologists (Klandermans, Sabucedo, and Rodriguez 2003; Licata and Klein 2002; Triandafyllidou 1998) have come up with evidence showing that a European identity is not certain to reduce anti-immigrant prejudice: some results point actually to the contrary. Nationalism is seldom studied at the individual level; generalizations from an individual to a group, and from a small group to society are the source of many errors and biases. Among other things, they generated the so-called paradox of "contact theory" (Forbes 1997). As phrased initially by Allport, contact theory claims that contact reduces prejudice among individuals from different groups (Allport 1954). Decades of amassed evidence show that *individuals* who enjoy more contact with individuals from another ethnic group tend to be less prejudiced, but that *groups* with more contact with other groups tend to perceive more ethnic conflict and to display prejudiced behavior. Generalizing from Allport's individual psychological approach to larger groups proved catastrophic. As is the case with many other variables that do not account for individuals but do matter for group behavior, groups are more than sums of individuals and societies cannot be reduced to the sum of social groups within them.

In this context, it is very important to distinguish between national identities at the individual level, which many studies found to coexist perfectly with European individual identities (Van Kersbergen 2000), and nationalism. The relation between the two is weak or nonexistent (Mungiu-Pippidi 2004). National identity is only the national self-ascription of an individual, whereas nationalism is the *individual subscription to the political ideology advocating the perfect congruity of the political unit with the national (ethnic) unit* (Barry 1987) and is therefore inseparable of a certain "exclusionary flavor" (Sidanius and Pratto 2000). Patriotism itself, attachment to the nation, is not necessarily nationalistic, as patriots, unlike nationalists, might well conceive the nation as a political, not ethnic, community. Social identity theory is sometimes invoked in the context of European identity (Hooghe and Marks 2004; Triandafyllidou 2002). Social identity theory postulates that "identity" arises through social comparison, and that we tend to discriminate other groups in favor of our own, as the main drive of groups is to be high on self-esteem (Brewer 1997; Tajfel 1981).

On the basis of this theory we would expect Europeans to start developing a common identity only as opposed to, for example, Americans, but we would not expect any tension between national and European identity, on two grounds: first, because from the national standpoint, there are no "Europeans" to compare with; second, because the European identity is endowed with high social esteem, so it is reasonable for individuals to "add" this new and valuable identity to their "old" national or ethnic ones. We would, on the contrary, expect *nationalism* to be in some tension with European integration. EU poses a challenge to national sovereignty, as it transfers some of it to European institutions and governing bodies. The national territory is no longer the locus of the exclusive and absolute national sovereignty. Moreover, national laws and the decisions of the national government have to be consistent with European rulings (Triandafyllidou 2002, 42). If this is right, then we should find evidence of a relationship between nationalism and Euroskepticism, but we should *not* find a negative association between support for Europe and patriotism or national identification.

The situation of the Balkans is indeed worth checking in this respect. Western Europe was terrified by the resurgence of nationalism after communism in Eastern Europe, and the Balkans, due to their proximity

Table 8.1 Nationalism as a Broad Regional Phenomenon

Country	Territorial nationalism (% agree)	Minorities a threat (% agree)
Romania	76	44
Bulgaria	67	43
Kosovo	81	78
Serbia	50	75
Slovakia	—	72
Montenegro	22	35
Macedonia	71	85
Hungary	60	—

Sources: Bulgaria, Romania, Macedonia, Montenegro 2003 (Gallup IBEU Project) Slovakia 2000, Serbia 2002 (Freedom House); Kosovo 2002 (UNDP); Hungary 1995 (MODUS).

to the core of Europe, are seen as the most nationalistic. However, as table 8.1 shows, the Balkans is rather on the average of postcommunist Europe when it comes to nationalistic *attitudes*. Nevertheless, the same attitudes that do not matter in Hungary, practically an ethnically homogenous country, might strongly matter in the Balkans due to the poor match between state and ethnicity that marks their most important Ottoman legacy.

Governance and Elite Intermediation

In a Western context, the factors relevant for this category are increased media consumption and government support, as the support to Europe seems mediated by the country leaders (Franklin, Van der Eijk, and Marsh 1995) and by the media. Party cues and the national political system were also discussed in this context, as in Rohrschneider's democratic performance model (Rohrschneider 2002). Again the situation of the East requires some qualifications here. While they are democrats, East Europeans are extremely critical toward their national political systems. Trust in political parties and parliaments is lower in Eastern Europe than in Western Europe, majorities across postcommunist Europe would prefer experts to political governments and the public perceives political elites as a privileged and unaccountable class. Indeed most instruments of accountability that function in consolidated democracies are only at their beginnings in postcommunist Europe. On the important question of preference of national democracy over Brussels democracy, East Europeans are on average in favor of

Brussels, exactly the opposite of Western Europeans (see figure A4 in the Internet appendix). Romania and Bulgaria, alongside Poland and Slovakia, top the list. The unaccountable and bureaucratic Brussels as seen from the West is perceived as a technocratic paradise from the East. Especially in the Balkans, survey data show that publics are unhappy with the persistence of particularism, notably in relation with the civil service and the administration, and the improper functioning of the rule of law. Majorities deny that citizens are indeed equal in front of the law, and complain of corruption of the political elites, according to the IBEU survey data. By contrast, Western Europe is seen as a society based on fairness and the principle of universalism.

This is an important category. The rather uncritical stance of East Europeans toward Brussels may explain, among others, their very low turnout in the first round of European elections, as their vote in favor of EU in the referenda meant entrusting some of their government to be managed by Westerners, not their own MPs recycled as European MPs. It may also explain why governments that fared well in the process of EU integration lost the elections in new member countries. The publics support their governments on the EU, but as this is a nonspecific policy, shared across political spectrum as the "mission" of the whole political class, success on the EU means little compared to perceived accountability and fairness.

More Distant Historical Factors

Traditional Western Europe has always been richer than the East, and is only Catholic or Protestant. Although these factors were less invoked in conjunction with EU integration than in connection with democracy and development, EU integration can succeed only in democratic and developed countries. Moreover, after Samuel Huntington invoked the border with the Orthodox denomination to the East and Southeast as the border of the European civilization, considerable paranoia flourished in the Balkans, dissipated only in part by the invitations to join given to Bulgaria and Romania in 1999.

However, it is difficult to see how these historical factors can play out today. The poorest immigrants who come to Europe, for instance the Albanians (also from an extremely pro-European country) show that one needs no development to discern that one's self-interest is better served by Europe than by a poor original country. Romanians and Bulgarians are overwhelmingly Orthodox, but they are in the lead in favorable attitudes toward the EU. However, a test of the older historical legacies, such as Orthodox denomination or development is worth considering.

Explaining Confidence in Europe

I will now proceed in two steps, using two different databases. First, I want to test Romania and Bulgaria comparatively with Central European countries, their former Warsaw Pact fellows. The last 50 years of history were quite similar in these countries, and despite different transition modes, their subsequent reform trajectories have also been comparable. The comparison excludes, therefore, former Yugoslav and former Soviet Union countries, which enjoy different historical backgrounds, and includes Hungary, Poland, Czech Republic, and Slovakia on one side (the formal Central Europe alliance known as "Vishegrad countries") and Romania and Bulgaria, two Orthodox and Balkan countries, on the other side. Pooling together all Warsaw Pact East European countries also allows us to test whether the general factors explaining pro-European attitudes in the East are similar to the Western models reported in literature. In another version, the data for Croatia and Slovenia were also pooled, allowing comparison of four Balkan countries against four Central European ones. These analyses are based on the World Values Survey 1998.[4]

In the second step I moved the analytical framework to the Balkans, using the recent (2003) data of the IBEU Fifth Framework survey in Romania, Bulgaria, Serbia, Montenegro, and Macedonia. This panel of countries allows a comparison between the Eastern Balkans and Western Balkans. The same data are used to build national separate models for Romania and Bulgaria. More than explaining the maximum variance for each sample (Romanian, Bulgaria, and pooled), I tried to test exactly the same predictors in order to allow a fair comparison across countries and the region.

The dependent variable I used for all the models was not support for EU integration, as countries are in different stages of integration or—as in the case of Serbia—they have not yet started at all the process. In the case of Romania and Bulgaria, support for integration is in any case so high that the tiny minority against joining is mostly made of people who are not aware of the existence of the EU and the prospects of joining. East Europeans are more specific, however, when it comes to the evaluation of the EU in general, regardless of whether they are in favor of joining or not. For these reasons, I use as the dependent variable how much confidence people feel in the European Union. Not only in former Yugoslavia are people quite critical of the EU on this measure. Also in Warsaw Pact countries, there is more variation when measuring confidence in the EU, where some criticism or scepticism is displayed, than when measuring support for EU, perceived as a historical fatality and therefore endorsed by large majorities. The two variables of confidence in European Union varied slightly in wording, the World Values Study question asking simply whether people trust EU, whereas the IBEU questions asking more explicitly, "Do you trust EU to want the best for your country?"

Former Yugoslavia differs sharply here from Central Europe. In the last decade, the EU failed to prevent and contain in a timely way the Yugoslav wars, brokered peace arrangements that left many frustrated, and was on the side of NATO when bridges and other buildings used mostly by civilians were bombed in Serbia and Montenegro. While the EU has developed relations recently by sending EU troops to Macedonia, and initiating the Stability and Accession process for former Yugoslavia, unlike the smooth partnership with Romania and Bulgaria, there remain mixed feelings in Western Balkans. In Serbia, less than a third believes Europe wants what is best for them; in Montenegro the figure falls to less than a fifth (see figure A5 in the Internet appendix). While Eurobarometer data show that a referendum on accession would pass in any of these countries if organized today, the current policy of EU toward them is viewed with moderate enthusiasm. The Western Balkans still face a long transition. Bulgaria felt its exclusion from the first wave of enlargement as unjust. Only Romanians feel that they are treated about right. So the first conclusion is that the specific relationship between a country and Europe, the treatment Europe reserves for a country, is of great importance when creating a constituency for Europe.

Table A13 in the Internet appendix shows the results of an analysis of the various determinants of EU support discussed above. Prior to discussing determinants by categories and across countries, the model considers effects across the Warsaw Pact countries as a whole and confirms the specificities of Eastern Europe, while supporting some findings from the Western European publics research. Dislike for the former communist regime and endorsement of a government by experts, together with an array of other antipolitics feelings not included in the final model (available from the author) indicate that integration is viewed as the final act of the 1989 revolution. Comparison of the

Orthodox with the rest of respondents shows that *there is no significant difference between them and the Western denominations* when it comes to Europe. Also, no significant difference was found among the four Balkan countries in the larger pooled sample and the Vishegrad countries. So it is the recent, not the distant, history that explains the European constituencies of Eastern Europe.

The Romanian and Bulgarian models (see table A14 in the Internet appendix) endorse even more the idea that Euroenthusiasm in the East is a different animal than in the West. The one predictor overwhelming all others and accounting for most of the explained variance, well above the usual level at such numbers, is trust for NATO (see also chapter 10 by Loveless and Rohrschneider on this issue). Trust for EU and trust for NATO in Romania and Bulgaria are so deeply linked that it is clear that respondents consider them two parts of the same whole, the West. The idea of a disagreement between NATO and EU is inconceivable in Eastern Europe, where accession to the two bodies was also presented as one process in two complementary parts, security first and development after. East Europeans value NATO for its security guarantee and its symbolic winning of the cold war as much as they value the EU. Their elites share these feelings, and it is important to mention to what extent these are widespread grassroots attachments. The EU and NATO are part of the same emotional and cognitive edifice, the West, built in decades of frustrations. Weakening of any of the parts might alter the whole.

A review of the factors' performance in the seven models presented in tables A13 and A14 allows a general picture of the European constituents.

Security and Historical Trauma

This factor emerges as very powerful. Trust for NATO in the Balkan sample and rejection of the former communist regime in the Warsaw Pact countries sample show that the confidence in Europe among people in accession countries has deep historical roots. Europe means more for these people than just the Europe of treaties and regulations. Belonging to Europe is belonging to the West, an ideal people dreamed of during the decades of communism. This makes, of course, the main difference between Eastern and Western pro-Europe constituencies. Western countries joined the EU sensibly and rationally, and their publics are eternally divided over calculations of costs versus benefits, whereas Eastern ones "returned to Europe" as the last stage of a revolution. There is also a strong link between being on the right and being in favor of Europe, as we expected. The most committed Europeans are the anticommunists.

Personal Expected Benefits

People who are active, young and middle aged, reside in urban areas, and are more educated emerge in most models as more pro-European. The relation between household economic situation and support for Europe is confirmed in the Warsaw Pact sample only. People who travel more frequently trust Europe more in the Bulgarian sample, a robust predictor in all variants of the model, but which is not replicated in the Romanian sample. The explanatory value of these predictors is small, except for Bulgaria.

Governance and Elite Intermediation

There is important confirmation of the hypothesis that perception of poor national governance feeds trust in the EU. Preference for expert governments is a robust predictor in the Warsaw Pact sample, and various items of distrust in politicians and discontent with the rule of law surface in the Balkan sample. *People trust Europe to be less corrupt and more competent in governing their societies than their own political elites and this adds to the attraction of Europe.* However, there is also a correlation between interest in politics and trust in Europe in the Warsaw Pact sample. For Romania and Bulgaria, the correlation is weak. In the Romanian sample, there is also a correlation between trust in government and trust in Europe, but it is not robust enough to hold in more complex variants of the model.

Nationalism

Findings on nationalism endorse the results published by social psychologists. National pride is not a significant determinant of trust in Europe. Patriotism, using as proxy the willingness to fight for one's country, is *positively* associated with confidence in Europe. In postcommunist Eastern Europe, they seem both to be indicators of a general attitude of civic engagement. Nationalism, however, is negatively correlated as we expected it to be. *People who have territorial claims on neighboring countries and are paranoid toward ethnic minorities tend to have less confidence in Europe.* This is a robust finding, surfacing in Romania, Bulgaria, and the Balkan sample. (Clear-cut questions on nationalism were not included in the World Values Survey, so this predictor is missing from the Warsaw Pact countries' sample.) Nationalist politicians can find some lever against Europe in these attitudes, so it becomes all the more important to convert the elites to the European project that will render these borders and territorial claims less and less important.

Development and Other Historical Legacies

Romania and Bulgaria show more confidence in Europe than the rest of the Balkans. Europe has been good to them in recent years, a perception not yet shared by inhabitants of Macedonia or Montenegro. I found no relation between regional development and European trust, despite testing complex indexes of local development included in the Balkan sample (aggregates of various infrastructure items in respondent's town or village).

Conclusion

Despite the different speeds at which they are integrating with the European Union, it seems that citizens of the Eastern Balkans are quite similar to Central Europeans. Specific postcommunist features mark strongly their confidence in the European Union and their grounds to join Europe. They are likely to be enthusiastic Europeans, although not very participative Europeans, at least for the generations that still remember communism. As these memories fade, we may expect these new European citizens to become more like Western Europeans, judging Europe by its performance, submitting it to what Ernest Renan called "a daily plebiscite". The more Europe replaces the nation as the political community, the more it will have to undertake this daily test. It is likely that as time goes on, opinions on Europe might become more differentiated than they are today and a more critical stance will develop gradually.

It is unlikely that European integration will so dramatically change these countries that universalism will reign the day after accession or even a decade after. The example of Greece shows that while Europe brings about development, it can be slow in changing culture. However, given that in the recent past Southeastern Europe had leaders like Ceausescu and Milosevic, the Greek example can and should be read as grounds for optimism. If all Balkan countries can copy the European path of Greece, the term "Balkans" itself will fade and become futile, and this part of Europe will lose the negative specificity that made its sad fame for so long.

Notes

1. Atlas method. GNI per capita is new term for GNP per capita.
2. Speech of the prime minister of Slovak Republic, Mikulas Dzurinda, at the Fiftieth Anniversary of the EPP-ED Group in Strasbourg, July 1, 2003.
3. The Internet appendix can be found at http: //www.indiana.edu/~iupolsci/ rrohrsch/ PalgraveTables+Figures.pdf
4. Courtesy of Hans-Dieter Klingemann.

CHAPTER 9

Support for the European Union in the Baltic States

Stephen Whitefield, Robert Rohrschneider, and Rasa Alisauskiene

Introduction

This chapter, as with others in this book, considers and empirically tests a range of competing explanations of the bases of public support for European integration. But it does so in the particular context of the Baltic States, whose recent histories, national composition, and geographical location suggest the possibility that a distinctive set of factors may be at play shaping attitudes and political mobilization on European issues.

Historically, these states were part of the Western Christian (Protestantism in Estonia and Latvia, Catholicism in Lithuania) and political world (linked to Poland, Hapsburg, and Germany), and there are strong identities among the titular nationalities in each state linked to the idea of Europe. In this sense, they resemble other parts of East–Central Europe. However, though all the East European states discussed in this book were subject to enormous Soviet influence, the Baltic States were forcibly incorporated into the Soviet Union in 1940 after a brief period of interwar independence, where they remained until 1991, and experienced large-scale (though varying degrees of) in-migration of Russians, as well as industrialization on the Soviet model. These states continue to directly border—and indeed have remaining unresolved territorial disputes with—Russia.

Given these conditions, therefore, we consider whether support for the EU in the Baltic States may comprise an intermediate set of cases between the pattern in East–Central Europe (see chapters 6, 7, and 5 by Jasiewicz, Fölsz and Tóka, and Kopecký, respectively), where the "return to Europe" is more geographically secure, and other states of the former Soviet Union such as Russia and Ukraine (see chapter 11 by Whitefield), where historical and cultural links to Europe are much more attenuated. In particular, we investigate whether the histories, locations, and ethnic composition of the Baltic States may not result in support for European integration that is shaped and mobilized in distinctive ways, in particular by the impact of nationalism and ethnic divisions that may work alongside—or in place of—the economic and political factors that have been shown to operate in other states.

All East European states have been faced with a potential dilemma about European integration. After decades of domination by one external power, the Soviet Union—and varied forms of national resistance to it—why should citizens move quickly to cede national sovereignty to another supranational institution, the European Union? The answers to that question appear to be various: for personal and national economic gain, for political and military security, for reasons of European identity. At the same time, in many postcommunist states, the issue remains contentious.

Each of these reasons for supporting European integration makes sense in the context of the Baltic States. Many commentators point to the importance of European identity to ethnic Estonians, Latvians, and Lithuanians (Tiilikainen 2003); to the strength of the link between European integration and national security concerns, particularly regarding the influence of Russia (Krickus 1997); and to the importance of the European Union and the West for economic recovery (Kaitila and Widgren 2003); and, on the side of opponents of integration, to a sense of alienation from an elite political process reflected in a sense of distance from national political institutions (Riak 2003). Indeed, these links may be even stronger in the Baltic States by comparison with other parts of Eastern Europe. As Graeme Herd has put it,

> While in the other central and east European states, the European idea has occasionally been undermined by the perceived threat of supranational integration after 50 years of totalitarianism, such a debate has not characterised nationalist rhetoric in the Baltic

States. Indeed, as one analyst [Joan Lofgren] succinctly remarked, rather the opposite is true: "Emphasising the Europeanness of Baltic cultures serves to heighten what many see as a clear cultural contrast with Russian 'Eastern' culture. 'Rejoining the European family' is seen by many as a way to bolster national identity rather than threaten it. Thus in the Baltic States, nationalists embrace EU integration as an opportunity to fulfil and further national interests." (Herd 1999, 261)

At the same time, the fact that the Baltic States were constituent parts of the former Soviet Union creates further special features of its relationship to the European Union. This may be expressed most clearly in the politicization of ethnic divisions. During the Soviet period, particularly in Estonia and Latvia, there was significant Russian in-migration such that the titular majority comprises approximately 65 percent of the population of Estonia (with 28 percent Russians), 57 percent in Latvia (with 30 percent Russians), and 81 percent in Lithuania (with 9 percent Russians, and 7 percent Poles).[1] This migration, moreover, was associated with postwar Soviet industry, which was seen by many of the titular nationalities as inimical to their countries' economic interests. Particularly in Estonia and Latvia, therefore, the struggle against Soviet power frequently involved political mobilization on ethnic lines that was subsequently attached to ethnically defined citizenship laws in the new states (Pettai 2001).

As is well known, these citizenship laws and more broadly the legal and human rights bases of ethnicity in the Baltic States became part of the discussion about European accession (Galazis 2003). However, the existing literature is ambiguous in its effects. While EU concern about ethnic issues should not be overstated (de Witte 2002), its intervention may have complicated the relationship of both titular nationalities and ethnic minorities to European integration. On the one hand, titular nationalities may see European integration as a hindrance to using national institutions to ensure cultural survival (Plakans 1997), while allowing minorities to use the EU as a means to mobilize to improve their own status (Liebich 2002). On the other hand, however, these international influences may mitigate the effects of ethnic divisions from the Soviet and transition periods, precisely because they provide external sources for resolving disputes (Pettai 2001).

The rest of the chapter, therefore, considers the influence of various sources of influence on support for the European Union—economic, political, nationalist/ethnic—drawing on data from the Candidate

Countries Eurobarometer (CCEB) surveys conducted between 1999 and 2003—with a primary focus on 2001, 2002, and 2003 when the CEEB included a broader range of measures that allow some of the most important hypotheses about support for European integration to be tested.[2] In particular, we present analyses of the social and attitudinal bases of support for European integration in the three Baltic States, as well as how this issue connects with the electoral preferences and referendum behavior of citizens.

Support for Europe in the Baltic States

Observers of attitudes toward European Union integration in the Baltic States in the 1990s have noted a dynamic from very high initial levels of support to increasing skepticism in the mid-1990s that appears largely the result of political concern about when, with whom, and how quickly accession talks could commence (Ehin 2001). Once these were resolved after 1997, levels of support then improved.

Our analysis takes up the story in 1999 and shows how support changes between then and 2003. Responses to two questions from the CCEB are shown in table 9.1. The first asks respondents generally whether they believe that the EU would be a good or bad thing for their country. The second asks more specifically about whether people expect advantages or disadvantages for the country in integrating with the EU.

Four things stand out in the results. First, and not surprisingly, there is a preponderance of EU supporters over opponents on both measures. Nonetheless, there is also a significant minority, particularly when respondents are asked to consider the advantages and disadvantages, that is skeptical about European integration. This picture fits with much of the evidence presented in other chapters. Second, and contrary to some evidence elsewhere, support between 1999 and 2003 increases significantly in all countries, although we note that it declines somewhat in Latvia in the intervening years. The increase in support is especially evident between 2002 and 2003 as accession approaches. Third, of the three states, Lithuania moves to being a clear outlier in terms of the extent of public support for the EU from levels comparable to the other states in 1999. These last two dynamics raise questions about the "cost mobilization" model discussed in chapter 1, and we return to the subject in the fourth section below.

Table 9.1 Support for European integration in the Baltic states, 1999–2003 (percentages)

	Estonia				Latvia				Lithuania			
	'99	'01	'02	'03	'99	'01	'02	'03	'99	'01	'02	'03
EU a good/bad thing												
Good	28.8	34.1	34.3	41.3	38.4	33.9	35.6	46.8	31.7	40.9	47.9	59.4
Bad	13.5	14.0	15.1	15.9	9.1	17.0	21.0	16.2	19.4	10.8	12.5	8.6
EU will bring advantages/disadvantages												
Advantage	30.4	34.9	33.1	38.5	39.4	35.5	37.6	45.4	34.0	46.0	45.5	60.2
Disadvantage	22.4	19.5	22.1	21.1	17.0	23.3	30.2	21.5	26.7	18.8	16.9	12.5

How then do we explain support for European integration in the Baltic States? Unfortunately, the CEEB surveys do not include measures of many of the normative factors that have been shown—from other data sources—by the authors (Rohrschneider and Whitefield 2004a) and in other chapters in this volume (Jacobs and Pollack [chapter 4], Jasiewicz [chapter 6], and Whitefield [chapter 11]) to be of great importance to public opinion on European integration. Nonetheless, a number of specific hypotheses are tested below. In line with the discussion in other chapters about what may be general determinants of support for integration, and the discussion above about the particular context of the Baltic States, we focus here on four types of factors and their hypothesized relationship to EU support.

1. *Economic factors.* European integration is supported by those who have more positive economic experience and higher expectations about personal and/or national economic gains from the integration process—the "winners" and opposed by the economic "losers" in the transition process (Cichowski 2000; Ehin 2001; Tucker, Pacek, and Berinsky 2002).
2. *Political factors.* European integration is supported by those with a greater sense of political engagement and by those who find greater satisfaction in national political institutions—and opposed by those who are alienated and dissatisfied with the EU as an elite level project (Ehin 2001).
3. *Ethnic and national factors.* These may cut both ways. On the one hand, titular nationalities may see the EU as a means of defending ethnic and national interest against Russian intrusion and may furthermore see the EU as a means of affirming the "Europeanness" of their ethnic identity. Against this, ethnic minorities in the Baltics, particularly Russians, whose identities may be less "European" and whose cultural, economic and family ties may be more oriented to Russia, may be less pro-European in outlook. Alternately, ethnic minorities may see the EU as a mechanism to redress grievances about discriminatory national laws, and titular nationalities in this context may see the EU as intrusive in areas of great concern to them.
4. *Partisan and electoral factors.* In line with the "cost mobilization" model discussed in chapter 1, these are factors that are argued to work at the national rather than the individual level to explain differences in levels of support across countries. We expect that higher levels of party competition over the EU may result in reduced average levels

of support for integration, as citizens in more mobilized states are made more aware of the costs of integration and to a greater degree see EU issues as attached to other fundamental political and economic values.

The Social and Attitudinal Bases of Support for the EU

In light of the above hypotheses, we consider first the social and attitudinal bases of support for European integration. The measure of integration used in the analysis that follows is based on a combined scale of the two items shown in table 9.1, which correlated at $r = .73$. Two models are shown for each year country and each year. The first, in table A15 in the Internet appendix,[3] includes only demographic and social characteristics—ethnicity, employment status, income, education, age, religiosity, and gender. The second, in table 9.2, looks at the attitudinal variables. Because social factors may be causally related to the attitudinal predictors and are less conceptually connected to the dependent variable, running two models in this way allows us to see the effects of social factors that may otherwise be removed or reduced when included alongside the more proximate effect of attitudes.

The results in table A15 point in a number of ways to the hypotheses. First, we find significantly stronger support among students, who appear to be clearly more supportive of integration. This "student" effect in a number of cases combines with significantly increased support among younger citizens, and (less consistently) among the more highly educated. Though we find some evidence that increased support is associated with higher income—Estonia, Lithuania in 2003—there appear to be no effects for employment status. The EU may be attractive to younger and more educated people in the Baltic States, but the evidence does not point clearly in favor of hypothesis 1 above, namely that integration is attractive mainly to the economic winners in demographic terms.

Second, the largest and most consistent sociodemographic predictors of integration support are the measures of ethnic identity. Among both Russians and other ethnic minorities—including, for example, Poles in Lithuania—support for EU integration is significantly and consistently lower than among the titular nationalities. With regard to hypothesis 3, therefore, the evidence points toward the great importance attached by the majority group to Europe as a means of securing national interests against the threat of external influence, and not toward the recognition by other ethnic groups that the EU might be a means for securing minority interests.

Further clarification of the hypotheses above can be gleaned from the evidence about the impact of attitudinal factors in table 9.2. Contrary to some accounts that exclusively stress the importance of economically instrumental calculations (Cichowski 2000; Tucker, Pacek, and Berinsky 2002), our results point to a much more balanced picture. They also suggest continuity from previous years in the attitudinal bases of support for the EU in the Baltics.[4]

First, we do find a clear and consistent relationship between those who expect their personal financial situation and the country's economy to do well in the near and medium term. These future expectations, however, are stronger than economic evaluations of the past. It is not so much that the EU is supported by the economic "winners" from the transition than a case of people having expectations that the EU will turn them (and their country) into winners in future.

Second, we find that political factors are at least—if not more—important than economic considerations. As hypothesis 2 above suggested, the EU is supported by those who are more engaged with national politics, and especially by those who are satisfied with the democratic institutions of the state. Or, put the other way, the evidence supports Riak's contention that there may be a "second Estonia" that feels alienated from a national administration that it sees as intent on selling out national interests at any price to obtain entry to the EU (Riak 2003). For these opponents of European integration, national institutions are of questionable legitimacy.

Third, we again find support for one side of hypothesis 3, namely that the EU is a project supported by those who most strongly identify with the nation. In this sense, Baltics nationalism may be more like liberal nationalism in the nineteenth century or, for that matter, like Scottish nationalism today; small nations see their best chance of securing their national interests against the negative impact of powerful neighbors by alliances with larger supranational entities, even if this entails some loss of sovereignty.

The European Union, Electoral Choices, and Referendum Behavior in the Baltics

We turn next to analyses that pertain more directly to the impact on EU support of partisan and electoral factors, outlined in hypothesis 4

Table 9.2 Regression of EU support onto attitudinal factors, 2002 and 2003 (standardized coefficients)

	Estonia		Latvia		Lithuania	
	2002	2003	2002	2003	2002	2003
Economic factors						
Country economy in next year	.11**	.23***	.12***	.24***	.14***	.11**
Household finance in next year	.08*	.03	.02	−.02	−.03	.03
Country employment in next year	.09**	.05	.06	.10**	.05	−.00
Personal employment in next year	−.01	−.04	.02	−.07	.03	.05
Personal economy five years ago	.11***	.07*	.08*	.06	.06	.04
Personal economy five years on	.11**	.19***	.13***	.14***	.19***	.19***
Political factors						
Attention to politics in country	.07*	.08**	.03	.01	.08**	.10**
Satisfaction with democracy in country	.27***	.23***	.21***	.22**	.19***	.19***
Nationalism	.06	.09**	.08**	.14***	.14***	.15***
Adjusted r^2	.27	.34	.20	.30	.26	.29

Notes: * Significant at $p<.05$, ** $p<.01$, *** $p<.001$.

above. Again, we expect that the impact of the EU on partisan choices should (1) increase as the reality and costs of accession draw closer and (2) that this increased connection should reduce actual support for the EU itself, as political parties point out the costs to voters.

The results of a series of multinomial logistic regressions for each country in the years 2001, 2002, and 2003 are shown in table 9.3. This regression technique is appropriate for dependent variables consisting of multiple classes—in this case, voters support for particular parties. (For comparative purposes over time and states, and to simplify somewhat the large number of parties in each system, we have coded parties in the analysis into party families.) Does the EU have a significant impact on party choice? Is it particularly supported or opposed by some types of parties over others? And has the EU become more or less of a factor affecting party choice over time? We deal with each of these questions in turn.

First, as the chi^2 statistics in the last row show, views of EU integration do indeed constitute a significant basis for discrimination in voters' partisan choices in all states and (almost) all years. The EU, in other words, matters. This does not mean that the EU matters most. Clearly, partisan choices are affected by a broad variety of attitudinal and social factors. In Estonia and Latvia, for example, other analysis (not shown but available) indicates that ethnic divisions are vastly more important to partisan choice than the EU is. However, even when other factors are included in the model, the EU remains a significant predictor.

Second, support for the EU appears to be associated with support for right-wing parties; in Estonia and Lithuania with liberals, in Latvia with conservatives and Christian democrats. This evidence fits both with perspectives on the EU that highlight its connection to market liberalism (Hooghe 2001) and with literature on postcommunist party systems that point to the connection of markets and European integration (Rohrschneider and Whitefield 2004b). By contrast, supporters of social-democratic parties in Estonia and Lithuania (which tend to represent ethnic minorities), and those choosing ethnic parties directly in Latvia, are clearly less likely than supporters of parties of the right to favor integration. What is also very clear in table 9.3 is that those without party attachments are also much less likely in general to support integration, a finding that meshes with the evidence above about lack of support among those who are relatively alienated from national politics and institutions.[5]

Third, the impact of the EU on partisan choice is increasing in Estonia and Latvia but actually declining in Lithuania. In Estonia, the

Table 9.3 Multinomial logistic regression of party vote intention onto EU support (unstandardised betas), 2001, 2002, 2003

	Estonia			Latvia			Lithuania		
	2001	2002	2003	2001	2002	2003	2001	2002	2003
Social democrats	-.75***	-.48***	-.74*1**	-.07	-.33*	-.57**	-.59***	-.47***	-.45**
Conservatives	-.49*	-.73***	-.72***	—	—	—	-.17	-.19	-.34
Ethnic parties	NA	NA	NA	-.02	-.56***	1.17***	NA	NA	NA
Will not vote	-.98***	-1.02***	-1.08	-.22	-.37**	-.99***	-.97***	-.71***	-.80***
Liberals	—	—	—	NA	NA	NA	—	—	—
Cox and Snell Pseudo r^2	.05	.08	.11	.01	.05	.19	.10	.05	.06
EU chi^2	35.32***	60.73***	88.40***	4.35ns	41.53***	144.63***	61.54***	33.37***	35.43***

Notes: Reference party in each country is indicated by—
* significant at $p < .05$, ** $p < .01$, *** $p < .001$
NA, not available; ns, not significant

chi^2 increases from 35.32 in 2001 to 88.40 in 2003; in Latvia, the increase is enormous, from 4.35 in 2001 to 144.63 in 2003. But in Lithuania, the figures are 61.54 and 35.43, respectively. These results match the descriptions provided of party politics in these states by a number of commentators (Ehin 2001). But they also speak in an important way to the effects of party competition and cost mobilization on relative support for the EU and help resolve a potential discrepancy between the findings of table 9.1 that show growing support for the EU and the premises of the "cost mobilization" model. Where party competition is least developed on EU issues, as it is in Lithuania, voters only weakly relate the issue to partisan choices and this elite consensus and lack of mass division sustains the particularly large increases in support for the EU in that state. By contrast, where party competition is greater—as it is in Estonia and Latvia—it may have the effect of significantly reducing the growth in support for the EU. No doubt citizens in the Baltic States have strong reasons to support EU entry, but these basic dispositions are less activated when party competition and partisan choice on this issue is greater.

We conclude this section by looking at the actual behavior of Baltic citizens in the referendum on accession held in these states in 2003.[6]

We consider first, the impact of important social and attitudinal factors on two choices by citizens: whether to vote yes or no, and whether to vote in the referendum at all. The results for these choices are shown for each country in table A16 in the Internet appendix. Two conclusions emerge. First, as was the case with support for integration, political and national factors are at least as important as economic ones in shaping choices among those voting yes or no. In Estonia and Latvia, those with more positive expectations about the immediate future of the national economy are more likely to vote yes, but this does not hold true in Lithuania. By contrast, in all three states, there is a clear impact on yes voters of greater satisfaction with national democracy. Second, economic factors have almost no impact on the decision not to vote at all. Not surprisingly perhaps, this appears to relate much more to engagement with national politics. But, particularly in what we know to be the more ethnically divided states of Estonia and especially Latvia, nonparticipants in the referenda are also found among ethnic minorities.

Finally, we can see the impact of partisanship on referendum behavior. Again, the results largely match the evidence above. Not surprisingly, those who have no partisan attachment are both more likely to vote no and to abstain from voting altogether. Second, supporters of right-wing parties are more likely than others to vote yes.

Conclusions

The evidence and discussion above tends to support many of the expectations about the sources of public support for the EU in the Baltic States. These countries do appear to be distinct from others in the way in which ethnic inheritances from the Soviet period impact on views of European integration. For the titular nationalities, particularly in Estonia and Latvia where "Russification" and negative Soviet influence went furthest, the return to Europe is clearly seen as a mechanism to advance national interests. For the Russian and other minorities, in these states, however, support for Europe is weaker. These ethnic differences, moreover, spill over into partisan choices and into political behavior, including nonparticipation, in ways that may be politically problematic as EU integration moves forward, particularly since those opposed to integration are also the ones who feel least regard for national democratic institutions. And economic progress, if this comes with EU membership, may not be a major factor in changing attitudes or in building support for democracy at home, since economic calculations appear to be only one part of the basis for EU support to begin with in these states.

We must also distinguish among the three Baltic States. Support is highest in Lithuania and this may be because of greater elite consensus that has to a large degree removed the EU as an issue from mass level partisan choices. Lithuania, of course, is also the state in which ethnic divisions are least pronounced in the party system. The cost mobilization model we developed, therefore, appears to have traction in the Baltic context, but in ways that suggest a broader basis for its application. Costs may be mobilized not just on economic terms, but as in the case of Estonia and Latvia, by reference to the differential impact of the EU on ethnic and national aspirations.

In so far as the EU, therefore, may become more important as the realities of accession become clear, we may speculate about its effects on these ethnic political cleavages. Much may depend on the perception of Russia, both among the titular nationalities and the Russian minorities. If Russia continues to move away from democracy, the threat perception among the titular nationalities may increase, exacerbating ethnic divisions. The EU, in turn, will then face the challenge in its own policies of how to manage a potentially problematic relationship with Russia.

Despite these regional characteristics, two general patterns clearly fit the general theme of the other chapters. First, whereas economic conditions have some effect on how the EU is being perceived, they are not the strongest determinant of EU support. In the case of the Baltic States, ethnicity is the driving force behind these evaluations. Neither do other sociodemographic characteristics, which might reflect the status of citizens as winners or losers, structure perceptions of the EU. Second, our longitudinal analyses support the cost mobilization argument: when political elites are most unified in support of the EU, publics are the least critical of it (as in Lithuania); when parties are more skeptical about it, public support for the EU is reduced. The model thus not only receives support from the accumulated cross-national evidence but also fits the temporal pattern we found in the three Baltic States.

Appendix: The Survey Measures

Dependent Variables

Generally speaking, do you think that (your country's) membership of the European Union would be . . . a good thing, neither good nor bad, a bad thing.

Do you think that (your country) would get (1) much more advantages than disadvantages, (2) more advantages than disadvantages, (3) as much advantages as disadvantages, (4) more disadvantages than advantages, or (5) much more disadvantages than advantages from being a member of the European Union?

These two items correlated at $r = .73$ and were combined in a single scale in the regression analyses.

Independent Variables

Social Demographics

Age, employment status (manual workers, self-employed, professionals and managers, at home, unemployed, retired), ethnicity (majority, first minority, second minority in each state), education (high, medium, low), income, church attendance, age, gender.

Economic Evaluations

What are your expectations for the year to come: will (the next year) be better, worse, or the same, when it comes to

1. the economic situation in (your country)
2. the financial situation of your household
3. the employment situation in (your country)
4. your personal job situation

If you compare your present situation with that of five years ago, what would you say? It has improved, stayed about the same, or gotten worse?

In the course of the next five years, do you expect your personal situation to improve, to stay about the same, or to get worse?

Political Evaluations

On the whole, are you ... with the way democracy works in (our country)? Are you (1) very satisfied, (2) fairly satisfied, (3) not very satisfied, or (4) not at all satisfied.

In general, do you pay attention to news about national politics?

Nationalism

Would you say you are very proud, fairly proud, not very proud, or not at all proud to be [nationality—*refer to citizenship*].

Notes

1. *Source:* CIA World Fact Book http://www.cia.gov/cia/publications/factbook/
2. Information on sampling and fieldwork can be found at: http://europa.eu.int/comm/public_opinion/cceb_en.htm/
3. The Internet appendix can be found at http://www.indiana.edu/~iupolsci/rrohrsch/PalgraveTables+Figures.pdf
4. Ehin (2001) does not, however, find significant effects for ethnicity in her study of support in 1999, which we may attribute to the fact that she includes both sociodemographic and attitudinal measures in a single model, thus crowding out the ethnic effect with other more proximate attitudinal factors such as nationalism.
5. Our interpretation about the greater elite consensus in Lithuania is supported by the results from the expert survey described in the Conclusion. Lithuania has the highest mean scores on West integration (Lithuania = 5.4, Latvia = 5.2, and Estonia = 5.0); political integration (Lithuania: = 5.0, Latvia = 4.9, and Estonia = 4.8), and market integration (Lithuania = 5.4, Latvia = 5.2, and Estonia = 5.0).

6. The actual results in each referendum and the reported behavior by respondents in the surveys, at least in the aggregate, appear to be a closely related. Moreover, in line with the discussion above about party competition and the importance of the EU as a mass level predictor of vote, it is also notable that by far the largest yes vote was obtained in Lithuania.

CHAPTER 10

Attitudes toward European Integration and NATO in Hungary, Bulgaria, and the Ukraine

Matthew Loveless and Robert Rohrschneider

Introduction

This chapter examines the determinants of support for integration into the European Union (EU) by citizens in Hungary, Bulgaria, and the Ukraine. It asks the following questions: Do individuals' attitudes regarding NATO membership build support for the enlargement of the EU? That is, can positive or negative experience with one international organization provide a reservoir of "good will" (Easton 1975) for another international organization? Although some analyses posit that NATO membership provides a positive reservoir for EU expansion (Kostadinova 2000), we know surprisingly little about this linkage.

Another important question is whether this process—the experiential process—works similarly for different levels of integration. Does NATO membership, or its prospects, affect citizens' attitudes the same way at different levels of abstraction? For example, do positive attitudes about NATO generate support for both EU membership in principle and for the specific integration policies? Prior research suggests that publics in postcommunist societies evaluate the idea of European integration quite differently from the specific aspects of it, such as the ownership of land by foreigners or the ownership of industrial enterprises by foreign companies. We thus examine whether NATO, which is typically positively evaluated, affects support for different aspects of EU enlargement.

The selection of these cases is to delineate between different levels of both EU integration and NATO membership.[1] Of the three cases, Hungary represents the most "Western" state. Its start toward integration with the West began simultaneously with the collapse of the former Soviet Union (if not in nascent form during the pretransitional period). Hungary's subsequent membership in Western and international organizations has been an orderly and rapid affair. Bulgaria has been following the same trajectory as Hungary although at a markedly slower pace. The first rounds of Bulgarian parliamentary elections maintained an authoritative regime, if not hostile, then reserved toward Western integration. Only slowly has it emerged in the past decade as a potential partner to the West.

In contrast to the overriding economic concerns of citizens in CEE toward integration and direct political and economic experience, Ukraine has the least direct integration experience with the West in the form of international organizational membership and may be subject to regional, or Eurasian, integrative pressure, particularly with the Russian and other former Soviet states.[2] Situated at the frontiers of the West, Ukraine, with the onset of true national existence and autonomy, has faced added historical and cultural challenges to cultivating prointegrative attitudes. Intraregional concerns, including ethnic and national identities, and the long shadow of Russian history may play heavily into citizens' attitudes regarding the West. Extant political and economic concerns may be eclipsed by cultural traditions, as has been alluded to in political competition (Pravda 1996). In the language of the EU literature, we are least likely to see cost/benefit calculations and economic ideals shape the integration views among the citizens of Ukraine and more likely to see evidence of the powerful undertow of social and cultural traditions. This is particularly relevant to this examination as direct or indirect experience with the West, or the lack thereof, may weigh in on Ukrainian attitudes toward Western integration. That is, domestic concerns may outweigh the distant, albeit crucial, concerns of international political, economic, and social relationships.

This chapter, therefore, reviews the theoretical determinants of EU support and distinguishes the difference between abstract support for integration and the support for specific components of integration in the region (see the introduction by Rohrschneider and Whitefield in this volume). Second, we introduce individuals' orientation toward

NATO membership as a reservoir of support for both broad and specific forms of support for integration. Finally, other relevant factors are addressed, including the theoretically important socioeconomic variables, but particularly the role of individuals' identification with nationalist sentiments, as they have been argued to affect support for both abstract and specific processes of integration.

Understanding Support for EU Expansion in East–Central Europe

When the iron curtain shattered, the EU quickly began to establish bilateral ties with a number of Central and Eastern European countries, including Hungary and Bulgaria. Citizens of these countries have demonstrated continual support for EU membership for roughly the first decade. However, more recently, publics began to voice criticisms about the EU, including the perception that foreigners supposedly gain too much influence within countries (Rohrschneider and Whitefield 2004a). At the outset, it appears that publics have supported integration in principle, that is, broadly, but demonstrate opposition to specific instruments of it.

There is a parallel in the democratic transitions literature that is applicable to the supranational institution of the EU as well. Evidence suggests that while many new democrats support for general democratic values, they are less likely to demonstrate the same level of support when these ideals are measured in more concrete terms (Evans and Whitefield 1995). In the EU context, publics may become aware of and demonstrate some resistance to the difficulty when they are asked to ponder it in the context of domestic institutions. For example, the foreign ownership of domestic enterprises may involve economic interests for some or invoke nationalist sentiments in others. In contrast, the domestic consequences of EU membership are more difficult to see when individuals are asked to evaluate the EU as an abstract entity. Therefore, our study incorporates two conceptual levels of attitudes regarding integration. One is at the most general level of integration, a generalized support for EU membership. The other is a specific and eventual component of this integration, views about foreign investment.

Empirically, the relevance of this distinction is evident from the different levels of support for integration (see figure A6 in the Internet appendix).[3] When publics are asked to evaluate whether a "[country] should join the European Union," we find considerable support for the statement. For example, we see that 68 percent of the Hungarian public respond in the affirmative, as do 74 percent in Bulgaria and even in the Ukraine (52 percent). Thus, there is a majority of support for EU membership, certainly in Hungary and Bulgaria, when individuals are not asked to ponder the domestic repercussions of EU membership.

In contrast to the broad "re-Europeanization" of EU integration seen above, one specific outcome of integration—foreign investment—is a key issue involving a specific domestic market player and thus conveys to citizens more drastically the potential consequences of further integration. In short, the costs are more easily seen when one asks publics to evaluate integration in light of the domestic transformation it may entail.

Another indicator asks whether "foreign investments in a [country] are a threat to our country," and this difference substantially reduces support for a specific aspect of integration (see figure A7 in the Internet appendix): only about 38 percent of the Hungarian public believe that foreign investments are not harmful for Hungary—a drop of nearly 30 percent when we compare it with the support for EU membership in principle. We find a similar drop in Bulgaria (21 percent) and even in the Ukraine (22 percent). Thus, there is a substantial difference in support for the EU, depending on the aspect of integration that individuals are asked to evaluate.

These patterns raise the following questions. To what degree does a country's membership in NATO affect support for the EU at these different levels? Specifically, can NATO provide a source of support for the EU at these different levels? The next section addresses this question.

The North Atlantic Treaty Organization (NATO) and Support for the EU

The expansion of NATO encouraged by the ethnic conflict in the former republic of Yugoslavia[4] and the concerns of the new geopolitical balance given the collapse of the former Soviet Union sought to incorporate these countries into the Western alliance structure as a means to regional stability. Mass public attitudes regarding NATO membership in Central Eastern Europe (CEE) has gone largely overlooked

(Lunak 1994). The few attempts that have been made to discern mass public support for NATO at the individual level explain support for NATO to be related to gender, political affiliation (Bruce 1992), residence (urban versus rural) (Kostadinova 2000), generational differences and education (Eichenberg 1989). Although one scholar has recognized the strong relationship between individuals' support for the EU and NATO (Kostadinova 2000), she does not develop a theoretical account for this relationship. All in all, we therefore know little about whether citizens connect the two integration dimensions.

We hypothesize that NATO provides a positive source of EU support in CEE for the following reasons. We know from transition studies that perceptions of a nation's regime performance has been a strong predictor of institutional support (Evans and Whitefield 1995). This effect is not limited to economic factors, which clearly do matter, but when citizens perceive that national institutions deliver human rights, or the political process works well, support for national institutions increases even more than when individuals believe that the economy works well. This research suggests, then, that the political performance of a regime, not just its economic outputs, substantially affects how a regime is appraised.

It is possible, indeed has been suggested, that NATO membership may have an analogous, beneficial effect for the EU at the level of supranational institutions. NATO was widely seen as a positive force in postcommunist societies. It integrated new democracies into the Western alliance structure, thus providing some protection against any potential Russian threat. Beyond the explicit security aspects, NATO membership also promised to link postcommunist countries closer with the West, thus undergirding the initial efforts by the EU to establish economic ties with countries in the region. In other words, the activities of NATO and the EU started at a similar point, involved mostly the same countries, and involved intertwined goals.

It is thus highly plausible to expect that individuals' approval for international regimes, in this case NATO, may spillover into support for other international regimes. After all, both NATO and the EU are closely associated with the West, particularly Western Europe. Since NATO membership was initiated much earlier than potential EU membership, our *experiential* argument thus suggests that prior positive experience with one international institution will extend to other international organizations as well. Generally, then, we anticipate a "spillover" from individuals' support for NATO into support for EU membership (Easton 1975).

Hypothesis 1: Both support for EU membership and foreign investment are positively correlated with attitudes regarding NATO.

The experiential account also suggests a hypothesis about the relative importance of NATO evaluations for EU support. Although Hungary has been a full member of NATO for most of the previous decade, only recently has Bulgaria been one. Ukraine remains a member of the Euro-Atlantic Partnership Council (EAPC), partners with but not members of NATO.[5] Therefore, if experience is indeed the driving factor, then the influence should be strongest in countries with longer experience with NATO membership and somewhat weaker in nations with partnership status:

Hypothesis 2: The influence of NATO support is strongest in Hungary, then Bulgaria and finally Ukraine

A final consideration concerns the distinction between support for the principles of a regime versus support for specific aspects of it. We expect that NATO membership is primarily affecting EU support at the general level. For any positive experience with NATO may spillover to another international institutions, especially if individuals do not have to ponder the domestic costs of EU membership. In contrast, NATO membership is, according to our argument, less likely to increase support for foreign ownership given that it invokes the costs of EU membership. And this should reduce the beneficial effect of positive NATO membership.

Hypothesis 3: The NATO effect is especially strong for EU membership in principle, but weaker for foreign ownership

Controlling for Other Factors

We need to control for a number of factors that may confound the influence of NATO on EU support. Indeed, one factor deserves special attention: an individuals' commitment to nationalism. EU ascension has initially been resisted in these countries by nationalistic parties but, more recently, even mainstream parties in postcommunist countries increasingly voice opposition to either integration in general, or some specific aspect to it.[6] For example, foreign investment, though a means and process of economic integration, may also be seen as exporting economic control of domestic markets and industries. We thus hypothesize that EU expansion is reduced by nationalist orientations, especially for foreign ownership. The nationalism variable is an additive index of two questions concerning the influence of foreign countries.[7] We expect that an individual's self-reported level of national association will negatively influence attitudes regarding EU membership and foreign investment.

Hypothesis 4: Both support for EU membership and foreign investment are negatively correlated with strong nationalist orientations

Finally, our discussion about the positive effect of NATO indicates that views about it are tied up with economic expectations. In Western Europe, attitudes regarding EU membership have been explained by personal economic situations (Gabel 1998a), individuals' perceptions of their own economic well-being, and national economic performance (Eichenberg and Dalton 1993; Gabel and Whitten 1997). Likewise, the classification of citizens into integration "winners" and "losers" affect EU support in the West (such as education and occupational groups) (Gabel 1998a) but less so in the East (Rohrschneider and Whitefield 2004a). Essentially, these explanations rest on the notion that support for EU membership comes from the outcomes of individuals' considerations of the personal economic benefit to be gained from integration.

Therefore, to control for the competing hypotheses of economic determinants and ideological orientations of CEE citizens, we include respondents' self-reported sociotropic and egocentric economic satisfaction.[8] We also use a measure of economic system preference to gauge respondents' ideological orientations.[9] Individual economic viability, that is, who is to benefit and lose from integration, is predicated on individuals' social position, education, occupation, income, and to some degree gender and age.

We model the influence of both attitudes toward NATO on attitudes toward EU membership and foreign investment in the following way.

Support for EU membership
$= \alpha + \beta_1(\text{NATO}) + \beta_2(\text{Market}) + \beta_3(\text{Nationalism}) + \beta_4(\text{Young}) + \beta_5(\text{National economy}) + \beta_6(\text{Living standard}) + \beta_7 (\text{Middle}) + \beta_8(\text{Income}) + \beta_9(\text{Education}) + \epsilon$

Support for foreign investment
= $\alpha + \beta_1$(NATO) + β_2(Market) + β_3(Nationalism)
+ β_4(Young) + β_5(National Economy) + β_6(Living standard)
+ β_7 (Middle) + β_8(Income) + β_9(Education) + ϵ

Measurement and Results

Using individual level, surveys in Hungary, Bulgaria, and Ukraine,[10] we examine the role of attitudes toward NATO membership in explaining attitudes toward EU membership.

From the first regression analysis of broad EU support, we find support for the hypothesized relationship between attitudes regarding NATO and EU membership (table 10.1). This relationship dominates the model, as individuals' positive attitudes regarding NATO substantially increase support for EU ideals. Note also that we see support for our second hypothesis as well, as the effect is most powerful in Hungary and diminishes as we move east.

Noticeably insignificant are the economic predictors of EU support. In both Hungary and Bulgaria, individuals' national economic evaluations and individual economic concerns demonstrated little power in shaping their attitudes toward EU membership. This is surprising given

Table 10.1 OLS regression on support for membership in the European Union

	Hungary	Bulgaria	Ukraine
NATO	.612 (.638)★★★	.518 (.626)★★★	.325 (.371)★★★
Market	.043 (.022)	−.020 (−.011)	.169 (.103)★★★
Nationalism	−.019 (−.033)	.011 (.021)	−.006 (−.011)
Young	.087 (.030)	−.023 (−.007)	−.065 (−.019)
National economy	.024 (.022)	−.004 (−.003)	−.168 (−.124)★★★
Living standard	.006 (.006)	−.041 (−.045)	.072 (.064)★
Middle	.026 (.010)	−.075 (−.031)	.106 (.041)
Income	.053 (.042)★	.078 (.073)★★	.073 (.067)★
Left/right	−.026 (−.055)★	.016 (.035)	.032 (.066)★
Education	−.013 (−.016)	.046 (.107)★★★	.075 (.118)★★★
Constant	1.653★★★	1.860★★★	1.90★★★
N	1828	1267	1167
Adjusted R^2	0.4320	0.4385	0.2325

Note: Unstandardized regression coefficients reported (standardized coefficients); statistical significance: ★★★ $p < .001$, ★★ $p < .01$, ★ $p < .05$.

economic predictors' consistent and powerful influence in the West-based models of understanding support for the EU.

However, in Ukraine, these economic variables do reach significance suggesting citizens' reliance on economic determinants as a foundation for shaping their attitudes regarding EU membership. For Ukraine, sociotropic concerns outweigh egocentric economic concerns; yet, the negative relationship between national economic performance and EU support in Ukraine suggests that as Ukrainians approve of the ability of their national economy, their support for integration decreases. This is in contrast to the other significant variable of economic system preference as we see the expected positive (and similarly as strong) relationship between the preference for a market economy and EU support. One way to interpret this seeming contradiction is that market ideals tap systemic views that are tied up with broader conceptions of democracy; on the other hand, however, individual economic perceptions may be limited to more immediate economic concerns.

Income and education, as sectoral locations, are expectedly positively correlated and significant predictors of EU support (with the exception of education in Hungary). This relationship lends support to the notion that individuals with higher levels of income and education are either more likely to be able to benefit from integration or at a minimum, not lose (Gabel's winner/loser hypothesis) (Gabel 1998a). Yet, their relative strength in comparison to the NATO variable should be noted. Finally, although a weak predictor, ideological orientation is included in Hungary and Ukraine. Although the directions of the coefficients are opposed, the substantive significance is weak enough to suggest that this relationship is not a core determinant of EU support.

In understanding support for EU membership in CEE, it is significant that economic concerns remain strongest in Ukraine, the country with the least amount of experience with international organizations. It seems that individual-level support for NATO, as a positive prior experience with an international organization, does create some "spillover" into support for the EU. Within these countries, traditional Western-based (primarily economic) predictors again find little purchase in competition with the direct experience of individuals with international organizations.

Does the influence of the NATO variable carry over into support for foreign investment that extends to the specific outcomes of integration? We find that this is not the case. Support for NATO membership shows greatly diminished power as a predictor of individuals' support for foreign investment (table 10.2), although positive, the predictive power of

Table 10.2 OLS regression on support for foreign investment

	Hungary	Bulgaria	Ukraine
NATO	.100 (.089)***	.190 (.203)***	.086 (.088)***
Market	.158 (.071)***	.074 (.037)	.330 (.178)***
Nationalism	−.243 (−.371)***	−.200 (−.355)***	−.288 (−.473)***
Young	.038 (.011)	−.061 (−.017)	−.003 (−.001)
National economy	.061 (.049)*	−.030 (−.023)	.018 (.012)
Living standard	.001 (.001)	.034 (.032)	−.011 (−.009)
Middle	.129 (.042)	.132 (.048)	−.082 (−.028)
Income	.033 (.023)	.137 (.113)***	.021 (.017)
Left/right	−.041 (−.074)***	.044 (.082)**	.005 (.010)
Education	.047 (.050)*	.036 (.075)**	.038 (.053)*
Constant	3.351***	3.202***	3.39***
N	1830	1262	1167
Adjusted R^2	0.1895	0.3388	0.3379

Note: Unstandardized regression coefficients reported (standardized coefficients); statistical significance: *** $p < .001$, ** $p < .01$, * $p < .05$.

NATO is weak on foreign investment. It does remain significant which lends some support for the direct experience argument however, for this specific dimension of integration, other variables, especially nationalism, are much more important.

Cross-nationally consistent and substantively (and statistically) significant, nationalism reduces support for foreign investment. For a specific process of integration, it seems that individuals draw less from a reservoir of direct international organizational experience and rely more on their national identity. Again, the nationalism variable taps a negative orientation of citizens toward foreign influences;[11] while insubstantial in shaping individuals' broad attitudes toward the EU, the specific and concrete processes of integration stoke the embers of the nationalism fire, and powerfully.

For Hungary and Ukraine, economic system preference also explains views about foreign investments: a preference for a market economy is positively correlated with support for foreign investment. While not a surprising finding, the absence of its role in Bulgaria is more perplexing. The income variable provides little insight as to the determinants of individuals' attitudes toward foreign investment in Hungary and Ukraine but so is it in Bulgaria. For Bulgarians, that individual income overpowers economic system preference suggests a disconnect between abstract ideological orientation and "money in pocket."

The left/right ideological orientation variable diminishes as we move east, suggesting either that individuals' development of more sophisticated ideological orientations is related to democratic progress[12] or, as we move from Hungary to Ukraine, that the specifics of integration remain to some degree divorced from the broader notion of integration (as the process is more removed and is thereby less politicized). Again, the opposite signs suggest opposition to integration from different ends of the ideological continuum in each country, the right in Hungary (more nationalist opposition) and the left in Bulgaria (more ideological opposition).

Discussion

For the countries of Hungary, Bulgaria, and Ukraine, this examination has demonstrated a disparity between the predictors of broad EU support and support for the specific processes of integration and the respective influence of previous international organizational experience and nationalism. The powerful influence of earlier international organizations on individuals' level of support for integration ideals is statistically clear. It is also clear that integration instruments are much more weakly linked to NATO. Theoretically, what does this tell us?

First, we draw attention to the under-whelming performance of the economic and sectoral variables. This analysis would suggest that direct experience with international organizations is more salient in shaping individuals' support for both EU membership and even foreign investment than economic performance variables. Only in Ukraine, the least internationally integrated of the three, do economic performance variables emerge—but in the opposite direction from what is predicted by Western-based models.

Second, for the citizens of new democracies, exposure to international organizations seems to imbue them with a preference for, or at least not an aversion to, further integration. Observation of NATO seems to have provided many citizens with direct, first-hand experience that spilled-over into support for further integrative organization, in this case, the EU. This seems to be the case for Hungary and Bulgaria although for Ukraine, while the experience was less comprehensive (as a partner rather than a member of NATO), the same effect (albeit marginally weaker) was observed.

Yet, while the spillover of support for nonspecific support across international organizations is supported, our experiential argument runs up against the results of the second analysis. Individuals' orientation to foreign investment is largely shaped by critical attitudes of nationalism. A citizen's opposition to foreign investment can be explained by attitudes of suspicion and fear of other countries. The question then is why does nationalism surface to influence a specific process of integration and show no influence on attitudes toward broader integration?

A partial answer is that not all foreign investment is exclusively from the West, and that respondents may react, in part, to the source of foreign investment. In 2002, there was a clear distinction in the level of foreign direct investment for these countries with Hungary more than tripling the levels in Bulgaria and Ukraine (Hungary: 2.4 billion, Bulgaria: 691.9 million, Ukraine: 792.0 million).[13] Additionally, as of 2000, Hungary had received a near negligible level of foreign investment from the East, most notably Russia proper. On the other hand, both Bulgaria and Ukraine have received approximately 7–8 per cent of their total foreign investment from Russia.[14] The nationalism variable may, therefore, capture some measure of citizens' historical experience with Russia rather than simply an overt rejection of the specific processes of integration.[15]

Therefore, analyses of the relationship between nationalism and the specific processes of integration (including foreign investments) may be guilty of simply assuming that a rejection of foreign investment is a rejection of the West. At least in the Ukraine, the fact that some foreign investment means investments from Russia may have increased the effect of nationalism. At the same time, the coefficients are quite strong in Bulgaria and Hungary as well, so while the specific source of foreign activities may accentuate the effect of nationalism, it is unlikely to be the sole, or perhaps even the major, reason for why nationalism is such a strong impediment to the specific dimension of integration.

More generally, the intangible payoffs of EU membership may be estimated in some part to individuals' experiences with other international organizations, such that, general orientations toward an organization of democracy spills over into general orientations toward another, in this case, future organization of democracy. Individuals seem willing to transfer their support, whether positive or negative, among these organizations.[16] Yet, attitudes toward the material requirements of the process of integration, in this case, foreign investment, may remind citizens of these countries of their disadvantaged position. Given this region's long history of contested borders and political proprietorship, citizens' resistance to specific dimensions of integration is arguably more susceptible to strongly held beliefs about the viability and sanctity of recently emerged nation-states.

Notes

1. Hungary signed the Treaty of Accession to the EU on May 1, 2004. Bulgaria is scheduled for the next round of ascension in 2007. Ukraine's relationship with the EU remains based on the Partnership and Co-operation Agreement (PCA) and is not yet being considered for membership.
2. See Stephen Whitefield's chapter 11 in this volume. He suggests that this may be the case as citizens' individual economic considerations are overshadowed by attitudes regarding the "old" Russia and economic norms.
3. The Internet appendix can be found at http://www.indiana.edu/~iupolsci/rrohrsch/PalgraveTables+Figures.pdf
4. Because of its geopolitical location as a neighbor of the former Yugoslav republic, Hungary was a heavy recipient of NATO infusion.
5. Along with Slovakia, Slovenia, Romania, Latvia, Lithuania, and Estonia, Bulgaria was invited to become a full member of NATO on March 18, 2004. Bulgaria's parliament overwhelmingly ratified pending membership into the North Atlantic Treaty (226 to 4). Ukraine has yet to be invited for full membership.
6. In all three countries, adamant nationalist (on the right) or anti-integration parties (typically on the left) retain significant constituencies in each election cycle. For example, in Bulgaria, the Bulgarian Socialist Party (BSP including the Coalition for Bulgaria (KzB); in Hungary, the Hungarian Workers' Party (MMP), Hungarian Justice and Life Party (MIEP), and Independent Party of Smallholders (FKgP); in Ukraine, both the Communists (KPU) and Socialist Party (SPU). See chapter 3 by Marks et al. and Rohrschneider and Whitefield in this volume.
7. The questions ask how strongly the respondent agrees with these statements, "Foreign conspiracies are responsible for most of the country's problems" and the second, "Foreign influences are a threat to our culture."
8. Individuals' satisfaction with the national economic performance and their personal economic situations are the responses to the questions "How satisfied are you with the economic situation in [your country] these days?" and "How satisfied are you with your own standard of living?" Both questions were followed by a 5-point scale ranging from very satisfied to not at all satisfied.
9. Economic system preference is captured by the question "Which of the following do you favor for [your country]? Market economy, mixed economy (market & planned), or planned economy." More broadly, we included a measure of individual's general political orientation as well: "In political matters, people talk of the 'left' and the 'right.' How would you place your views on this scale?" Left = 1, right = 10.

10. *Bulgaria.* InterMedia National Survey in 2002; conducted by the Center for the Study of Democracy, Sofia. Face-to-face interviews, raw sample size: 2,052. September 29 to October 11 and October 22–31, 2002. *Hungary.* InterMedia National Survey in 2002; Conducted by MEMRB/Synovate. Face-to-face interviews, raw sample size: 2,000. July 31 to August 20, 2002. *Ukraine.* InterMedia National Survey in 2002. Conducted by KIIS. Face-to-face interviews, raw sample size: 2,019. November 6–19, 2002.
11. These questions include references to foreign conspiracies and threatening foreign influences; see previous footnotes for the exact wording of these questions.
12. This is essentially the argument that individuals have developed a stable and coherent political heuristic from which to evaluate political issues and phenomena.
13. These are net inflows into (country) in current USD, according to World Bank On-line (2002 data) http://www.worldbank.com/data/country-data/countrydata.html
14. Hungary: http://www.fifoost.org/ungarn/hung.pdf; Bulgaria http://www.fifoost.org/bulgarien/bulg.pdf; Ukraine http://www.fifoost.org/ukraine/ukra.pdf. These documents were drafted by the European Bank for Reconstruction and Development (EBRD) Country Promotion Programme team assisted by the respective countries' authorities.
15. It may prove to be a fertile hypothesis to assess individuals' direct experience with foreign investment as it relates to this specific component of integration in order to further support this experiential argument. However, this is beyond the scope of the data available here.
16. Certainly, EU membership most likely confers the wide acceptance of the completion of the transitional period of political and economic transformation for these countries.

CHAPTER 11

Between East and West: Attitudes toward Political and Economic Integration in Russia and Ukraine, 1993–2001

Stephen Whitefield

Introduction

Russia and Ukraine are marginally democratic and market states on the border of the EU. Progress toward their inclusion in Europe and the West is, therefore, of great potential importance, both to the democratic and economic consolidation of these states themselves and to the broader security and stability of Europe. However, the character and over-time dynamics of public support for Western integration, and how these may interact with elite politics in each country, remain relatively obscure.

Accounts of popular support for political and economic integration in Western countries generally point to the importance of cost–benefit analyses by individuals, located in different sectors of the economy, in making their judgments (Gabel 1998b; Scheve and Slaughter 2001). Some studies of support for integration in postcommunist states have also worked within this instrumentalist framework (Cichowski 2000; Tucker, Pacek, and Berinsky 2002). In postcommunist states, however, information about cost and benefits may be sparse, and recent analysis (Rohrschneider and Whitefield 2004a) points to the importance of economic norms, rather than expected losses or benefits as the main basis for citizens' judgments about integration.

Support for Western integration in Russia and Ukraine may be affected by another set of factors. As states on the border of European and Western integration that have long been integrated with one another in a variety of ways, the question of Western integration in Russia and Ukraine, however, may not be so much "will we benefit?" or even "will it help bring about a desirable economic system?" Rather, attitudes toward Western integration may be fundamentally related to the relationship of these states to one another, and therefore by ethnic and national identities and social ties.

This chapter investigates the effects of these attitudinal and social factors and seeks to determine whether Soviet legacies and views of the role of contemporary Russia significantly alter the nature and dynamics support for Western integration in both countries.

Most postcommunist states in Eastern Europe have embraced—and been embraced by—European and Western institutions and their inclusion has changed the economic, political, and security situation in Europe dramatically, though arguably the full impact of the accession of these states to the European Union is only emerging (Rohrschneider and Whitefield 2004a). International institutional engagement with Russia and Ukraine has also clearly increased dramatically since the collapse of the Soviet Union, through bodies such as the Organisation for Security and Cooperation in Europe (OSCE), the Council of Europe, and of course in Russia's case in membership in the G8 and the UN Security Council. But neither Russia nor Ukraine is scheduled for entry into the European Union or NATO, and neither is currently a full member of the WTO—Ukraine has observer status. Though there has been considerable discussion in Europe and the West about developing appropriate relationships with the two states—and clear differences in assessments and approach to each—nonetheless, for Western policy makers, Russia and Ukraine are defined at the limits of the European integration process (Zielonka 2002).

This marginality of Russia and Ukraine reflects not just Western interests but also features of the domestic politics of each state where, to be sure in differing ways and degrees, there exist strong divisions between political camps about the appropriate stance for the country to adopt vis-à-vis the international community (Kuzio 1999; Morozov 2003). This political divide in both states has had many labels but is often characterized as one between "Westernizers," on the one hand, and "Eurasianists" or "Slavophiles" on the other—Eurasianist is the term adopted here (Baranovsky 2000; Kassianova 2001; Kuzio 1999; Pravda 1996). As the names suggest, the former have tended to be supportive of Western integration, while the latter have focused on other historical and potential foci of regional integration, particularly to the south and east. Arguably, differences between Westernizers and Eurasianists (and other anti-Westernizers) are centuries old and reflect deep cultural differences sustained both normatively and by the ongoing geostrategic interests of these states.

Attitudes toward the West were important in the Soviet period, where opponents of Soviet power, often younger and more educated with a connection to Western culture, associated integration with the West with democratic and market reforms. By contrast, supporters of Eurasianism have tended to place much less emphasis on democratic and market reforms. Historically and today, they have focused on the potential for integration between, among others, Russia and Ukraine themselves and stress national independence and distinctive non-Western cultural values. In making this connection, contemporary Eurasianists in both countries have emphasized the common Soviet (and pre-Soviet) past of both states, current membership in the CIS, and other post-Soviet initiatives such as the 2003 declaration by Russia, Ukraine, Belarus, and Kazakhstan of their intention to create a single economic space (Wilson 2000). The legacy of the Soviet Union (and indeed of the Russian Empire before it) also connects with the question of Russia's role in the post-Soviet space. As is well known, around 19 million Russians live outside Russia in the newly independent states, including around 11 million in Ukraine.[1] Many of these Russians are in areas of long-standing Russian settlement and occupation—particularly in Eastern Ukraine and Crimea—and their historical and personal links to Russia and the persistence of Russian and Soviet identities have been factors in both Ukrainian and Russian politics driving support and opposition to "Eurasianism."

Citizens of Russia and Ukraine in these circumstances are subject to efforts by politicians to mobilize support for both Western and "Eurasian" integration process. The existence of these alternative programs for political and economic integration, each of which is rooted in long-standing cultural traditions, social and regional identities, and divergent conceptions of state interests, has also powerfully politicized the issue of Western integration in the party systems of both states (Parfionov 1999; Pravda 1996) made most obvious in Ukraine's "Orange Revolution" in December 2004. In this respect, the centrality of foreign policy to voters' electoral choices is unusual for democratic politics.

One perspective on the efforts at further integrating Russia and Ukraine with Western institutions, therefore, is that the character of public opinion is such that it would create a further source of potential instability for the market and democracy and in the two countries—neither of which has managed to create successful or fully functioning market or democratic systems—and for the international security of Europe and the West more generally.

Developments over the last decade in the two states, however, may have had an effect on ideological and social bases of attitudes toward Western and Eurasian models of integration and on their salience to electoral choices. These changes, moreover, may have lessened the distinctiveness of attitudes in Russia and Ukraine and thereby the problematic relationship of these states to Western integration may also have been reduced. (A contrary suggestion should also be considered that the economic difficulties of the post-Soviet period in both states may have intensified anti-Westernism; Blacker 1998.)

First, historical distance from the Soviet Union has opened and citizens have acquired experience of their newly independent states. Soviet identities, therefore, may have diminished and a greater sense of national identity with independent Russia or Ukraine grown, and with this the appeal of integration with the other state may also have declined (Kuzio 2002).

Second, despite the relative limitations of integration of each state with Western Europe, ties of this sort have grown over time economically (with market development and increased foreign investment and availability of Western goods), politically (with the end of the communist bloc and the development, however imperfectly, of democratic politics), in terms of security (with the acceptance of NATO expansion), and personally (as citizens of both countries have developed personal ties with the West). With greater experience of the realities of integration with the West, opposition to it—and support for its Eurasian alternative—may also have declined and the attitudinal and social associations of pro-Western attitudes may also have altered, away from normative bases for judgments rooted in social identities toward cost–benefit calculations rooted in economic locations.

Third, Russian and Ukrainian politicians have been faced with the realities of running their domestic economies and ensuring the territorial integrity of their states (Molchanov 2002). This has entailed acknowledgment of the need for Western support or, at least, engagement with new transnational economic, political, and security institutions. The shift in policy orientation of ruling politicians has therefore been toward greater pragmatism in relation to the West and to one another, and away from the extremes of either Westernist or Eurasianist camps (Pravda 1996; Sherr 1998). Alongside this, candidates for office from the ruling "parties of power" in both states have increasingly pursued ideological and electoral strategies with reduced emphasis on pro-Western and pro-Eurasian sentiments.

The nature of the attitudinal and social bases of pro- and anti-Western feeling in each country, however, may limit the success of political elites in mobilizing public opinion in either direction, which may also have consequences for the democratic and market development of each state. Pinning down the causal relationship between elite framing and public opinion is notoriously difficult—and ultimately will not be resolved here. However, the character and stability of responses to the question of Western integration may give some indication of the potential for elite framing to radically alter—in one direction or another—attitudes toward the West. Stability in attitudes that are based in fundamental normative orientations may make it less likely that elites have been or will become capable of shaping public opinion to any great degree. This, in turn, may make it less likely that ruling elites may wish to engage in democratic politics in these states, if they perceive public opinion to be divided in ways that, if mobilized, would run counter to elite interests. The great upheavals in Ukraine's "Orange Revolution" may, in this regard, be the exception that proves the rule. On the other hand, development in public attitudes toward a more instrumental view of the integration process and diminished salience to the issue of the West may reflect the effects of increased pragmatism among ruling parties in both countries, which could have positive consequences for their willingness to engage further in the democratic process. Understanding the nature and dynamics of popular support for Western integration is therefore an important political as well as political science question.

The discussion above should not be seen to preclude the existence of important differences between Russia and Ukraine in the character of pro-Western or pro-Eurasianist perspectives, and these will be considered throughout the analysis that follows. For example, in historical terms, a large part of western Ukraine was politically and culturally part of Central East Europe, and geopolitically today, Ukraine is much more committed to entry into Europe than Russia, which has to deal with the reality of its Eurasian territorial stretch. On the other hand, the appeal of Eurasianism and therefore anti-Westernism, may be greater to many of the large numbers of Russians in Ukraine and to those in the Eastern part of the country who find themselves in a state that is no longer connected to their historic motherland.

Using data obtained from national random probability surveys organized by the author and colleagues at Oxford University (particularly Geoffrey Evans) in Russia (1995, 1996, 1998, 2001, 2003) and Ukraine (1995, 1998),[2] the next section shows the basic distribution of attitudes in both states and how these may have changed on the main integration items of relevance; attitudes toward the West and toward internationalism more generally, toward the role of Russia in the newly independent states, and toward the Soviet Union. The issues discussed above are then tested as a set of specific hypotheses in the third and fourth sections below. The concluding section discusses the implications of the findings for the prospects of greater Western integration of Russia and Ukraine and for the general literature on political and economic integration.

Trends in Support for Integration

The discussion above has pointed to a variety of ways in which the issue of state integration presents itself to Russians and Ukrainians—with the West, with one another, with nostalgia for the integrated space of the Soviet Union. We consider next how citizens in both countries view the attractiveness of each of these integration modes, and how their responses changed over time. The results are shown in table 11.1. (Exact question wording for these items is provided in appendix I.)

First, respondents were asked for their position on the question of integration with the West. They were posed a choice between supporting integration for their country as far as possible with the West or with supporting the alternative that their country should remain as isolated as far as possible from the West. The question therefore takes into account people's estimations of the real-world possibilities of integration and isolation, and therefore can be treated as a measure of respondents' normative commitments to Western integration. The results show a preponderance of support for Western integration in Russia and essentially majority support for it in Ukraine. Opposition in both states is between 15 and 20 percent. In both countries, support for Western integration peaks in 1995, and in Russia, for which there are longer term data available, the lowest point reached is in 1998 which then increases somewhat in 2001 and 2003.

Second, respondents were asked their views on the issue of integration in general, regardless of which other states were involved. Did they

Table 11.1 Support for forms of integration in Russia (1995–2003) and Ukraine (1995–1998)

	Russia					Ukraine	
	1995	1996	1998	2001	2003	1995	1998
Integration with West							
Support	48.0	43.2	37.5	43.0	41.9	63.8	49.4
Oppose	15.4	17.3	17.5	18.9	23.3	14.2	16.6
General integration							
Support	37.0	28.0	28.7	39.2	41.1	57.9	50.2
Oppose	36.9	42.5	41.7	30.7	30.9	19.4	26.4
Integration with Russia							
Support	27.6	27.0	25.1	32.5	35.9	12.0	13.1
Oppose	36.3	30.0	25.5	26.6	20.9	52.3	55.3
Integration in Soviet Union							
Support	70.6	62.3	69.4	64.0	59.3	58.1	53.4
Oppose	9.7	13.3	7.2	9.9	13.2	20.1	23.1

favor their country cooperating with other countries if this involved giving up some independence? Support here is more limited in Russia, particularly in 1996 and 1998, though again it increases thereafter. However, more noticeably, opposition to cooperation at the expense of some independence is much greater, with no less than 30 percent against in all years, though opposition too declines over time. In Ukraine, responses are much more positive, with the majority in favor in both 1995 and 1998 and lower levels of opposition.

Third, respondents—both citizens of Russia and citizens of Ukraine—were asked whether they favored the expansion of Russia's contemporary borders to include areas of ethnic Russians in the newly independent states, including—obviously—parts of Ukraine. Support for this proposition in Russia, while never nearly a majority, clearly increases over time, from 28 percent in 1995 to 36 percent in 2003, and opposition that initially outweighed support declines from 36 percent to only 21 percent. The situation in Ukraine, perhaps not surprisingly, is quite different, with a majority of respondents in both 1995 and 1998 expressing opposition to the proposition, and relatively small numbers of respondents (12–13 percent) in favor.

Finally, respondents were asked whether they thought that the dissolution of the Soviet Union was a good thing. While not directly asking whether reintegration of Russia or Ukraine within the Soviet Union was desirable—no such question was asked—the wording does connect with the actual historical form of political and economic integration available as experience to respondents. Here, responses are striking: in both Russia and Ukraine in all the years, the majority of respondents view the dissolution of the Soviet Union as an undesirable thing. These views are slightly less prevalent in Ukraine. And in Russia, levels of opposition to Soviet dissolution have tended to decline over time but still amount to 59 percent of respondents.

These data, therefore, provide an ambiguous picture of aggregate levels of support for various forms of international integration. Support for Western integration appears to be relatively high in Russia and in Ukraine, but this goes along with a great amount of nostalgia for the Soviet Union. Support for integration generally, however, is much lower in Russia, where the population also appears divided on the question of the expansion of Russia's borders. Ukrainians appear less divided about integration issues more generally and more broadly pro-Western.

The broader issue that this chapter addresses, however, concerns the determinants of pro- and anti-Western sentiments, since whether these are instrumental or normative, economic or nationalist, electorally salient or not, may have a far greater impact on the integration process and on associated democratic and market developments in each country than can be discerned from the aggregate figures just shown. These issues are addressed next.

The Social and Attitudinal Determinants of Support for Western Integration

As was pointed out in the introduction, much of the literature on support for political and economic integration in both Western states and in Eastern Europe has focused on the importance of instrumental calculations by citizens about the integration process, with differential views of costs and benefits arising particularly from citizens' employment status and sector, and economic experiences. Recent analysis (Rohrschneider and Whitefield 2004a), however, has cast doubt on this instrumental account in postcommunist states—including Russia and Ukraine—and has refocused attention on the importance of normative commitments, particularly to the type of economic system. The peculiarities of Russia and Ukraine discussed above suggest another possible basis for citizens' judgments about the value of Western integration, namely a relationship to the alternative forms of integration available and being attempted in the region. These do not apply elsewhere in Eastern Europe where the locus for the integration process—and indeed actual experience of integration—is clearly fixed on the West and its institutions such as NATO and the EU. Clearly, the collapse of communist power and the dissolution of the Soviet Union are associated with a package of public attitudes, so that there is a positive relationship between support for market norms, on the one hand, and Western integration and the dissolution of the Soviet Union, on the other ($r = .30$ and $.22$ in Russia and $.27$ and $.24$ in Ukraine). But it is important to establish whether there are independent effects on views of Western integration from both economic norms and views of the Soviet legacy and Russian expansion, and to establish which has the sharpest connection.

It is also important to bear in mind not only the relative importance of instrumental or evaluative factors as Russians and Ukrainians begin to consider Western engagement, but also to consider the development of these factors over time. Citizens' experiences since the collapse of the Soviet Union may have reduced the importance both of economic norms and of alternative forms of integration to judgments about the desirability of integration with the West. As time from the Soviet Union has passed, it may have become less associated with an alternative form of integration to the West and become more simply an expression of nostalgia. Similarly, as state-to-state relations between Russia and Ukraine have stabilized—for example, over such questions as Crimea—concerns about the real prospects of Russian expansionism may have also declined. Finally, the reality of some level of involvement with the West among political elites in each state may also have lessened the connection made politically in these relatively undemocratic states of Western integration to other state or national level concerns.

These points suggest a number of specific hypotheses about both the social and attitudinal bases of support for Western integration.

Hypothesis 1a: The social bases of support for political and economic integration with the West are weakly connected to economic locations and, so far as they have a social basis, are rooted in those with a cultural openness to the West (young and educated).

Hypothesis 1b: However, over time the social bases of support for Western integration have become more associated with economic locations.

Hypothesis 2a: The attitudinal bases of support for political and economic integration with the West are mainly associated (negatively) with stances toward the Soviet Union and toward Russia's relationship to the newly independent states; and, conversely, that evaluative or cost–benefit attitudes and normative views of the ideal economic and political system play a relatively minor role.

Hypothesis 2b: However, over time support for Western integration has become less connected to views of the Soviet Union and Russia and more rooted in economic and evaluative judgments.

These hypotheses are tested by a series of multivariate regression models that treat support for Western integration as the dependent variable and estimate the independent effects of a number of predictor variables:

1. a set of sociodemographic measures that operationalize the main identity and economic factors in hypotheses 1a–b;
2. a set of attitudinal measures that operationalize the alternative forms of integration and—along with these—other predictor variables that measure economic and political norms and economic and political evaluations and expectations.

Details of the question wordings for these measures are provided in appendix I. The results of these analyses for Russia are shown in table 11.2 and for Ukraine in table A17 in the Internet appendix.[3]

Two models are shown for each year. The first includes only demographic and social characteristics—including whether respondents have relatives in the CIS or in the West, ethnicity, language at home, employment status, sector, social class,[4] as well as education, age, and gender. The second adds the attitudinal variables. Because social factors may be causally related to the attitudinal predictors and are less conceptually connected to the dependent variable, running two models in this way allows us to see the effects of social factors that may otherwise be removed or reduced when included alongside the more proximate effect of attitudes.

The results for the demographic models in both countries and all years show a consistent picture. First, economic locations generally appear to be weakly explanatory of Western integration attitudes. There are some effects for class in the expected direction, particularly with the upper service class more likely to be pro-West in some years, though there is no consistent pattern. Other measures of economic location are

Table 11.2 Russia: Regression of support for Western integration onto social characteristics and attitudes toward alternative integration, political, and economic norms, and economic experience (standardized beta coefficients)

Models	1995		1996		1998		2001		2003	
	1	2	1	2	1	2	1	2	1	2
Family members in West	.03	.00	.02	−.00	.07**	.05*	.03	.03	.01	.02
Family members in CIS	.05*	.06**	.01	.02	.07**	.06*	.01	.02	−.06*	−.05*
Russian ethnic	.01	.02	−.01	.02	−.00	.00	−.03	−.04	−.01	−.02
Russian language at home	−.02	−.01	.04	.02	.01	.01	.01	.02	.01	.02
Employed	—	—	—	—	—	—	—	—	—	—
Student	.03	.01	−.01	−.05*	.00	−.04	.04	.02	.01	−.00
Unemployed	.04	.05*	−.03	−.02	−.03	−.04	.05	.03	−.01	−.01
Retired	−.07*	−.03	−.10**	−.05	−.02	−.01	−.00	−.01	−.06	−.03
At home	.02	.09	.03	.01	.01	.00	−.06*	−.03	−.02	−.02
State industry	—	—	—	—	—	—	—	—	—	—
Private sector	.03	.03	.06*	.00	−.03	−.05	−.01	−.01	.05	.02
Farm	.02	.03	−.02	.00	.02	.01	.05	.06*	.01	.01
Budget sector	.03	.04	.00	−.01	−.04	−.03	.02	.04	−.03	−.01
Working class	—	—	—	—	—	—	—	—	—	—
Upper service	.10**	.07*	.05	.02	.09**	.05*	.06*	.04	.03	−.00
Routine nonmanual	.05	.03	.04	.02	.03	.00	.07**	.05*	.04	.03
Petty bourgeois	.03	−.01	.04	.01	.05*	.05*	.00	−.00	−.01	−.03

Continued

Table 11.2 Continued

Models	1995 1	1995 2	1996 1	1996 2	1998 1	1998 2	2001 1	2001 2	2003 1	2003 2
Agricultural workers	.04	.01	-.02	-.02	.05*	.05*	.05	-.05	-.01	-.00
Age	-.11**	-.02	-.14**	-.04	-.17**	-.05	-.12**	-.05	-.09**	-.03
Education	.05	.01	.10**	.04	.06*	.03	.05	.01	.08**	.06*
Gender	.08**	.06*	.08**	.03	.06*	.04	.05*	.05*	.06*	.05*
Cooperate with other states		.05*		.03		.09**		.10**		.12**
Russia should expand borders		.08**		.05*		.03		.07**		.00
Dissolution of the Soviet Union a good thing		.10**		.10**		.07**		.07**		.08**
Democracy as ideal system		.07**		.10**		.02		.13**		.05*
Market as ideal system		.14**		.15**		.14**		.09**		.10**
Role of state norms		.16**		.20**		.16**		.13**		.11**
Democracy evaluation		-.00		.09**		.06*		-.01		-.00
Market evaluation		.02		-.05*		-.01		-.01		-.03
Household living standards past five years		-.01		.01		.06**		-.02		.03
Household living standard next five years		.00		.03		-.01		.02		.01
Adjusted r^2	.06	.17	.11	.26	.08	.19	.06	.14	.04	.10

Notes: * $p < .05$, ** $p < .01$.

even less linked to the dependent variable. There are essentially no effects for employment status or employment sector in either country. The results therefore show very weak evidence for the sorts of economic locations that are privileged in many accounts of support for international integration in other contexts.

Strikingly, the effects of ethnic and linguistic factors that might be expected to be important are also absent, even in Ukraine where the population is clearly differentiated on these items. Being or speaking Russian or Ukrainian does not appear to affect Western integration attitudes. However, one significant social factor also emerges in the Ukraine analyses, namely the sharp differences in support for Western integration between regions of the country, with those in Eastern Ukraine and Crimea, where historical links to Russia are strongest, less supportive and, in 1998, those in Western Ukraine where historical links to the West (and relatively recent incorporation into Russia) are strongest.

The most important social determinants of support for Western integration are, first, age (younger people are more supportive) and education (more educated the more supportive). There is also an effect in all years except 2001 in Russia and in 1995 in Ukraine for gender, with men more supportive than women. The question of how to interpret age, education, and gender effects is clearly problematic. Since these are possibly strongly connected with economic status and (dis)advantage, particularly at a relatively early stage in the market transition (Kitschelt 1992), their inclusion in these models may explain why the other economic variables capture so little of the variance. On the other hand, they may be more connected to cultural commitments, especially openness or otherwise to Western cultural influences. To test this—analysis available but not shown—the regressions were run again excluding age, education, and gender to see whether the effects of the economic variables were boosted as a result. Apart from a big increase in the coefficients for retired people—which clearly replaces age—the effects for all other sector, employment, and class variables remain essentially stable, from which we may infer that age, education, and gender are in this context more cultural than economic.

The overall picture provided by the analyses of the social bases of support for the West, therefore, points toward confirmation of hypothesis 1a. The data, however, show no support for hypothesis 1b. The effects of the economic location variables do not increase over time (even in the truncated models that exclude age, education, and gender). Rather, the relationships appear to be generally stable over time.

Turning next to the attitudinal determinants of Western integration (shown in model 2 for each year and country), the results show modest confirmation for hypothesis 2a but clearly speak against hypothesis 2b. As was the case in other postcommunist states, in Russia, the main predictors of support for the West are connected to economic norms, both views of the market as an ideal system, and normative judgments about the role of the state in the economy. Democratic norms are also consistently significant. As was pointed out above, support for the West is positively associated with promarket and prodemocratic stances. Nonetheless, even controlling for the effects of economic and political norms, there remain strong and consistent effects for attitudes toward the Soviet Union—those who regret its passing are less likely to support Western integration. There are also significant effects for attitudes toward Russian expansion in three of the five years. Interestingly, there also appears to be a growing relationship in Russia over time for a more generalized orientation toward cooperation with other states and Western integration.

What is notably absent from the analysis, however, are consistently significant or strong effects for evaluations of Russian democracy and the market in practice, or for Russians' perceptions of trends in their living standards past or future. As was the case with the social bases, therefore, economic calculations do not appear to play a significant direct role in generating support and neither is there any indication that such calculations are coming to mean more with growing experience of the West and the market. Even the fact of greater historical distance from the Soviet Union does not appear to have reduced the effects of attitudes toward the Soviet past. Rather, the attitudinal basis of Russians' judgments about Western integration has remained remarkably stable over time.

Much the same picture emerges from the analysis of Ukraine, where economic perceptions and market evaluation are also insignificant for both years. Here, however, the effects of the Soviet legacy and contemporary relationships to Russia are, if anything, stronger than was the case in Russia, and rival the importance of economic norms.

We can summarize this section, therefore, by noting that contrary to many accounts of support for integration, economic locations and calculations are of little importance. As with other postcommunist states, normative judgments, particularly regarding the economy, are of considerable significance. However, the legacy of the Soviet Union as an alternative locus of integration continues to play a major role in shaping opinion toward integration with the West in both Russia and

Ukraine, as do attitudes toward the integration of parts of Ukraine in Russia for attitudes toward the West in Ukraine.

International Integration and Electoral Choice

Establishing the precise direction in the causal relationship between public opinion and party positioning is, of course, a vexed issue scientifically and an important one for assessing the possibilities of change in public attitudes. At least at the beginning of electoral competition in postcommunist states, parties probably had a limited capacity to shape public attitudes and so the relationship initially may have been "bottom-up" in character (Evans and Whitefield 2000). Over time, however, as parties develop relationships with voters, their ability to shape public opinion may increase, and in Russia and Ukraine, there is some evidence that ruling politicians who might have the greatest capacity to do so have also had an interest in reducing the salience of Western integration to electoral competition. Their success in doing so might also result from the fact that elites in Russia and Ukraine were much less democratic than those of other postcommunist states (Rohrschneider and Whitefield 2004a). Competing and potentially offsetting influences, however, were not wholly absent, as other politicians and parties sought to increase the salience of West versus Eurasia to public opinion, especially in Ukraine in 2004. Moreover, the strongly normative bases of judgments just shown, which tend to be "sticky" over time, may also point to limitations on the capacities of parties to shift public opinion in one direction or another. So, while the specific causal flow cannot be fully sorted out here, evidence about the importance of Western and other forms of integration to partisanship, and how this has changed since 1995, may cast some light on the capacity of elites to shape public opinion, as well as on the political possibilities and consequences of further Western integration in these states.

Again, two hypotheses are considered.

Hypothesis 3a: The issue of Western integration, the dissolution of the Soviet Union, and the role of Russians in the newly independent states are strongly salient to the partisan choices of Russians and Ukrainians.

Hypothesis 3b: However, as elite level state-to-state relationships have stabilized over time, so too have the issues of Western integration, the dissolution of the Soviet Union, and the expansion of Russia's borders become less important to electoral choice in both countries.

These hypotheses are tested using data on intended vote for political parties as the dependent variable in a series of multinomial logistic regression models that allows for estimates of the overall effect of various integration factors on vote choice and also for the relationship of these factors to support for particular parties. Because of the great number of (often small) parties in both countries, blocs have been created based on their general ideological orientation and relationship to the "party of power" in both countries (Parfionov 1999; Pravda 1996). Following a broad consensus in the party literature on these states, the exact nature of the blocs differs somewhat between the two countries; in particular, in Ukraine, nationalism is associated with support for reform, whereas in Russia, this is much less the case, where nationalism appears divided between the left and the antidemocratic right. (Details of each bloc can be found in appendix II.) Party rather than presidential choice is used because parties are organizationally relatively more stable over time; the distribution of support for presidential candidates is much more prone to change because at the point of any given survey, the availability of presidential candidates is often unknown. However, analysis using presidential choice (available but not shown), is generally compatible with the picture that emerges below.

The results for Russia are shown in table 11.3. First, the chi-square statistics show the difference in fit between a full model and a reduced one that leaves out the given effect; the null hypothesis would be that all parameters of that effect are 0. However, as table 11.3 shows, attitudes toward Western integration are a significant factor for vote choice in all the years. Moreover, while the effect fluctuates somewhat in strength, there appears to be no overall decline over time. There are also strong effects in all the years for views of the Soviet past and in two years—to a much lesser degree—for attitudes toward the expansion of Russia's borders too.

Table 11.3 also shows the effects of attitudes toward integration on support for particular party blocs, with the "center bloc" as the reference category. Not surprisingly, these are most striking in the case of the communist dominated left bloc, which is significantly more opposed to Western integration (than the center bloc) in 1995, 1998, and 2003, and whose relative opposition to the dissolution of the USSR is strongly significant in all years. Supporters of the national-authoritarian bloc (mainly those who would vote for Zhirinovsky's Liberal

Table 11.3 Russia: Multinomial logit regressions of intended party choice onto views of integration, political and economic norms, and evaluations

	1995 B (S.E.)	1996 B (S.E.)	1998 B (S.E.)	2001 B (S.E.)	2003 B (S.E.)
National-authoritarian					
Western integration	NS	−.23 (.11)★	NS	−.24 (.12)★	NS
Russia's borders	NS	NS	−.33 (.15)★	NS	NS
Soviet Union	NS	NS	NS	−.34 (.14)★	NS
Democratic norms	NS	NS	−.33 (.15)★	NS	NS
Market norms	NS	NS	NS	NS	NS
State role	.41 (.17)★	NS	NS	NS	NS
Democracy evaluation	NS	−.38 (.17)★	NS	NS	−.41 (.15)★★
Market evaluation	NS	−.46 (.13)★★	−.38 (.16)★	.32 (.15)★	NS
Right					
Western integration	NS	NS	NS	.29 (.10)★★	NS
Russia's borders	NS	NS	NS	.20 (.09)★	.19 (.09)★
Soviet Union	.29 (.09)★★	NS	NS	NS	NS
Democratic norms	.25 (.09)★★	NS	NS	NS	NS
Market norms	NS	.33 (.13)★	NS	NS	NS
State role	.26 (.11)★	NS	NS	.41 (.13)★	.34 (.12)★★
Democracy evaluation	NS	−.40 (.16)★	NS	NS	NS
Market evaluation	NS	−.33 (.12)★★	−.36 (.14)★	NS	NS
Left					
Western integration	−.20 (.09)★	NS	−.44 (.13)★★	NS	−.24 (.07)★★
Russia's borders	NS	NS	−.36 (.14)★	NS	NS
Soviet Union	−.27 (.13)★	−.80 (.13)★★	−.52 (.14)★★	−.26 (.09)★★	−.57 (.09)★★
Democratic norms	NS	−.39 (.12)★★	−.36 (.15)★	−.32 (.09)★★	−.33 (.09)★★

Continued

Table 11.3 Continued

	1995 B (S.E.)	1996 B (S.E.)	1998 B (S.E.)	2001 B (S.E.)	2003 B (S.E.)
Market norms	−.51 (.10)**	−.34 (.12)**	NS	−.21 (.12)*	NS
State role	NS	−.48 (.15)**	−.62 (.18)**	NS	−.43 (.12)**
Democracy evaluation	NS	−.60 (.17)**	−.43 (.22)*	NS	NS
Market evaluation	NS	−.55 (.13)**	−.50 (.16)**	NS	−.31 (.10)**
Cox and Snell pseudo r^2	.23	.45	.39	.20	.26
Chi square					
Western integration	11.25*	9.69*	16.05**	20.11**	13.71**
Russia's borders	NS	NS	7.91*	9.02*	NS
Soviet Union	27.62**	65.16**	24.98**	17.89**	49.04**
Democratic norms	12.63**	15.82**	28.15**	15.57**	22.55**
Market norms	29.74**	29.61**	13.20**	10.70*	NS
State role	12.27**	22.48**	14.14**	16.24**	28.79**
Democracy evaluation	NS	14.66**	NS	NS	9.32*
Market evaluation	NS	21.84**	10.95*	NS	14.87**

Notes: Reference category is "center parties."

* significant at $p < .05$, ** $p < .01$, NS = nonsignificant.

Democratic Party of Russia) are also less likely to favor Western integration than the center bloc in 1996 and 2001. It is also interesting to note that in 2001, supporters of the right bloc were more likely to favor Western integration than the center bloc and more likely to oppose the expansion of Russia's borders in 2001 and 2003.

While democratic, market, and state norms were also strongly significant in all years (with the exception of market norms in 2003), and distinguished the left bloc (antimarket, antidemocratic, and pro-state) on the one hand, and the right bloc (anti-state) on the other, it is clear that attitudes toward Western integration and the formerly integrated Soviet space were significant independently to a degree that is surprising in comparative terms for a foreign policy issue. It is also notable that support for right, left, and national-authoritarian blocs is regularly drawn from those who are more negative than those for the center about both democracy and the market in Russia in practice (Whitefield 2005).

Once again, we find similarities and differences in the picture for Ukraine in table A18 in the Internet appendix. First, there are big changes in the county comparing 1995 with 1998 in the extent to which most of the variables have an impact. Most accounts of the Ukrainian politics stress the slow development of the party system and party identification (Birch 1998; Miller et al. 2000) and these results may reflect that. Second, however, as the chi-square statistics show, views of the Soviet Union are of enormous significance to electoral choice, and may have grown in importance as the party system developed. In 1998, moreover, both views of Western integration and Russian expansion were also significant to the regression model, and particularly distinguished supporters of the left bloc (anti-West, pro-Russian expansion, pro-Soviet, antidemocratic, antimarket, prostate) from the center. The nationalist right, for its part, was more anti-Soviet than the center in 1998.

To return to our hypotheses, the analyses certainly confirm the centrality of integration issues both to the West and to the East (and to the Soviet past) to political divisions; they do not confirm that these have become less salient over time.

Conclusions

The postwar process of European integration generally proceeded between states that shared geostrategic as well as economic interests based upon commonality of regime type. In that context, the basis by which citizens in these states made judgments about international integration appears to have related mainly to instrumental calculations, and the ability of these democracies to engage and consolidate the European Union was the result of the excess of perceived winners over losers among the public.

In postcommunist states, international integration occurs against the quite different background of systematic and revolutionary transformation in which the issue of Europe and the West is connected to where citizens stand on concepts of ideal forms of government. For this reason, support for international integration in these societies connects most strongly with economic and political norms—especially the former—rather than costs and benefits.

In Russia and Ukraine, however, these normative factors are supplemented by an additional set of concerns that is related to system-level considerations but have a further important independent effect. In these states, for historical and geostrategic reasons, large parts of the public have commitments to an alternative form of integration—which I have labeled Eurasianism—that provides a distinct reason to be opposed to Western integration. Opposition to Eurasianism, in turn, provides a separate reason to be pro-West. The impact of this division in public opinion is also consequential for each country's politics, as it connects significantly with the choices that voters make about parties.

The integration of Russia and Ukraine with the West, and most obviously with Europe, is therefore particularly challenging for politicians in these countries and in the West who have a strategic and economic interest in achieving it. From the perspective of Western institutions, the further integration of Russia and Ukraine is difficult to avoid. As states outside a common security and economic structure, Russia and Ukraine raise many potential problems. However, it is instructive too to consider what difficulties might arise if they were to have the status of other postcommunist states. The problems for the governance of the European Union that may arise from enlargement including East European states whose populations appear strongly divided from Western Europe by ongoing normative commitments to economically socialist norms and relatively weak commitments to democracy are only now coming into focus. The difficulties that would arise from the inclusion of Russia and Ukraine, where anti-Westernism appears to have a more complex and deeper historical and geostrategic base would be much greater.

Russia and Ukraine may be most likely, therefore, to remain border states between East and West, with all of the division and possibility of conflict and instability that this status entails. Certainly, there are strong constituencies in favor of Western integration in both countries, especially among younger and more educated people. However, the process does not appear to depend on stable economic interests but much more on normative and cultural commitments that may be much more difficult for politicians to shift. The issue of the West and of Eurasianism appears embedded in the party system, and attempts to integrate are likely to remain highly contested in democratic politics. This results in a double-edged problem. On the one hand, to the extent that those in power in these states wish to engage with the West and may have sought to diminish its political salience, its status as an ongoing political cleavage may reduce the incentive to elites to improve democracy in their countries—and so far as the West wants their engagement, it may be incentivized to close its eyes to Russia and Ukraine's democratic weaknesses. On the other hand, to the extent that Russia and Ukrainian leaders may not wish to engage with the West, the character of public opinion may give them incentives to anti-Western populism. Neither alternative is highly satisfactory for democratic and market development in Russia and Ukraine or to international stability in Europe. Over time, it might be hoped, exposure to the West and the market may produce new popular economic interests or a cultural change to shift the balance more strongly toward the West. But there are few signs that this has occurred to any significant degree over the last decade.

Appendix I: Survey Items

All variables use 5-point agree–disagree scales.

Integration

Western integration. Either: [Country] should integrate as far possible into the Western world. Or: [Country] should remain isolated as far as possible from the Western world.
General integration. [Country] should cooperate with other countries even if it means giving up some independence.
Russian integration. The borders of Russia should be expanded to include ethnic Russians in "the near abroad."
Soviet integration. The dissolution of the Soviet Union was a good thing.

Political Norms

Democracy. How do you feel about the *aim* of building democracy in the country in which political parties compete for government?

Markets. How do you feel about the *aim* of creating a market economy with private ownership and economic freedom to entrepreneurs.

Government intervention. Four-item scale comprised of

Either: The government should see to it that every person has a job and a good standard of living. Or: The government should just let each person get ahead on his or her own.

Either: The government should not concern itself with how equal people's incomes are. Or: The government should try to make differences between incomes as small as possible.

Either: The government should take all major industries into state ownership. Or: The government should place all major industries in private ownership.

Either: The government should just leave it up to individual companies to decide their wages, prices, and profits.
Or: The government should control wages, prices, and profits.

Experience and Evaluations

Democracy. How would you evaluate the *actual practice* of democracy here in [*country*] so far?

Markets. How would you evaluate the *actual experience* of the market economy so far?

Household living standards past. Compared with *five years ago*, has your household's standard of living fallen a great deal, fallen a little, stayed about the same, risen a little, or has it risen a lot?

Household living standards future. And looking ahead over the *next five years*, do you think that your household's standard of living will fall a great deal from its *current* level, fall a little, stay about the same as it is now, rise a little, or rise a lot from its current level?

Appendix II: Party Blocs

Russian Party Blocs

1993: *National-authoritarian bloc*: Liberal-Democratic Party of Russia; *Right bloc*: Future of Russia, Democratic Choice, Yabloko, supporters of

Svyacheslav Fyodorov and Boris Fyodorov; *Center bloc*: Our Home is Russia, Movement for Democratic Reforms, Democratic Party of Russia, Civic Union, Women of Russia, Cedar, Dignity and Charity, supporters of Shakhray; *Left bloc*: Communist Party of the Russian Federation, Agrarian Party, supporters of Tuleev.

1996: *National-authoritarian bloc*: Liberal-Democratic Party of Russia, Congress of Russian Communities, Derzhava, Fatherland, My Fatherland; *Right bloc*: Yabloko, Forward Russia, supporters of Gaidar; *Center bloc*: Our Home is Russia, Women of Russia, Cedar, Social Democrats, supporters of Rybkin; *Left bloc*: Communist Party of the Russian Federation, Agrarian Party.

1998: *National-authoritarian bloc*: Liberal-Democratic Party of Russia, Congress of Russian Communities, Derzhava, Fatherland, My Fatherland; *Right bloc*: Yabloko, Forward Russia, supporters of Gaidar; *Center bloc*: Our Home is Russia, Women of Russia, Cedar, Social Democrats, supporters of Rybkin; *Left bloc*: Communist Party of the Russian Federation, Agrarian Party.

2001: *National-authoritarian bloc*: Liberal-Democratic Party of Russia, Congress of Russian Communities and Boldyrev Movement, Russian Conservative Movement, Spas; *Right bloc*: Yabloko, Union of Right Forces; *Center bloc*: Unity, Fatherland-All Russia, Our Home is Russia, Women of Russia, Cedar, Dignity; *Left bloc*: Communist Party of the Russian Federation, Communists for the Soviet Union.

2003: *National-authoritarian bloc*: Liberal-Democratic Party of Russia; *Right bloc*: Yabloko, Union of Right Forces; *Center bloc*: United Russia; *Left bloc*: Communist Party of the Russian Federation, Agrarian Party.

Ukrainian Party Blocs

1995: *Left bloc*: Rural Democratic Party, People's Party of Ukraine, Rural Party of Ukraine, Front of Workers of Ukraine, Union of Communists of Ukraine, Party of National Salvation, Party of Free Peasants, Communist Party of Ukraine, Party of Slavic Unity; *Centrist bloc*: Liberal Party, Socialist Party, Labour Party, Party of Justice, Social Democratic Party, Constitutional Democrats, Party of Solidarity and Social Justice; *Nationalist bloc*: Republican Party, Green Party, Ukrainian Christian-Democratic Party, Conservative Republican Party, Christian-Democratic Party of Ukraine, Congress of Ukrainian Nationalists, People's Rukh, Nation-wide Rukh.

1998: *Left bloc*: Agrarian Party, Communist Party of Ukraine, Soyuz, All-Ukrainian Party of Workers, Progressive Socialists; *Centrist bloc*: Labour and Liberal Bloc, Party of Regional Rebirth of Ukraine, Hromada, Ahead Ukraine, Labour Party, Social Democratic Party, National Democratic Party, Socialist Party, Social Democratic Party-United; *Nationalist bloc*: Republican Christian Party, Ukrainian National Assembly, Green Party, People's Rukh, Christian Democratic Party of Ukraine.

Notes

1. Proportionally, the number of Ukrainians living in states of the former Soviet Union may be even greater.
2. Data used in this chapter were obtained from surveys conducted by the author and colleagues at Oxford University funded by the British Economic and Social Research Council's East-West Research Program, Phase II (G. Evans, S. Whitefield, A. Heath, and C. Payne, Grant no. Y 309 25 3025 "Emerging Forms of Political Representation and Participation in Eastern Europe"); INTAS (S. Whitefield and G. Evans, "Ethnicity, Nationalism and Citizenship in the Former Soviet Union"); the UK ODA Know-How Fund (G. Evans and S. Whitefield, "The Development of Social Class in Post-Communist Russia"); and the British Economic and Social Research Council (G. Evans and S. Whitefield, "The Development of Social Class in Post-Communist Russia"). A survey was also conducted in both Russia and Ukraine in 1993, but to ensure comparability of all questions over time, these have been omitted from this study. However, more limited analysis that includes 1993 (available from the author) points to the same pattern of results as that found in 1995.
3. The Internet appendix can be found at http://www.indiana.edu/~iupolsci/rrohrsch/PalgraveTables+Figures.pdf
4. Class is measured here using the Erikson-Goldthorpe scheme (Erikson and Goldthorpe 1992), which can be best understood as a related set of occupational characteristics uniting workers in different sectors of the economy, especially those of employed versus self-employed, salaried versus waged (or piece-rated or commissioned), supervisory versus supervised, with benefits versus without, which give rise to differentiated economic strategies and life-chances. For a validation of the Goldthorpe scheme in Russia, see Evans and Mills (1999) and Evans and Whitefield (1999).

Conclusion: The Political Consequences of Postcommunist Accession

Robert Rohrschneider and Stephen Whitefield

Introduction

The evidence and argument presented in the previous chapters have clear implications for the politics of integration in postcommunist states. Accession to the EU of 10 postcommunist states—and the ongoing exclusion of some others—will have major effects on the dynamics of political competition in East European states themselves and may raise significant challenges for EU governance.

We see two reasons for this. First, public attitudes toward integration, and their interaction with the democratic process in postcommunist states, differ in politically consequential ways from other integration experiences in established democratic and market environments. So far as the public is concerned, integration appears to be judged in highly normative rather than in instrumental terms as is more common in Western Europe. Postcommunist citizens remain divided by their ideological attachments to socialist versus market and democratic versus antidemocratic system ideals (see chapter 4 by Jacobs and Pollack, this volume). If integration is contested on the basis of ideological factors, rather than mainly on the basis of a utilitarian calculus, debates are likely to be more intense, issues more far-reaching, and compromise less easily reached.

Second, party competition in East European states may also have a powerful effect on the politicization of integration issues because, all else being equal, support for integration appears to be reduced and the connection of integration to citizens' normative commitments appears to be greater in more democratic countries where political parties are better able to mobilize support for and opposition against integration. It happens to be the case that the more democratic countries are also the ones who first joined the EU in 2004. In so far as parties constrain governments' engagement with the EU, therefore, they may also pose a challenge to international institutions such as the EU.

For these reasons, it is vital to know how political elites frame the integration process and we turn our attention in this conclusion to a further elaboration of this question in the context of the arguments developed in the introductory chapter and as these issues have been developed in the empirical chapters that followed.

The Sources of Party Positions on Integration

As the book has made clear at various points, two important distinctions capture many of the complexities of the politics of integration in postcommunist states. First, we distinguish ideal stances from instrumental considerations. Second, we distinguish among dimensions of the integration process and, in particular, between economic and polity considerations. We consider these distinctions important because they reflect the characteristics and dynamics of mass opinion discussed above, and because they relate to the multidimensional nature of the transition in Eastern Europe that is simultaneously economic (market), democratic, geostrategic (security), and national-ethnic. One theoretical implication of these distinctions, therefore, is that they allow for many of the differences across countries we observed in the empirical chapters in the ways in which integration is politicized in the party systems, and over time as the realities of integration become apparent.

Theoretically, however, it is also important to analyze why parties adopt a specific stance on European integration. There are numerous factors at various levels that we hypothesized in the introductory chapter have an effect on the stances taken by parties in different contexts: country characteristics, such as transition paths, ethnic composition; party characteristics, such as party family, party organization, faces of party power, and the like. These, we argue, make themselves evident in connection with two facets of the way in which parties position themselves on integration issues. First, in differences between levels of support versus salience ascribed to ideal versus instrumental aspects of integration. Second, in the relationship between accession status and how parties frame the EU and are divided on integration issues. Because integration ideals are distinct from instrumental factors, the economic and political realities of integration fall most strongly on those states that are closest to accession, so parties frame relationships among political and economic as well as ideal and performance aspects differently in countries that have to deal with these realities.

We referred in the introduction to the "cost mobilization" model in explaining the dynamics of this process, the premise of which is that the issue of integration becomes particularly salient to parties and citizens when countries are presented with greater opportunities to evaluate it. The greater relevance of integration in accession countries stimulates political parties on both sides of the policy. Political entrepreneurs, who oppose integration, for example, mobilize mass sentiments against the general ideals of a single market or they mobilize against what they present as a loss of political sovereignty. Integration supporters, in turn, mobilize their camp in the opposite way. More specifically, integration opponents may mobilize opposition to accession criteria that include the expansion of foreign corporate entry, or the "diktat" of the EU on minority rights. Again, integration supporters may do the opposite.

The effects of greater party mobilization that results from proximity to accession are evident in the structure of relationships among integration issues. In particular, we note four characteristics of these relationships, which are not only theoretically plausible but also empirically supported by evidence from a survey of the stances of political parties in 13 postcommunist states that we undertook in late-2003/early-2004, comprising the states scheduled for accession in 2004 (Czech Republic, Estonia, Hungary, Latvia, Lithuania, Poland, Slovakia, and Slovenia), later accession (Bulgaria, Romania), as well as states that are not scheduled for entry at all (Moldova, Russia, and Ukraine).[1]

As the next section suggests, our evidence suggests that the levels of support for, and salience of, integration issues vary with context in ways that speak directly to the problematic ways in which these questions will impact on national and EU-level politics.

Party Position and the Salience of Integration

Ideals and Instruments

We begin the analyses with a broad overview of the degree to which various integration dimensions are politicized by political parties in the region (figure A8 in the Internet appendix).[2] (See the appendix for details of the results and for exact question wordings.) First, it is immediately apparent that parties on average support greater Western integration nearly everywhere. And for most parties this is an important issue as well. This holds as we move to party positions about more specific issues such as political integration and the common market, which parties tend on average also to view favorably (although there is quite a bit of spread around the mean). However, EU polity and an integrated market are somewhat less important to party appeals than general integration toward the West. It appears that integration dimensions that reaffirm further integration in the West are both supported and important to party appeals. However, as one moves toward actual European Union structures, we find that while support is still strong, the importance of it to party stances is reduced.

As was discussed in various previous chapters (chapter 8 by Mungiu-Pippidi, chapter 9 by Whitefield, Rohrschneider, and Alisauskene, and chapter 10 by Loveless and Rohrschneider), one possibility for this broad pattern is that Western integration stands for protection against the former Soviet empire. Consequently, parties view it as highly desirable to develop their ties with the West. However, the EU itself may be viewed with more ambivalence because EU membership not only implies ties with Europe but also points to the surrender of national and domestic institutions. This means that the reduced salience of EU integration ideals may signal the beginnings of some skepticism about integration given the complicated nature of the supranational transition. Thus, parties may not come out directly against European integration *in principle*; neither may they come out against market integration *in principle*. What parties may do, however, is to reduce their advocacy for integration in principle. That is, they say they are for it but don't make it a central plank in their appeals to mass publics.[3]

If this reasoning is correct, then we should see more skepticism about specific integration instruments *and* that these instruments are important to parties. In order to begin to test this possibility, figure A9 in the Internet appendix presents the position of parties about specific integration instruments. An important instrument—a means to implement integration with specific institutions—is the foreign ownership of land and industrial enterprises. If the lower salience of integration ideals in party appeals reflects reservations on the part of parties, it should emerge when we plot the position and importance of integration instruments.

Let us begin with the foreign ownership of land and industrial enterprises. In terms of the position of parties, there is more skepticism over these integration instruments than there is over integration ideals.[4] The salience of these integration instruments is somewhat higher than for market integration, albeit by a narrow margin.[5] What is especially noteworthy is that there is greater polarization over integration instruments than over market integration (see also below).[6] Importantly, this pattern is not limited to just the minor, splinter parties. For example, the Bulgarian Socialists (BSP) and the Hungarian conservative party (Fidesz) are among the skeptics, even though they support market integration in principle.

We also find that support for other integration instruments is lower than for integration ideals, including the migration of people and the EU directives over minorities. These issues are not relevant to all countries, and may in general terms be less polarizing than the other integration instruments. Still, we find roughly the same pattern when we compare how parties position themselves on these instruments: support is lower and polarization is greater when compared with integration ideals.[7] The only difference to foreign ownership concerns the relatively low salience of these two instruments in a number of countries: nations with few minorities are presumably less concerned with these dimensions, and the issues are thus not as relevant as the other integration instruments.

Overall, what we observe in these broad patterns are a number of significant developments that support our conclusions and concerns about how integration issues have entered party competition in post-communist Europe and in turn frame issues to voters. First, support for integration ideals is higher than for integration instruments. Second, support for Western integration is higher than support for EU-related integration. Third, the salience of integration instruments is, on average higher, than the salience of EU-related ideals. We may infer from this, therefore, that as integration moves from ideals to reality, support will fall and the salience of these issues will rise in party competition, with significant consequences for public opinion.

The Effects of Accession Proximity on Party Support and Party Polarization

To what extent do we already find that proximity to accession has had an impact on party stances? Are party positions influenced by the accession date? From the cost mobilization model, our prediction is that, regardless of the particular integration element that is at issue, support will decline with greater proximity to accession and polarization of parties will increase. This is exactly what we observe in action already.

Accession Status and Levels of Integration Support

To repeat, in broad terms, parties are on average somewhat more prointegration than against it (see table 12.1). This is true across all waves and regions, including the CIS states included in the study that are not scheduled for accession at all.[8] We may draw from this a relatively optimistic conclusion about the general positive disposition of party systems as a whole in postcommunist states towards European and international integration.

The evidence shows, however, that there is considerable variation across waves and regions. First wave countries—Czech Republic, Estonia, Hungary, Latvia, Lithuania, Slovakia, and Slovenia—show levels of support for integration that are clearly lower on average than those in second wave states—Bulgaria and Romania—across every dimension of integration that is considered. Differences are most pronounced on the items that tap into broad integration ideals, such as attitudes

Table 12.1 Mean scores on integration issues by accession wave and region

	First wave	Second wave/ Southeast Europe	CIS	Central Europe	Baltics	All
West in general	5.19	6.26	4.69	5.16	5.23	5.21
EU political integration	4.89	6.23	—	4.83	4.98	5.06
Single European market	4.93	5.70	—	4.74	5.24	5.00
Euro currency	4.95	5.70	—	4.78	5.22	5.04
EU directives on minorities	4.79	5.01	—	4.76	4.81	4.81
Foreign ownership of land	3.58	4.74	3.88	3.32	4.02	3.76
Foreign ownership of enterprises	4.47	5.34	4.02	4.32	4.72	4.48
Migration	4.09	4.34	4.12	4.12	4.04	4.12
NATO expansion	5.21	6.34	4.09	5.04	5.50	5.12

Note: A "1" indicates opposition to a policy and "7" indicates support.

toward the West in general and toward the broad ambition of a politically integrated Europe. This relationship also obtains even when the first wave states are disaggregated by region into the Baltics and Central East Europe. In this case, levels of support for integration are lower in Central Europe, but even so support for integration also remains lower in the Baltic States than in Southeast European second wave countries. The evidence indicates, therefore, that levels of support do indeed fall with proximity to accession, at least so far as the comparison between first and second wave states is concerned.

The situation is less straightforward regarding the CIS countries, where support for integration is clearly lower than that found even in first wave states. This outcome is in line with other research (see chapter 11 by Whitefield) that points to the problematic character of attitudes toward the West in CIS states, which have not in any case been involved in the European Union accession process. We consider, then, that the dynamics of integration support may work in different ways in postcommunist states. On the one hand, there are those countries with relatively low support for integration that have neither consistently sought nor been sought out for accession because integration is too politically and economically problematic. On the other hand, there are those countries that show sufficient support for the EU and international integration to be brought into the accession process; once in the process, however, proximity to the realities of integration may work to reduce support.

Party Polarization on Integration Issues

The results of the previous section show differences in levels of integration support across accession waves in line with the cost mobilization theory discussed in the introduction. A second element of this theory, however, points to the importance of party polarization. Proximity to accession, we argue, stimulates political entrepreneurs to build constituencies in the public who are increasingly aware of the pros and cons of integration. A consequence of this constituency building is that political parties increasingly define their policy stances across a spectrum of opinion. Moreover, as they engage in debate about integration issues, differences between parties become more evident. Indeed, the very fact of increased contestation of integration issues is likely to reduce support, as parties (and the public) move away from relatively weakly understood positions to greater awareness of costs and benefits. The corollary of lower support for integration in first wave states, therefore, should be greater party polarization on the same issues.

Table 12.2 shows measures of the range of party positions on each of the integration items for each country, as well as averages overall for the three waves. The results point immediately to the diversity of perspectives presented to the electorate of postcommunist states by political parties, and not just small or politically marginal ones. With few exceptions, it is clear that integration questions are not valence issues over which parties are undivided; the electorate is generally faced with real policy choices. Even where party differences are very limited on some questions—as, for example, over migration in Moldova and Ukraine, or over EU directives on minorities in Lithuania—there exist other significant party divisions over integration issues in these states; for example, over NATO and foreign ownership of land.

Table 12.2 also shows, however, that there are strong differences by region in the degree to which political parties are divided on integration questions. We see clearly that there is a relationship between party support, party polarization, and accession proximity. Among those states that are in the first wave, support is lowest and parties are most polarized; in the second wave, support is highest and parties least polarized; and among nonaccession states, support and polarization is intermediate. Again we point to the dynamics of the cost mobilization approach. In states that are part of the accession process, proximity leads to greater awareness of costs and benefits and to greater action by parties that must define themselves on integration issues. This process in turn reduces support. In those states that are outside the accession process, divisions over whether to be in or out have considerable political importance in a divisive way, though the realities of the accession process are less clear and therefore parties have less need and incentive to make clear their policy differences.

Conclusions

The findings of this chapter and of the book more generally lend support to the cost mobilization model that encapsulates our broad theoretical perspective on integration. Dealing with real policy choices that will produce winners and losers is more difficult for parties and citizens to support than the broad ideals of integration, but as a result we should expect them to be more salient. As the realities of the process of integration become more concrete, so must parties define themselves

Table 12.2 Party polarization on integration issues by accession wave (range from 1 to 7)

	West	EU polity	EU market	Euro	Minorities	Land	Enterprises	Migration	NATO	Average of all
First wave										
Czech Rep.	4.56	4.22	4.61	4.63	4.25	3.50	4.25	3.50	5.56	
Estonia	3.24	2.86	1.71	3.67	2.93	4.43	3.00	2.98	4.57	
Hungary	5.75	5.75	5.73	4.88	2.74	4.88	5.63	4.17	5.50	
Latvia	4.38	2.67	2.72	2.39	4.88	2.25	2.34	2.13	5.38	3.93
Lithuania	3.32	2.65	3.28	1.62	1.13	4.44	2.38	1.81	2.50	
Poland	5.38	4.88	4.88	5.00	4.60	4.25	5.00	4.80	3.14	
Slovakia	4.30	4.10	4.10	3.65	5.60	4.10	4.10	3.30	5.79	
Slovenia	4.64	3.55	3.86	3.96	3.23	4.00	4.00	4.00	4.63	
Average	4.45	3.84	3.86	3.73	3.67	3.98	3.84	3.35	4.63	
Second wave										
Bulgaria	1.75	0.75	1.93	2.45	3.25	3.98	2.50	1.95	2.25	
Romania	3.33	3.50	2.82	2.86	5.22	4.78	4.11	3.13	3.33	3.00
Average	2.54	2.13	2.38	2.66	4.24	4.38	3.31	2.54	2.79	
CIS										
Moldova	2.80	—	—	—	—	3.25	1.80	0.60	5.00	
Russia	5.06	—	—	—	—	4.86	4.00	4.41	4.30	3.74
Ukraine	5.50	—	—	—	—	4.13	4.00	0.93	5.50	
Average	4.45	—	—	—	—	4.08	3.27	1.98	4.93	

Note: Entries are mean scores where "1" represents opposition to a policy and "7" support for it.

and compete with one another, and the effect of this is likely to be negative for support and will increase political divisions among parties.

Importantly, however, the results also highlight the potential difficulties for EU governance that may result from accession. While the integration of postcommunist states after 1989 proceeded with great speed and consensus, the realities of the enlarged EU are likely to be much more disputed by governments emerging from party systems in Eastern Europe that are based in quite different ideological and electoral cleavages to those found in Western Europe. We expect, therefore, that policy disputes in the enlarged EU will be increasingly contested.

At the same time, our findings also point to the difficulties that may obtain from leaving states out of the accession and integration process. A satisfactory solution to many important issues in Europe, from security to migration to crime to economic development to the democratic consolidation in many postcommunist states, depends to a significant degree on finding a way to integrate CIS states. However, as our analysis shows, the stances of parties in these states may also act as an impediment to such an outcome.

All in all, then, the essays in this volume point to two crucial factors that we need to consider when trying to understand the EU's recent (and future) enlargements. First, we need to know how parties frame integration in domestic political debates. Second, we need to know how citizens perceive the integration process, and what the underlying causes are of these perceptions. Given what the essays in this volume tell us, we are less sanguine about the prospects of Europe's further integration than many policy makers appear to be, both in Brussels and in Europe's national capitals.

Appendix: Party Stances on Integration

All questions use a 7-point scale. Policy stance: 1 = strongly opposed and 7 = strongly supportive. Salience: 1 = not important at all and 7 = very important.

West Integration

What about the parties' positions on integration with the West in general? (All countries.) And how important is the issue to how the party appeals to the public?

EU Polity

How about the EU? Regardless of the specific form that integration may take, where do parties stand on creating a politically unified Europe? (Not asked in Moldova, Russia, and Ukraine.) And how important is the issue to how the party appeals to the public?

Market Ideals

Where do the parties in (country *x*) stand on creating a Europe-wide, integrated market for the European Union? (Not asked in Moldova, Russia, and Ukraine.) And how important is the issue to how the party appeals to the public?

Euro

And what would you say is the position taken by parties on the introduction of the Euro in (country *x*)? (Not asked in Moldova, Russia, and Ukraine.) And how important is the issue to how the party appeals to the public?

EU Directives Concerning Minorities

And what about parties' positions on EU directives on the rights of ethnic minorities? (Not asked in Moldova, Russia, and Ukraine.) And how important is the issue to how the party appeals to the public?

Foreign Ownership of Land

And where do parties stand on the question of foreign ownership of land? (All countries.) And how important is the issue to how the party appeals to the public?

Foreign Ownership of Industrial Enterprises

And what about foreign ownership of industrial enterprises? (All countries.) And how important is the issue to how the party appeals to the public?

Migration of People

And what about parties' positions on migration of people in and out of (country x)? (All countries.) And how important is the issue to how the party appeals to the public?

NATO

And now what about their position on NATO? (All countries.) And how important is the issue to how the party appeals to the public?

Notes

1. For further details of the Rohrschneider/Whitefield survey and for an analysis demonstrating the reliability of the evidence collected by this method, which cross-validates measures from the Rohrschneider/Whitefield and Marks/Chapel Hill study utilized in chapter 4 of this volume, see Whitefield et al. (2006). Data for the Rohrschneider/Whitefield expert survey were obtained with a grant from the Nuffield Foundation Project, "Political Mobilization and Elite Framing in Generating Support for Supra-National Institutions and European Union Enlargement in Post-Communist Eastern Europe," Grant no.: SGS/00827/G. We would like to thank Matt Loveless for his superb research assistance.
2. The Internet appendix can be found at http://www.indiana.edu/~iupolsci/rrohrsch/PalgraveTables+Figures.pdf
3. Statistically, the mean for the importance of West integration to parties (4.9) is substantially greater than for the EU polity (3.1) or market integration (3.7) on the 7-point indicator.
4. The mean support for land ownership (3.8) and industrial enterprises (3.9) is a full point below that for West integration (5.2) and market integration (5.0).
5. Salience of land (3.8) and enterprises (4.0) compares with that of market integration (3.7), and it is substantially higher than that for EU polity (3.1).
6. The variance over market integration (.76) is substantially small than that for land (1.3) and industrial enterprise (.98).
7. Again, the variances are higher for both variables than for integration ideals (1.4 and 1.3 for directives and minorities, respectively).
8. There is in fact only one exception to this rule: the mean score for parties in Central Europe on the issue of foreign ownership of land. Even on this politically vexed issue in the CIS states, however, the average party score is above the midpoint on the 7-point scale.

NOTES ON CONTRIBUTORS

Rasa Alisauskiene received her PhD in Psychology from Leningrad State University and Vilnius University in 1987. She has been an associate professor in both the Departments of Social Theory and Sociology at Vilnius University, where she heads the Sociological Laboratory. Since 1992, she has been the director general of "Baltic Surveys Ltd."/The Gallup Organization. For the EU, she has been a national expert for OECD program on social exclusion evaluation (1998) and national coordinator and program leader on PHARE research program on social welfare system reform in Lithuania (2000).

Jack Bielasiak is a professor at Indiana University's Department of Political Science. Most recently, he has published articles on two main themes. One concerns party system institutionalization in new democracies: "The Institutionalization of Electoral and Party Systems in Post-Communist States" (*Comparative Politics* 34:2, January 2002, pp. 189–210) and "Party Competition in Emerging Democracies: Representation and Effectiveness" (*Studies in Public Policy* 382, Center for the Study of Public Policy, University of Strathclyde, Glasgow, December 2003). The second theme focuses on Poland's trajectory toward democratization: "Determinants of Public Opinion Differences on EU Accession in Poland" (*Europe-Asia Studies* 54:8, December 2002, pp. 1241–1266), and "Past and Present in Transitional Voting: Electoral Choices in Post-Communist Poland" (*Party Politics* 8:5, September 2002, pp. 563–585).

Erica Edwards is a PhD candidate in Political Science at the University of North Carolina at Chapel Hill. Her dissertation focuses on internal party dissent over issues of European integration. Her research interests include political parties, public opinion, European integration, and gender and the welfare state.

Attila Fölsz is an assistant professor in the Political Science Department at Central European University in Budapest, Hungary. His work has primarily focused on macroeconomic concerns of East European transition and eventual integration. He has been a research partner and research fellow with the Phare-ACE research projects "Monetary Policy and European Accession" and the "Monetary Policy and Transmission Mechanisms in Transition Economies." He currently maintains an European Integration Online Papers series, "The Monetary Framework after Accession: A Political Economy Analysis of ERM2" (March 2003).

Liesbet Hooghe is professor of Political Science at the University of North Carolina, Chapel Hill, and is professor in the chair in Multilevel Governance at the VU Amsterdam. Her recent books include *The European Commission and the Integration of Europe: Images of Governance* (CUP, 2002), *Multi-Level Governance and European Integration* (Rowman & Littlefield, 2001, with Gary Marks), and *Cohesion Policy and European Integration: Building Multi-Level Governance* (OUP, 1996). Her interests are in theories of European integration, multilevel governance, political parties, political elites, and public opinion.

Jörg Jacobs is currently a research fellow at Viadrina University's Department of Comparative Cultural Sociology. His research interests include political sociology, empirical politics policy, transition research, and methods of empirical social research. Obtaining a degree in Political Science from the University of Bamberg, he finished his PhD in 2002 at Viadrina. Among his recent publications are *Political Culture in Post-Communist Europe* (edited together with Detlef Pollack et al.) and *Tuecken der Demokratie—Antisystemeinstellungen und ihre Determinanten in sieben post-kommunistischen Transforationslaendern*.

Krzysztof Jasiewicz is currently a professor of Sociology at Washington and Lee University in Lexington, VA and a research fellow at the Polish Academy of Sciences, Institute of Political Studies in Warsaw, Poland. Most recently he has published "Poland: Party System by Default" in Paul P. Webb, David M. Farrell, and Stephen White (eds.) *Political Parties in Transitional Societies* (Oxford: Oxford University Press, forthcoming), and "Elections and Voting Behaviour," in S. White, J. Batt, and P. G. Lewis (eds.) *Developments in Central and Eastern European Politics 3* (Basingstoke, UK, and New York: Palgrave, 2003, pp. 173–189).

Petr Kopecký is currently a research fellow of the Netherlands Organization for Scientific Research (NWO) and assistant professor of Political Science in the Department of Political Science at the University of Leiden. He was a senior lecturer at the Department of Politics in the University of Sheffield. His research interests include comparative political institutions and organizations, in particular, parliaments and political parties, and regime change and democratization, particularly the role of civil society in democratization. He is currently working on a research project concerning party financing and party patronage in new democracies. He has recently published the book (coedited with C. Mudde) *Uncivil Society? Contentious Politics in Eastern Europe* (London: Routledge, 2003) and two articles: "Rethinking Civil Society," *Democratization* 10(3), 2003, pp. 1–14 (with C. Mudde) and "An Awkward Newcomer. EU Enlargement and Euroscepticism in the Czech Republic," *European Studies: A Journal of European Culture, History and Politics*, 19, 2003.

P. Matthew Loveless received his PhD from Indiana University, Bloomington in Political Science (2005) and is the research manager at the Council of Graduate Schools providing data management and research consultation on completion and attrition in doctoral programs. Before this, he was a researcher at the *Mannheimer Zentrum für Europäische Sozialforschung* (MZES) in Mannheim, Germany where he co-managed the European Elections Study 2004 (EES2004). In ongoing participation, he continues to be involved on both the EES2004 and the *Prospects for EU Democracy after Eastern Enlargement* projects. His personal research interests include political behavior and political communication in Central and Eastern Europe; he has published in edited volumes and peer-reviewed journals.

Gary Marks is Burton Craige professor of Political Science at the University of North Carolina, Chapel Hill, and is professor in the chair in Multilevel Governance at the VU, Amsterdam. His recent books include *European Integration and Political Conflict*, coedited with Marco Steenbergen (CUP, 2004); *Multi-Level Governance and European Integration*, with Liesbet Hooghe (Rowman & Littlefield, 2001); and *It Didn't Happen Here: Why Socialism Failed in the United States*, with Seymour Martin Lipset (Norton, 2000).

Alina Mungiu-Pippidi, with a PhD in Social Psychology from the University of Iasi, Romania, is a political scientist and a journalist trained both in Romania and the United States. She held various media management positions in the past, most notably as director in charge of reform of the Romanian public television. She is currently chairing the Romanian Academic Society, the largest think-tank in Romania and works as a consultant on governance and public opinion for UNDP and the European Commission.

Moira Nelson is a PhD candidate at the University of North Carolina, Chapel Hill. Her interests are in theories of welfare state reform, employer organization, and political parties.

Detlef Pollack is currently a professor of Comparative Sociology of Culture at the European University of Frankfurt (Oder). He received his PhD in 1984 with a doctoral thesis on the theory of religion by Niklas Luhmann, and completed his "Habilitation" in 1994 at the Faculty of Sociology of the University of Bielefeld. He was a professor of Sociology of Religion at Leipzig University in 1994. In 1996/97, he was a fellow at the Institute of Advanced Study (Wissenschaftskolleg) Berlin, and is the 2003/05 holder of the Max Weber Chair at New York University. His research focuses on sociology of religion, political culture in reunified Germany, democratization in Eastern Europe, new social movements, and systems theory. His recent publications include *Religiöser Wandel in den postkommunistischen Ländern Mittel- und Osteuropas* (Würzburg: Ergon, 1998, edited together with Irena Borowik and Wolfgang Jagodzinski); *Politischer Protest: Politisch alternative Gruppen in der DDR* (Opladen: Leske+Budrich, 2000); *Political Culture in Post-Communist Europe. Attitudes in New Democracies* (Aldershot: Ashgate, 2003, edited together with Jörg Jacobs, Müller und Gert Pickel); *Säkularisierung—ein moderner Mythos? Studien zum religiösen Wandel in Deutschland* (Tübingen: Mohr, 2003).

Robert Rohrschneider is a professor of Political Science at Indiana University. He received a PhD in Political Science from Florida State University in 1989. His teaching and research interests center on comparative politics of advanced industrialized democracies with a concentration on Europe. Currently, he is involved in two projects: One examines popular support for a European government in Western Europe. Another, with Stephen Whitefield, examines the policy stances of parties about integration in East–Central Europe. His publications include *Learning Democracy: Democratic and Economic Values in Unified Germany* (Oxford: Oxford University Press, 1999) that won the 1998 Stein Rokkan Prize for Comparative Social Science Research. He also coedited the spring 2003 issue of *German Politics and Society* about the 2002 Federal election in Germany. He spent the 2004–2005 academic year as a Transatlantic Fellow at the Brussels' office of the German Marshall Fund of the United States.

Beate Sissenich (PhD, Cornell, 2003) studies regional integration with a focus on the European Union and its eastward enlargement. She joined Indiana University's faculty in the fall of 2003, after spending a year as a lecturer at Rutgers University and the two previous years as a visiting scholar at Columbia University. Her work looks at how international and domestic politics interact. In particular, she investigates whether and how rules spread across national borders and what role nonstate actors play in this process. She uses network analysis to trace the cross-border links of nonstate actors. Professor Sissenich has a chapter ("The Diffusion of EU Social Policy in Poland and Hungary") in Ronald Linden, ed., *Norms and Nannies: The Impact of International Organizations on Central and East European States* (Rowman & Littlefield, 2002) and another in a 2005 volume on "Europeanization," edited by Ulrich Sedelmeier and Frank Schimmelfennig. Professor Sissenich's current projects deal with mechanisms of rule transfer, EU state-building in Central and Eastern Europe, and transnational networks and the state.

Gábor Tóka is associate professor and head of the Department of Political Science at Central European University in Budapest, Hungary. He studied history and sociology at the Eötvös University, Budapest, which was also the site of his doctoral studies. He is coauthor of *Post-Communist Party Systems* (CUP, 1999), editor of three volumes and author of a few dozen scholarly articles and book chapters on electoral behavior, public opinion, political parties, and democratic consolidation. He has directed about 30 opinion surveys and elections studies in Hungary and other East Central European countries since the early 1990s, and is the principal investigator for the Hungarian surveys in the Comparative Study of Electoral Systems, the 2004 European Election Study. His most recent research focuses on information and deliberation effects on political attitudes and behavior and attitudes toward European integration.

Joop J. M. van Holsteyn is associate professor at the Department of Political Science, Leiden University, the Netherlands. His most recent books are *Democratie in verval?* (Democracy in Decay? Amsterdam: Boom, 2002; coedited with Cas E. Mudde) and *Blijft dan niets hetzelfde? Nederlandse kiezers en verkiezingen in het begin van de 21e eeuw* (Will Nothing Stay the Same? Dutch Voters and Elections at the Beginning of the 21st Century, Amsterdam: Aksant, 2005; coauthored with Josje M. Den Ridder). He has published various articles on public opinion and opinion polls, right-wing extremism and elections, and voting behavior in the Netherlands. On behalf of the Dutch Parliamentary

Election Study Foundation, he has served as codirector of the 2002 and 2003 national election studies.

Stephen Whitefield is a Rhodes Pelczynski Tutorial Fellow in Politics at Pembroke College, Oxford University. He has written on issues such as democratic commitment, electoral cleavages, class development, welfare reform, public representation, and support for environmentalism in postcommunist states. His book *Industrial Power and the Soviet State* (1993) won the Ed Hewett Prize. He is also commencing in 2006 a multicountry study of the character and political consequences of social inequality in postcommunist Eastern Europe, funded by the European Commission.

REFERENCES

Alexandre, Agnes and Xavier Jardin. 1997. "From the Europe of Nations to the European Nation? Attitudes of French Gaullist and Centrist Parliamentarians." *British Elections and Parties Review* 7: 185–206.
Allport, G. 1954. *The Nature of Prejudice*. New York: Addison-Wesley.
Almond, Gabriel and Sidney Verba. 1963. *The Civic Culture*. Princeton, NJ: Princeton University Press.
Anderson, Christopher J. 1998. "When In Doubt, Use Proxies: Attitudes toward Domestic Politics and Support for European Integration." *Comparative Political Studies* 31(5): 569–601.
Anderson, Christopher J. and Shawn Reichert. 1996. "Economic Benefits and Support for Membership in the EU: A Cross-National Analysis." *Journal of Public Policy* 15(3): 231–249.
Aspinwall, Mark. 2002. "Preferring Europe: Ideology and National Preferences on European Integration." *European Union Politics* 3: 81–111.
Bailey, David and Lisa De Propris. 2004. "A Bridge Too Phare? EU Pre-Accession Aid and Capacity-Building in the Candidate Countries." *Journal of Common Market Studies* 42(1): 77–98.
Baker, David, Andrew Gamble, David Seawright, and Katrina Bull. 1999. "MPs and Europe: Enthusiasm, Circumspection or Outright Scepticism?" *British Elections and Parties Review* 9: 171–185.
Baranovsky, V. 2000. "Russia: A Part of Europe or Apart from Europe?" *International Affairs* 76(3): 443–458.
Barry, B. M. 1987. "Nationalism." In *The Blackwell Encyclopaedia of Political Thought*, ed. David Miller. Oxford, UK: Blackwell.
Bartolini, Stefano. 2004. "Cleavages." Paper Presented at Workshop on the Analysis of Political Cleavages and Party Competition, Duke University, Durham, NC, April 2–3.
Bartolini, Stefano and Peter Mair. 1990. *Identity, Competition, and Electoral Availability: The Stabilization of the European Electorate, 1885–1985*. Cambridge, MA: Cambridge University Press.
Bátory, Ágnes. 2001. "Hungarian Party Identities and the Question of European Integration." SEI Working Paper No. 49, Sussex European Institute.
———. 2002a. "Attitudes to Europe: Ideology, Strategy and Issue of the European Union Membership in Hungarian Party Politics." *Party Politics* 8(5): 525–540.

———. 2002b. "The Political Context of EU Accession in Hungary." Briefing Paper, Royal Institute of International Affairs, November.
Bátory, Ágnes and Nick Sitter. 2004. "Cleavages, Competition, and Coalition-building: Agrarian Parties and the European Question in Western and Eastern Europe." *European Journal of Political Research* 43: 523–546.
Bell, J. 1997. "Unemployment Matters: Voting Patterns during the Economic Transition in Poland, 1990–1995." *Europe-Asia Studies* 49(7): 1263–1292.
Bernik, Ivan and Brina Malnar. 2003. "Political Culture in Post-Communist Europe." In *Political Culture in Post-Communist Europe: Attitudes in New Democracies*, ed. Detlef Pollack, Joerg Jacobs, Olaf Müller, and Gert Pickel, Burlington: Ashgate, 181–205.
Bielasiak, Jack. 2002a. "The Institutionalization of Electoral and Party Systems in Postcommunist States." *Comparative Politics* 34(2): 189–210.
——— 2002b. "Determinants of Public Opinion Differences on EU Accession in Poland." *Europe–Asia Studies* 54(8): 1241–1266.
Birch, Sarah. 1998. "Party System Formation and Voting Behavior in the Ukrainian Parliamentary Elections of 1994." In *Contemporary Ukraine: Dynamics of Post-Soviet Transformation*, ed. Taras Kuzio. London: Sharpe, 139–160.
Blacker, Coit D. 1998. "Russia and the West." In *The New Russian Foreign Policy*, ed. Michael Mandelbaum. New York: Council on Foreign Relations, 167–193.
Boeri, Tito and Herbert Brückner. 2001. "The Impact of Eastern Enlargement on Employment and Wages in the EU Member States." Brussels: Commission of the European Communities.
Börzel, Tanja A. 2001. "Non-Compliance in the European Union: Pathology or Statistical Artefact?" *Journal of European Public Policy* 8(5): 803–824.
Bozóki, András and Gergely Karácsony. 2003. "Membership without Belonging? Hungary into the European Union: A Historic Step Passively Approved." *Central European Political Science Review* 4(13): 21–41.
Brewer, M. B. 1997. "The Social Psychology of Intergroup Relations: Can Research Inform Practice?" *Journal of Social Issues* 53(1): 197–211.
Bruce, Erika. 1992. "NATO's Public Opinion Seminar Indicates Continuing, but Not Unshakeable, Support." *NATO Review* 40(2): 3–8.
Cameron, David R. 2003. "The Challenges of Accession." *East European Politics and Societies* 17(1): 24–41.
Campbell, Angus, Philip E. Converse, Warren Miller, and Donald Stokes. 1960. *The American Voter*. New York: John Wiley.
Carpenter, Michael. 1997. "Slovakia and the Triumph of Nationalist Populism." *Communist and Post-Communist Studies* 30(2): 205–220.
CBOS Public Opinion Research Center. 2003. "Opinions on the Preparation of Poland for the European Union Membership." *Polish Public Opinion*, November. <http://www.cbos.com.pl/Opinia/2003/11_2003.pdf. Last accessed on February 23, 2006.
Chan, K. K.-L. 1995. "Poland at the Crossroads: The 1993 General Elections." *Europe–Asia Studies* 47(1): 123–145.
Christin, Thomas. 2003. "The European Union from the Point of View of Candidate Countries: Economic and Political Basis of Attitudes towards EU (1991–1996)." Paper prepared for the ECPR Conference, Marburg, September 18–21.

Cichowski, Rachel A. 2000. "Western Dreams, Eastern Realities: Support for the European Union in Central and Eastern Europe." *Comparative Political Studies* 33: 1243–1278.

Commission of the European Communities. 1999. "Guidelines for Phare Programme Implementation in Candidate Countries for the Period 2000–2006 in Application of Article 8 of Regulation 3906/89." SEC (1999) 1596, October 13.

——— 2001a. "2001 Regular Report on Slovenia's Progress towards Accession." SEC (2001) 1755, November 13

——— 2001b. "The Phare Programme: Annual Report 2000." Brussels.

——— 2002. "Towards the Enlarged Union. Strategy Paper and Report of the European Commission on the Progress towards Accession by Each of the Candidate Countries." SEC (2002) 1400–1412, October 9.

——— 2003a. "Comprehensive Monitoring Report 2003." <http://europa.eu.int/comm/enlargement/report_2003/pdf/summary_paper2003_full_en.pdf> (accessed June 21, 2004).

——— 2003b. "Report on the Results of the Negotiations on the Accession of Cyprus, Malta, Hungary, Poland, the Slovak Republic, Latvia, Estonia, Lithuania, the Czech Republic and Slovenia to the European Union." Prepared by the Commission's departments. Brussels. <http://europa.eu.int/comm/enlargement/negotiations/pdf/negotiations_report_to_ep.pdf > (accessed March 30, 2004).

Converse, Philip E. 1964. "The Nature of Belief Systems in Mass Publics." In *Ideology and Discontent*, ed. David Apter. New York: Free Press, 206–61.

Dalton, Russell. J., Scott. C. Flanagan, and Paul A. Beck. 1984. *Electoral Change in Advanced Industrial Democracies: Realignment or Dealignment?* Princeton, NJ: Princeton University Press.

Dalton, Russell. J. and Martin P. Wattenberg. 2000. *Parties Without Partisans: Political Change in Advanced Industrial Democracies*. New York: Oxford University Press.

Dauderstädt, Michael and Britta Joerissen. 2004. "The European Politics of Left-Wing Parties in Post-Communist Accession Countries." Paper prepared for the Europolity Conference, International Policy Analysis Unit.

Davies, N. 1989. *Heart of Europe: A Short History of Poland*. New York: Oxford University Press.

de Witte, Bruno. 2002. "Politics vs. Law in the EU's Approach to Minorities." In *Europe Unbound: Enlarging and Reshaping the Boundaries of the European Union*, ed. Jan Zielonka. London: Routledge, 137–160.

Dimitrova, Antoaneta. 2002. "Enlargement, Institution-Building and the EU's Administrative Capacity Requirement." *West European Politics* 25(4): 171–190.

Duch, Raymond. 1993. "Tolerating Economic Reform: Popular Support for Transition to a Free Market in the Former Soviet Union." *American Political Science Review* 87(3): 590–608.

——— 2001. "A Developmental Model of Heterogeneous Economic Voting in New Democracies." *American Political Science Review* 95(4): 895–910.

Dunai, Marton. 2003. "Hungary Demands Role in Romania's EU Accession Talks." *Transitions Online*, July 26. www.tol.cz. Last accessed on February 23, 2006.

Duponcel, Marc. 1998. "The Europe Agreement between Hungary and the EU." *Russian and East European Finance and Trade* 34(1): 79–96.

Duverger, Maurice. 1954. *Political Parties, Their Organization and Activity in the Modern State*. New York: Wiley.
Easton, David. 1975. "A Re-assessment of the Concept of Political Support." *British Journal of Political Science* 5: 435–457.
Ehin, Piret. 2001. "Determinants of Public Support for EU Membership: Data from the Baltic Countries." *European Journal of Political Research* 40: 31–56.
Eichenberg, Richard. 1989. *Public Opinion and National Security in Western Europe*. Ithaca: Cornell University Press.
Eichenberg, Richard and Russell J. Dalton. 1993. "Europeans and the European Community: The Dynamics of Public Support for European Integration." *International Organization* 47(4): 507–534.
Ellison, David L. 2004a. "Politics and the Environment in Central Europe." Paper prepared for the 14th International Conference of Europeanists organized by the Council for European Studies in Chicago, IL, March 11–13.
——— 2004b. "Divide and Conquer: The EU Enlargement's Successful Conclusion." Paper presented at the panel on "Comparative European Political Behavior" at the 14th International Conference of Europeanists organized by the Council for European Studies in Chicago, IL, March 11–13.
Elster, Jon, Claus Offe, and Ulrich K. Preuss. 1998. *Institutional Design in Post Communist Societies: Rebuilding the Ship at Sea*. Cambridge, MA: Cambridge University Press.
Erikson, R. and J. H. Goldthorpe. 1992. *The Constant Flux: A Study of Class Mobility in Industrial Societies*. Oxford, UK: Clarendon Press.
Eurochambres. 2004. *Corporate Readiness for Enlargement in Central Europe* (4th edition). Brussels: Eurochambres.
European Commission. 2001. "Applicant Countries Eurobarometer 2001." December 2001. http://europa.eu.int/comm/public_opinion/. Last accessed on February 23, 2006.
——— 2002. "Candidate Countries Eurobarometer 2002.2." December 2002. <http://europa.eu.int/comm/public_opinion/>. Last accessed on February 23, 2006.
——— 2003. "Candidate Countries Eurobarometer 2003.4." Autumn 2003. http://europa.eu.int/comm/public_opinion/. Last accessed on February 23, 2006.
European Court of Justice. 2001. "Annual Report 2000." Luxembourg: European Court of Justice.
——— 2004. "Annual Report 2003." Luxembourg: European Court of Justice.
European Union. 2004. "Treaty Establishing a Constitution for Europe." Signed at Rome, October 29, 2004. http://europa.eu.int/constitution/. Last accessed on February 23, 2006.
Evans, Geoffrey ed. 1999. *The End of Class Politics? Class Voting in Comparative Context*. Oxford, UK: Oxford University Press.
Evans, Geoffrey and Colin Mills. 1999. "Are There Classes in Post-Communist Societies? A New Approach to Identifying Class Structure." *Sociology* 33: 23–46.
Evans, Geoffrey and Stephen Whitefield. 1993. "Identifying the Bases of Party Competition in Eastern Europe." *British Journal of Political Science* 23: 521–548.

——— 1995. "The Politics and Economics of Democratic Commitment: Support for Democracy in Transition Societies." *British Journal of Political Science* 24: 485–514.

——— 1999. "Class and Vote in Post-Soviet Russia." In *The End of Class Politics? Class Voting in Comparative Context*, ed. Geoffrey Evans. Oxford, UK: Oxford University Press, 254–280.

——— 2000. "Explaining the Formation of Electoral Cleavages in Post-Communist Democracies." In *Elections in Central and Eastern Europe: The First Wave*, ed. H.-D. Klingemann, E. Mochmann, and K. Newton. Berlin: Sigma, 36–70.

Flanagan, Scott C. 1987. "Value Change in Industrial Societies." *American Political Science Review* 81(4): 1303–1319.

Fodor, É., E. Hanley, and I. Szelényi. 1997. "Left Turn in Postcommunist Politics: Bringing Class Back In?" *East European Politics and Societies* 11(1): 190–224.

Forbes, H. D. 1997. *Ethnic Conflict: Commerce, Conflict and the Contact Hypothesis*. New Haven: Yale University Press.

Franklin, Mark. 1992. "The Decline of Cleavage Politics." In *Electoral Change: Responses to Evolving Social and Attitudinal Structures in Western Europe*, ed. Mark N. Franklin, Thomas L. Mackie, and Henry Valen. Cambridge, MA: Cambridge University Press, 383–405.

Franklin, Mark and Michael Marsh. 1994. "Uncorking the Bottle: Popular Opposition to European Integration in the Wake of the Maastricht." *Journal of Common Market Studies* 32(4): 455–472.

Franklin, Mark, Cees Van der Eijk, and Michael Marsh. 1995. "Referendum Outcomes and Trust in Government: Public Support for Europe in the Wake of Maastricht." *West European Politics* 18(3): 101–117.

Fuchs, Dieter and Edeltraud Roller. 1998. "Cultural Requisites of the Transition Process to Liberal Democracies in Central and Eastern Europe." In *The Postcommunist Citizen*, ed. Samuel H. Barnes and Janos Simon. Budapest: Erasmus Foundation and Institute for Political Science of the Hungarian Academy of Sciences, 35–77.

Fuchs, Dieter and Hans-Dieter Klingemann. 2002. "Eastward Enlargement of the European Union and the Identity of Europe." *West European Politics* 25(2):19–54.

Gabel, Matthew. 1998a. "Public Support for European Integration: An Empirical Test of Five Theories." *Journal of Politics* 60(2): 333–354.

——— 1998b. "Integration and Mass Politics: Market Liberalization and Public Attitudes in the European Union." *American Journal of Political Science* 42(3): 936–953.

——— 1998c. *Interests and Integration: Market Liberalization, Public Opinion and the European Union*. Ann Arbor: University of Michigan Press.

Gabel, Matthew and Harvey Palmer. 1995. "Understanding Variation in Public Support for European Integration." *European Journal of Political Research* 27: 3–19.

Gabel, Matthew and Guy D. Whitten. 1997. "Economic Conditions, Economic Perceptions, and Public Support for European Integration." *Political Behavior* 19: 81–96.

Gal, András. 2003. "Amended Hungarian Status Law Fails to Quiet Critics." *Transitions Online*, July 1. <www.tol.cz>. Last accessed on February 23, 2006.
Galazis, Nida M. 2003. "The Effects of EU Conditionality on Citizenship Policies and the Protection of National Minorities in the Baltic States." In *The Road to the European Union, Volume 2: Estonia, Latvia and Lithuania*, ed. Vello Pettai and Jan Zielonka. New York: Manchester University Press, 46–74.
Garrett, Geoffrey. 1998. *Partisan Politics in the Global Economy*. New York: Cambridge University Press.
Gebethner, S. 1992. "Partie, parlament i rząd w 10 miesięcy po wyborach." In *Wybory '91 a polska scena polityczna*, ed. S. Gebethner and J. Raciborski. Warsaw: FIS Polska w Europie, 191–202.
George, Stephen. 1996. *Politics and Policy in the European Union*. Oxford, London: Oxford University Press.
Gibson, James L. 1993. "Perceived Political Freedom in the Soviet Union." *Journal of Politics* 55(4): 936–974.
Gibson, J. and A. Cielecka. 1995. "Economic Influences on the Political Support for Market Reform in Post-Communist Transitions: Some Evidence from the 1993 Polish Parliamentary Elections." *Europe-Asia Studies* 47(5): 765–786.
Grabbe, Heather. 2001. *Profiting from EU Enlargement*. London: Centre for European Reform.
———. 2004. "Poland: The EU's New Awkward Partner." *CER Analysis*, February 10. London: Centre for European Reform.
Grabbe, Heather and Kristy Hughes. 1999. "Central and East European Views on EU Enlargement: Political Debates and Public Opinion." In *Back to Europe: Central and Eastern Europe and the European Union*, ed. Karen Henderson. London: University College London Press. 185–202.
Grabowska, M. 1991. "System partyjny—w budowie." *Krytyka* 37: 24–33.
———. 1993. "Political Parties in Post-Communist Poland: Disenchantments and Uncertain Chances." *Sisyphus* 1: 55–74.
———. 1997. "Partie polityczne: reprezentant spoleczenstwa czy tworca nowego ladu?" In *Pierwsza szesciolatka 1989–95: Proba bilansu polityki*, ed. M. Grabowska and S. Mocek. Warsaw: ISP PAN, 29–52.
Grabowska, M. and T. Szawiel. 2001. *Budowanie demokracji: Podziały społeczne, partie polityczne i społeczeństwo obywatelskie w postkomunistycznej Polsce*. Warsaw: PWN.
Gral-Iteo. 2002. "EU Index Survey," *Third Measurement*, April 2002.
Grzymala-Busse, Anna and Abby Innes. 2003. "Great Expectations: the EU and Domestic Political Competition in East Central Europe." *East European Politics and Societies* 17(1): 64–73.
Haerpfer, Christian. 2002. *Democracy and Enlargement in Post-Communist Europe: The Democratisation of the General Public in 15 Central and Eastern European Countries 1991–1998*. London: Routledge.
Hall, Peter A. and David Soskice, eds. 2001. *Varieties of Capitalism: The Institutional Foundations of Comparative Advantage*. Oxford: Oxford University Press.
Hanley, Sean. 2002. "Party Institutionalisation and Centre-Right Euroscepticism in East Central Europe: The Case of the Civic Democratic Party in the Czech Republic." Paper presented at the 29th ECPR Joint Sessions of Workshops, 22–27 March, Turin.

———. 2003. "The Czech EU Accession Referendum." Referendum Briefing No. 6, *OERN Research Network*, University of Sussex.
Hegedűs, István. 2001. "Premature European Identity and 'Europessimism' in the Hungarian Media." *Central European Political Science Review* 2(6): 201–211.
———. 2003. "After the Accession Talks, Facing the Referendum: Hungary and its Media Joining the European Union." *Central European Political Science Review* 4(11): 35–43.
Henderson, Karen. 2001. "Euroscepticism or Europhobia: Opposition Attitudes to the EU in the Slovak Republic." Paper presented at the Annual Meeting of the Political Studies Association, April 10–12, 2001, Manchester.
———. 2003. "The Slovak EU Accession Referendum." Referendum Briefing No. 7, *OERN Research Network*, University of Sussex.
Herd, Graeme. 1999. "The Baltic States and EU Enlargement." In *Back to Europe: Central and Eastern Europe and the European Union*, ed. Karen Henderson. London: University College London Press.
Hix, Simon and Christopher Lord. 1997. *Political Parties in the European Union*. New York: St. Martin's Press.
Hofferbert, Richard and Hans–Dieter Klingemann. 1999. "Remembering the Bad Old Days: Human Rights, Economic Conditions, and Democratic Performance in Transitional Regimes." *European Journal for Political Research* 36(6): 155–174.
Hooghe, Liesbet. 2001. *The European Commission and the Integration of Europe*. Cambridge, MA: Cambridge University Press.
Hooghe, Liesbet and Gary Marks. 1999. "Making of a Polity: The Struggle Over European Integration." In *Continuity and Change in Contemporary Capitalism*, ed. Herbert Kitschelt, Peter Lange, Gary Marks, and John Stephens. Cambridge, UK: Cambridge University Press, 70–97.
———. 2004. "Calculation, Community, and Cues: Public Opinion on European Integration." Paper Presented at the Conference *Redefining the European Project*, Halki, Greece, June 23–27.
Hooghe, Liesbet, Gary Marks, and Carole Wilson. 2002. "Does Left/Right Structure Party Positions on European Integration?" *Comparative Political Studies* 35(8): 965–989.
Hughes, James, Gwendolyn Sasse, and Claire Gordon. 2002. "Saying 'Maybe' to the 'Return to Europe.' Elites and the Political Space for Euroscepticism in Central and Eastern Europe." *European Union Politics* 3(3): 327–355.
Huntington, Samuel P. 1991. *The Third Wave: Democratization in the Late Twentieth Century*. Norman: University of Oklahoma Press.
Iankova, Elena and Peter J. Katzenstein. 2003. "European Enlargement and Institutionalized Hypocrisy." In *The State of the European Union Vol. 6: Law, Politics, and Society*, ed. Tanja A. Börzel and Rachel A. Cichowski. Oxford, UK: Oxford University Press, 269–290.
Inglehart, Ronald. 1970. "Public Opinion and Regional Integration." *International Organization* 24(4): 764–795.
———. 1977. *The Silent Revolution: Changing Values and Political Styles among Western Publics*. Princeton, NJ: Princeton University Press.
———. 1990. *Culture Shift in Advanced Industrial Society*. Princeton, NJ: Princeton University Press.

Inglehart, Ronald. 1997. *Modernization and Postmodernization: Cultural, Economic, and Political Change in 43 Societies*. Princeton, NJ: Princeton University Press.

Inglehart, Ronald, Jacques-Rene Rabier, and Karlheinz Reif. 1997. "The Evolution of Public Attitudes toward European Integration, 1970–1986." *Journal of European Integration* 10(2–3): 135–155.

Inotai, András. 1995. "From Association Agreements to Full Membership? The Dynamics of Relations between the Central and Eastern European Countries and the European Union." Institute of World Economics Working Paper No. 52. Budapest: Hungarian Academy of Sciences.

——— 1999. "Political, Economic, and Social Arguments for and against EU Enlargement." Institute of World Economics Working Paper No. 101. Budapest: Hungarian Academy of Sciences.

Iorga, Nicolae. 1929. *Le Caractère Commun des Institutions du Sud-Est de l'Europe*. Paris: J. Gamber.

Jacobs, Jörg. 2004. *Tücken der Demokratie Antisystemeinstellungen und ihre Determinanten in sieben post-kommunistischen Transformationsländern*. Wiesbaden: VS Verlag für Sozialwissenschaften.

Jasiewicz, K. 1988. "Zwischen Einheit und Teilung: Politische Orientierungen der Polen in den 80-er Jahren." In *Die Politische Kultur Polens*, ed. G. Meyer and F. Ryszka. Tübingen: Francke Verlag, 141–171.

——— 1993. "Polish Politics on the Eve of the 1993 Elections: Toward Fragmentation or Pluralism?" *Communist and Post-Communist Studies* 26(4): 387–411.

——— 1999. "Polish Politics after the 1997 Election: Polarization or Pluralism." *Soviet and Post-Soviet Review* 26(1): 93–114.

——— 2002. "Portfel czy różaniec? Wzory zachowań wyborczych Polaków w latach 1995–2001." In *System partyjny i zachowania wyborcze: dekada polskich doświadczeń*, ed. Radoslaw Markowski. Warsaw: ISP PAN/Friedrich Ebert Stiftung, 75–100.

——— 2003a. "Eurosceptycyzm, euroentuzjazm, euroapatia: postawy społeczne przed referendum akcesyjnym." In *Przed referendum europejskim: absencja, sprzeciw, poparcie*, ed. Lena Kolarska-Bobińska. Warsaw: Instytut Spraw Publicznych, 41–65.

——— 2003b. "Pocketbook or Rosary? Economic and Identity Voting in 2000–2001 Elections in Poland." *Studies in Public Policy*, Number 379. Glasgow: Center for the Study of Public Policy, University of Strathclyde, 26.

——— 2004. "Polska u progu Unii Europejskiej: referendum akcesyjne a deficyt demokratyczny." In *Populizm a demokracja*, ed. Radosław Markowski. Warsaw: PAN and Ebert Foundation, 95–122.

Jones, Erik and Niels van der Bijl. 2004. "Public Opinion and Enlargement." *European Union Politics* 5(3): 331–351.

Jordan, A. 1999. "The Implementation of EU Environmental Policy: A Policy Problem Without a Political Solution?" *Environment and Planning C: Government and Policy* 17(11): 69–90.

Kaitila, Ville and Mika Widgren. 2003. "Revealed Comparative Advantage in Trade between the European Union and the Baltic Countries." In *The Road to the European Union, Volume 2: Estonia, Latvia and Lithuania*, ed. Vello Pettai and Jan Zielonka. New York: Manchester University Press, 205–230.

REFERENCES

Kaminski, B. 1995. "The Significance of the Europe Agreements for Central-European Industrial Exports." *Russian and East European Finance and Trade* 31(1): 9–47.
Karpowicz, E., J. Osiecka, and A. Kojder. 2002. *Droga do Unii Europejskiej*. Warsaw: Sejm.
Kassianova, Alla. 2001. "Russia: Still Open to the West? Evolution of the State Identity in the Foreign Policy and Security Discourse." *Europe-Asia Studies* 53(6): 821–39.
Kitschelt, Herbert. 1988. "Left-Libertarian Parties." *World Politics* 40: 194–234.
——— 1992. "The Formation of Party Systems in East Central Europe." *Politics and Society* 20(1): 7–50.
——— 1995a. "Formation of Party Cleavages in Post-Communist Democracies: Theoretical Propositions." *Party Politics* 1(4): 447–472.
——— 1995b. "A Silent Revolution." In *Governing the New Europe*, ed. Jack Hayward and Edward Page. Durham: Duke University Press.
Kitschelt, Herbert, Zdenka Mansfeldova, Radoslaw Markowski, and Gabor Toka. 1999. *Post Communist Party Systems: Competition, Representation, and Inter-Party Cooperation*. Cambridge, MA: Cambridge University Press.
Klingemann, Hans-Dieter. 1994. "Die Enstehung wettbeweerbsorientierter Parteiensysteme in Osteuropa." In *Institutionenvergleich und Institutionendynamik*, ed. Wolfgang Zapf and Meinolf Dierkes. Berlin: WZB Jahrbuch.
Kolarska-Bobinska, L., ed. 2001. *Polacy wobec wielkiej zmiany*. Warsaw: ISP.
Kolarska-Bobinska, L., A. Rosner, and J. Wilkin. 2001. *Przyszlosc wsi polskiej*. Warsaw: ISP.
Kopecký, Petr. 2004. "An Awkward Newcomer: EU Enlargement and Euroscepticism in the Czech Republic." *European Studies: An Interdisciplinary Series in European Culture, History and Politics* 20: 225–246.
Kopecký, Petr and Cas Mudde. 2002. "The Two Sides of Euroscepticism: Party Positions on European Integration in East Central Europe." *European Union Politics* 3(3): 297–326.
Koseła, K., Tadeusz Szawiel, Mirosława Grabowska, and Małgorzata Sikorska. 2002. *Tozsamosc Polakow a Unia Europejska*. Warsaw: IBnPD.
Kostadinova, Tatiana. 2000. "East European Public Support for NATO Membership: Fears and Aspirations." *Journal of Peace Research* 37(2): 235–249.
Kostelecky, Tomas. 2002. *Political Parties after Communism: Developments in East-Central Europe*. Washington DC: Woodrow Wilson Center Press.
Krastev, Ivan. 2004. "The Anti-American Century?" *Journal of Democracy* April: 5–16.
Kreuzer, Marcus and Vello Pettai. 2003. "Patterns of Political Instability: Affiliation Patterns of Politicians and Voters in Post-Communist Estonia, Latvia, and Lithuania." *Studies in Comparative International Development* 38(2): 76–99.
Krickus, Richard J. 1997. "Democratization in Lithuania." In *The Consolidation of Democracy in East-Central Europe*, ed. Karen Dawisha and Bruce Parrott. Cambridge, MA: Cambridge University Press, 290–333.
Kuzio, Taras. 1999. "Slawophiles versus Westernizers: Foreign Policy Orientations in Ukraine." In *Between Russia and the West: Foreign and Security Policy of*

Independent Ukraine, ed. Kurt R. Spillman, Andreas Wenger and Derek Muller. Bern: Peter Lang, 53–74.

———. 2002. "European, Eastern Slavic, and Eurasian: National Identity, Transformation, and Ukrainian Foreign Policy." In *Ukrainian Foreign and Security Policy. Theoretical and Comparative Perspectives*, ed. Jennifer D. P. Moroney, Taras Kuzio, and Mikhail Molchanovs. London: Praeger, 198–225.

Lane, David, ed. 2002. *The Legacy of State Socialism and the Future of Transformation*. New York: Rowman & Littlefield Press.

Lawson, Kay, Andrea Roemmele, and Georgi Karasimeonov, eds. 1999. *Cleavages, Parties, and Voters. Studies from Bulgaria, the Czech Republic, Hungary, Poland, and Romania*. Westport, Connecticut: Praeger Press.

Levy, R. 2000. *Implementing European Union Public Policy*. Cheltenham: Edward Elgar.

Lewis, Paul, G. 2000. *Political Parties in Post-Communist Eastern Europe*. London: Routledge.

———. 2001. "The 'Third Wave' of Democracy in Eastern Europe: Comparative Perspectives on Party Roles and Political Development." *Party Politics* 7(5): 543–565.

Licata, L. and O. Klein. 2002. "Does European Citizenship Breed Xenophobia? European Identification as a Predictor of Intolerance towards Immigrants." *Journal of Community and Applied Social Psychology* 12: 1–15.

Liebich, Andre. 2002 "Ethnic Minorities and Long-term Implications of EU Enlargement." In *Europe Unbound: Enlarging and Reshaping the Boundaries of the European Union*, ed. Jan Zielonka. London: Routledge, 117–136.

Lipset, Seymour Martin, and Stein Rokkan. 1967. "Cleavage Structures, Party System and Voter Alignments: An Introduction." In *Party Systems and Voter Alignments: Crossnational Perspectives*, ed. Seymour M. Lipset and Stein Rokkan. New York: Free Press, 1–64.

Lunak, Pert. 1994. "Security for Eastern Europe: The European Option." *World Policy Journal* 11(3): 128–131.

Mainwaring, Scott. 1998. "Party Systems in the Third Wave." *Journal of Democracy* 9(2): 67–82.

Mair, Peter. 1997. *Party System Change: Approaches and Interpretations*. Oxford: Clarendon Press.

———. 2000. "The Limited Impact of Europe on National Party Systems." *West European Politics* 23(4): 27–51.

Mair, Peter and Cas Mudde. 1998. "The Party Family and Its Study." *Annual Review of Political Science* 1: 211–229.

Majone, Giandomenico. 2000. "The Credibility Crisis of Community Regulation." *Journal of Common Market Studies* 38(2): 273–302.

Markowski, R. and Toka, G. 1993. "Left Turn in Poland and Hungary Five Years after the Collapse of Communism." *Sisyphus* 1: 77–99.

Marks, Gary and Carole J. Wilson. 2000. "The Past in the Present: A Cleavage Theory of Party Response to European Integration." *British Journal of Political Science* 30: 433–459.

Marks, Gary, Carole Wilson, and Leonard Ray. 2002. "National Political Parties and European Integration." *American Journal of Political Science* 46(3): 585–594.

REFERENCES

Marks, Gary and Liesbet Hooghe. 2003. "National Identity and Support for European Integration." Discussion Paper SP IV 2003–202, Wissenschaftszentrum Berlin für Sozialforschung (WZB).
Marks, Gary and Marco Steenbergen, eds. 2004. *European Integration and Political Conflict*. Cambridge, MA: Cambridge University Press.
Mateju, P., B. Rehakova, and G. Evans. 1999. "The Politics of Interests and Class Realignment in the Czech Republic, 1992–96." In *The End of Class Politics? Class Voting in Comparative Context*, ed. Geoffrey Evans. Oxford, UK: Oxford University Press, 231–253.
Mayhew, Alan. 1998. *Recreating Europe: The European Union's Policy toward Central and Eastern Europe*. Cambridge, MA: Cambridge University Press.
McClosky, Harold and John Zaller. 1984. *The American Ethos: Public Attitudes toward Capitalism and Democracy*. Cambridge, MA.: Harvard University Press.
McLaren, Lauren. 2002. "Public Support for the European Union: Cost/Benefit Analysis or Perceived Cultural Threat?" *Journal of Politics* 64(2): 551–566.
McLean, Ian. 2001. *Rational Choice and British Politics: An Analysis of Rhetoric and Manipulation from Peel to Blair*. Oxford, UK: Oxford University Press.
Mertler, C. A. and R. A. Vannatta. 2001. *Advanced and Multivariate Statistical Methods*. Los Angeles: Pyrczak Publishing.
Meyer, Gerd. 2003. "Values, Small Life Worlds and Communitarian Orientations: Ambivalent Legacies and Democratic Potentials in Post-Communist Political Cultures." In *Political Culture in Post Communist Europe: Attitudes in New Democracies*, ed. Detlef Pollack, Jorg Jacobs, Olaf Müller, and Gert Pickel. Burlington: Ashgate, 169–205.
Michnik, Adam. 2001. "Confessions of a Converted Dissident." *Essay for the Erasmus Prize*, December 28, 2001. <http://www.eurozine.com/>. Last accessed on February 23, 2006.
Miller, Arthur H., Vicki Hesli, and William Reisinger. 1995. "Comparing Citizen and Elite Belief Systems in Post-Soviet Russia and Ukraine." *Public Opinion Quarterly* 59(1): 1–40.
Miller, Arthur H., Gwyn Erb, William M. Reisinger, and Vicki L. Hesli. 2000. "Emerging Party Systems in Post-Soviet Societies: Fact or Fiction?" *Journal of Politics* 62(2): 455–490.
Milward, Alan S. 1992. *The European Rescue of the Nation-State*. Berkeley: University of California Press.
Mishler, William and Richard Rose. 1997. "Trust, Distrust and Skepticism: Popular Evaluations of Civil and Political Institutions in Post-Communist Society." *Journal of Politics* 59(2): 418:451.
——— 2001. "What are the Origins of Trust?" *Comparative Political Studies* 34(1): 30–63.
Molchanov, Mikhail. 2002. "National Identity and Foreign Policy Orientation in Ukraine." In *Ukrainian Foreign and Security Policy: Theoretical and Comparative Perspectives*, ed. Jennifer D. P. Moroney, Taras Kuzio, and Mikhail Molchanov. London: Praeger, 227–261.
Moravcsik, Andrew. 1994. "Why the European Community Strengthens the State." Center for European Studies Working Paper No. 52. Cambridge, MA: Harvard University Press.

Moravcsik, Andrew. 1998. *The Choice for Europe: Social Purpose and State Power from Messina to Maastricht*. Ithaca, NY: Cornell University Press.
———. 2002. "In Defense of the 'Democratic Deficit': Reassessing Legitimacy in the European Union." *Journal of Common Market Studies* 40(4): 603–624.
Moravcsik, Andrew and Milada Anna Vachudova. 2003. "National Interests, State Power, and European Union Enlargement." *East European Politics and Societies* 17(1): 42–57.
Morozov, V. 2003. "In Search of Europe—Political Discourse in Russia." *Osteuropa* 53(9): 1501–1514.
Nicolaides, Phedon, Sylvia Raja Boean, Frank Bollen, and Pavlos Pezaros. 1999. *A Guide to the Enlargement of the European Union (II): A Review of the Process, Negotiations, Policy Reforms and Enforcement Capacity*, revised edition. Maastricht: European Institute of Public Administration.
Norpoth, Helmut. 1996. "The Economy." In *Comparing Democracies*, ed. Lawrence LeDuc, Richard Niemi, and Pippa Norris. London: Sage, 299–318.
O'Connor, Alison and Martha Kearns. 2002. "Use This Historic Chance, Leaders Implore." *Irish Independent*, October 16, 2002.
Parfionov, Aledsandr. 1999. "Foreign and Security Policy Views of Relevant Ukrainian Political Forces." In *Between Russia and the West: Foreign and Security Policy of Independent Ukraine*, ed. Kurt R. Spillman, Andreas Wenger, and Derek Muller. Bern: Peter Lang, 75–94.
Pavlowitch, Steven. 1999. *History of the Balkans, 1804–1945*. London and New York: Hurst.
Pennings, Paul. 2002. "The Dimensionality of the EU Policy Space." *European Union Politics* 3: 59–80.
Peters, Guy. 2000. "The Commission and Implementation in the EU: Is There an Implementation Deficit and Why?" In *At the Heat of the Union: Studies of the European Commission*, ed. Neill Nugent. Basingstoke: Palgrave. 190–225.
Pettai, Vello. 2001. "Estonia and Latvia: International Influence on Citizenship and Minority Integration." In *Democratic Consolidation in Eastern Europe. Volume 2. International and Transnational Factors*, ed. Jan Zielonka and Alex Pravda. Oxford, UK: Oxford University Press, 257–280.
Pienkos, Donald E. 2004. "Consensus and Division over Poland's Entry into the European Union." *East European Quarterly* 37: 461–473.
Plakans, Andrejs. 1997. "Democratization and Political Participation in Postcommunist Societies: The Case of Latvia." In *The Consolidation of Democracy in East-Central Europe*, ed. Karen Dawisha and Bruce Parrott. Cambridge, UK: Cambridge University Press, 245–289.
Pollack, Detlef. 1999. "Trust in Institutions and the Urge to Be Different: On Attitudinal Change in Eastern Germany." *German Politics* 8(3): 81–102.
Pollack, Detlef and Jörg Jacobs. 2002. "Bedingungen der Konsolidierung von politischen Systemen in Ostmitteleuropa—Demokratie, Rechtsstaatlichkeit, Marktwirtschaft und soziale Ungleichheit in den Augen der Bevölkerung postkommunistischer Länder." In Berliner Debatte *INITIAL* 13(3): 38–52.
Pollack, Mark. 1999. "A Blairite Treaty: Neoliberalism and Regulated Capitalism in the Treaty of Amsterdam". In *European Integration After Amsterdam: Institutional Dynamics and Prospects for Democracy*, ed. Karl-Heinz Neunreither and Antje Wiener. Oxford, UK: Oxford University Press, 266–289.

Powers, D. V. and J. H. Cox. 1997. "Echoes from the Past: The Relationship between Satisfaction with Economic Reforms and Voting Behavior in Poland." *American Political Science Review* 91(3): 617–633.
Pravda, Alex. 1996. "The Public Politics of Foreign Policy." In *Internal Factors in Russian Foreign Policy*, ed. Neil Malcolm, Alex Pravda, Roy Allison, and Margot Light. Oxford, UK: Oxford University Press, 230–285.
Rabkin, Jeremy. 2000. "Is the EU Eroding the Sovereignty of Non-Member States?" *Chicago Journal of International Law* 1(2): 273–291.
Radio Free Europe-Radio Liberty. 2000. "Orban says there is 'life outside EU,'" *RFE-RL Newsline*, July 10, 2000.
Ray, Leonard. 1999. "Measuring Party Orientations towards European Integration: Results form an Expert Survey." *European Journal of Political Research* 36: 283–306.
Rhodes, Martin and Bastiaan van Apeldoorn. 1997. "Capitalism versus Capitalism in Western Europe." In *Developments in West European Politics*, ed. Martin Rhodes, Paul Heywood, and Vincent Wright. New York: St. Martin's Press, 171–189.
Riak, Kristi. 2003. *Democratic Politics or the Implementation of Inevitabilities? Estonia's Democracy and Integration into the European Union*. Tartu: Tartu University Press.
Rohrschneider, Robert. 1996. "Cultural Transmission versus Perceptions of the Economy: The Sources of Political Elites' Economic Values in the United Germany." *Comparative Political Studies* 29(1): 78–104.
——— 1999. *Learning Democracy*. Oxford, UK: Oxford University Press.
——— 2002. "The Democracy Deficit and Mass Support for an EU-wide Government." *American Journal of Political Science* 46(2): 463–475.
Rohrschneider, Robert and Stephen Whitefield. 2004a. "Support for Foreign Ownership in Eastern Europe: Economic Interests, Ideological Commitments and International Context." *Comparative Political Studies* 37(3): 313–339.
——— 2004b. "Explaining Party Stances on Political and Economic Integration in Post-Communist Eastern Europe." Paper presented at the EPOP Conference, Oxford, September 2004.
Rose, Richard, William Mishler, and Christian Haerpfer. 1998. *Democracy and its Alternatives: Understanding Post-Communist Societies*. Baltimore: Johns Hopkins University Press.
Rose, Richard and Neil Munro. 2003. *Elections and Parties in New European Democracies*. Washington, DC: CQ Press.
Ross, George. 1995. *Jacques Delors and European Integration*. New York: Oxford University Press.
Rupnik, Jacques. 2003. "De l'élargissement de l'Europe à l'unification de l'Europe." *Pouvoirs* 106: 42.
Sanchez-Cuenca, Ignacio. 2000. "The Political Basis of Support for European Integration." *European Union Politics* 1(2): 147–171.
Scheve, K. F. and M. Slaughter. 2001. "Labor Market Competition and Individual Preferences over Immigration Policy." *The Review of Economics and Statistics* 83(1): 133–145.
Schimmelfennig, Frank, Stefan Engert, and Heiko Knobel. 2003. "Costs, Commitment and Compliance: The Impact of EU Democratic

Conditionality on Latvia, Slovakia and Turkey." *Journal of Common Market Studies* 41(3): 495–518.
Sherr, James. 1998. "Ukrainian Security Policy: The Relationship between Domestic and External Factors." In *Contemporary Ukraine: Dynamics of Post-Soviet Transformation*, ed. Taras Kuzio. London: M.E. Sharpe, 245–266.
Sidanius, J. and F. Pratto. 2000. *Social Dominance: An Intergroup Theory of Social Hierarchy and Oppression*. Cambridge, MA: Cambridge University Press.
Sissenich, Beate. 2003. *State Building by a Nonstate*. Ph.D. dissertation. Ithaca: Cornell University.
Sitter, Nick. 2002. "Opposing Europe: Euro-Skepticism, Opposition and Party Competition." Sussex European Institute Working Paper no. 56, October 2002.
Sniderman, Paul M., Richard A. Brody, and Philip E. Tetlock. 1991. *Reasoning and Choice: Explorations in Political Psychology*. New York: Cambridge University Press.
Steenbergen, Marco and Gary Marks. 2006. "Evaluating Expert Judgments," *European Journal of Political Research*.
Sükösd, Miklós and Péter Bajomi-Lázár. 2003. "The Second Wave of Media Reform in East Central Europe." In *Reinventing Media: Media Policy Reform in East Central Europe*, ed. Miklós Sükösd and Péter Bajomi-Lázár. Budapest: CEU Press, 13–27.
Szawiel, T. 1999. "Zroznicowanie lewicowo-prawicowe i jego korelaty." In *Wybory parlamentarne 1997 roku*, ed. R. Markowski. Warsaw: Ebert Foundation Press, 111–148.
Szczerbiak, Alex. 1999. "Interests and Values: Polish Parties and Their Electorates." *Europe-Asia Studies* 51(8): 1401–1432.
——— 2001. "Polish Public Opinion: Explaining Declining Support for EU Membership." *Journal of Common Market Studies* 39: 105–122.
——— 2003. "Old and New Divisions in Polish Politics: Polish Parties' Electoral Strategies and Bases of Support." *Europe-Asia Studies* 55(5): 729–746.
Szczerbiak, Alex and Paul Taggart. 2001. "Parties, Positions and Europe: Euroscepticism in the EU Candidate States of Central and Eastern Europe." SEI Working Paper No. 46, Sussex European Institute.
——— 2002. "The Party Politics of Euroscepticism in EU Member and Candidate States." SEI Working Paper No. 52, Sussex European Institute.
Szilágyi-Gál, Mihály. 2003. "Press Coverage of the EU and NATO Accession Processes in Hungary and Romania in the late 1990s." In *Reinventing Media: Media Policy Reform in East Central Europe*, ed. Miklós Sükösd and Péter Bajomi-Lázár. Budapest: Central European University Press, 137–52.
Taggart, Paul. 1998. "A Touchstone of Dissent: Euroscepticism in Contemporary Western European Party Systems." *European Journal of Political Research* 33(3): 363–388.
Taggart, Paul and Alex Szczerbiak. 2004. "Contemporary Euroscepticism in the Party Systems of the European Union Candidate States of Central and Eastern Europe." *European Journal of Political Research* 43: 1–27.
Tajfel, H. 1981. *Human Groups and Social Categories*. Cambridge, New York: Cambridge University Press.
Terestyéni, Tamás. 2001. "Magyarország és az Európai Unió a sajtó tükrében" (Hungary and the European Union in the Mirror of the Press). *Szociológiai Szemle* 2: 16–34.

Tesser, Lynn M. 2003. "The Geopolitics of Tolerance: Minority Rights under EU Expansion in East Central Europe." *East European Politics and Societies* 17(3): 483–532.

Thomassen, Jacques and Hermann Schmitt. 1997. "Policy Representation." *European Journal of Political Research* 32: 165–184.

Tiilikainen, Teija. 2003. "The Political Implications of the EU's Enlargement to the Baltic States." In *The Road to the European Union, Volume 2: Estonia, Latvia and Lithuania*, ed. Vello Pettai and Jan Zielonka. New York: Manchester University Press, 14–24.

Tilkidjiev, Nikolai. 2001. "The King as a Prime-Minister: Peculiarity of the Bulgarian Case or a Lesson to Post-Communist Transformations." FIT-discussion papers, December 2001, Frankfurt (Oder).

Todorova, Maria. 1996. "The Ottoman Legacy in the Balkans." In *Imperial Legacy. The Ottoman Imprint on the Balkans and the Middle East*, ed. Carl L. Brown. New York: Columbia University Press.

——— 1997. *Imagining the Balkans*. Oxford, UK: Oxford University Press.

Tóka, Gábor. 2004. "Hungary." In *Handbook of Political Change in Eastern Europe*, 2nd revised and updated edition, ed. Sten Berglund, Joakim Ekman, and Frank H. Aarebrot. Cheltenham: Edgar Elgar.

Töller, Annette. 1995. *Europapolitik im Bundestag: eine empirische Untersuchung zur europapolitischen Willensbildung im EG-Ausschuss des 12. Deutschen Bundestages*. Frankfurt: Lang.

Triandafyllidou, Anna. 1998. "National Identity and the 'Other'." *Ethnic and Racial Studies* 21: 593–612.

——— 2002. *National Identity Reconsidered: Images of Self and Other in a "United" Europe*. Lampeter: Edwin Mellen Press.

Tucker, Joshua A., Alexander C. Pacek, and Adam J. Berinsky. 2002. "Transitional Winners and Losers: Attitudes toward EU Membership in Post-Communist Countries." *American Journal of Political Science* 46: 557–571.

Tverdova, Yulia V. and Christopher J. Anderson. 2004. "Choosing the West? Referendum Choices on EU Membership in East-Central Europe." *Electoral Studies* 32(2): 185–208.

Tworzecki, H. 1996. *Parties and Politics in Post-1989 Poland*. Boulder, CO and Oxford: West view Press.

Vachudova, Milada Anna. 2004. *Revolution, Democracy, and Integration*. Oxford: Oxford University Press.

——— 2005. *Europe Undivided: Democracy, Leverage, and Integration after Communism*. Oxford: Oxford University Press.

Van de Velde, Mike. 2003. "Public Opinion towards EU Accession in Slovakia: The Relation between Socio-demographic Profiles and Party Affiliation, and Support for EU Membership." Unpublished M.A. dissertation. Brussels: Universite Libre de Bruxelles.

Van Kersbergen, Kees. 2000. "Political Allegiance and European Integration." *European Journal of Political Research* 37: 1–17.

Van Meurs, Wim and Alexandros Yannis. 2002. *The European Union and the Balkans: From Stabilisation Process to South-Eastern Enlargement*. Gutersloh: Bertelsmann.

Večerník, Jirí and Matějů, Petr. 1999. *Ten Years of Rebuilding Capitalism: Czech Society after 1989*. Prague: Academia.

Vetik, Raivo. 1999. *Estonian Human Development Report 1999*. Iloprint. New York: UN Development Program.
────── ed. 2004. "Barriers of Democratic Consolidation: The Estonian Case." In *Democratic Values in Central and Eastern Europe*, ed. Detlef Pollack, Jörg Jacobs, Olaf Müller, and Gert Pickel. FIT Research Report, Frankfurt (Oder). 49–62.
Vlaams Blok. 2004. (Accessed July 18, 2004) <http://www.vlaamsblok2004.be/pdf/europa.pdfVlaamsblok.be>
Wade, L. L., P. Lavelle, and A. J. Groth. 1995. "Searching for Voting Patterns in Postcommunist Poland's Sejm Elections." *Communist and Post-Communist Studies* 28(4): 411–425.
Wessels, Bernhard. 1995. "Evaluations of the EC: Elite or Mass-Driven?" In *Public Opinion and Internationalized Governance*, ed. Oskar Niedermayer and Richard Sinnott. Oxford, UK: Oxford University Press.
Wesołowski, W. 2000. *Partie: nieustanne kłopoty*. Warsaw: IFiS PAN.
Whitefield, Stephen. 2002. "Political Cleavages and Post-Communist Politics." *Annual Review of Political Science* 5: 181–200.
────── 2005. "Putin's Popularity and Its Implications for Democracy in Russia." In *Ruling Russia: Putin in Perspective*, ed. Alex Pravda. Oxford, UK: Oxford University Press, 139–160.
Whitefield, Stephen, M. Anna Vachudova, M. Steenbergen, R. Rohrschneider, G. Marks, P. Loveless, and L. Hooghe. 2006. "Do Expert Surveys Produce Consistent Estimates of Party Stances on European Integration? Comparing Expert Surveys in the Difficult Case of Central and Eastern Europe." *Electoral Studies*, forthcoming.
Whitefield, Stephen and Geoffrey Evans. 2001. "Attitudes towards the West, Democracy and the Market." In *Democratic Consolidation in Eastern Europe Volume 2: International and Transnational Factors*, ed. Jan Zielonka and Alex Pravda. Oxford: Oxford University Press, 231–254.
Wiatr, J. J. 2000. "Lasting Cleavages and the Changing Party System in Poland." In *Between Animosity and Utility: Political Parties and Their Matrix*, ed. J. Wiatr and H. Kubiak. Warsaw: Scholar, 11–30.
Williams, A. M., V. Balaz, and S. Zajac. 1998. "The EU and Central Europe: The Remaking of Economic Relationships." *Tijdschrift voor Economische en SocialeGeografie* 89(2): 131–149.
Williams, Margit Bessenyey. 2001. "Exporting the Democratic Deficit: Hungary's Experience with EU Integration." *Problems of Post-Communism* 48(1): 27–38.
Wilson, Andrew. 2000. *The Ukrainians: Unexpected Nation*. New Haven: Yale University Press.
Wolff, Larry. 1994. *Inventing Eastern Europe*. Stanford: Stanford University Press.
Wnuk-Lipński, E. 1993. *Left Turn in Poland*. Warsaw: ISP PAN.
Zaller, John. 1992. *The Nature and Origins of Mass Opinion*. Cambridge, MA: Cambridge University Press.
Zielinski, Jakub. 2002. "Translating Social Cleavages into Party Systems: The Significance of New Democracies." *World Politics* 54: 184–211.
Zielonka, Jan. 2002. *Europe Unbound: Enlarging and Reshaping the Boundaries of the European Union*. London: Routledge.
Żukowski, T. 1994. *Wybory 1993: Wyniki i ich uwarunkowania*. Warsaw: UW Press.

INDEX

accession
  conditions and conditionality, 19, **20**, 22, **25**, 26, 27, 32, 36, 37, 38, 45, 60, 75, 88, 113, 122. *See also* Copenhagen criteria
  negotiations, 13, 20, 27, **32**, 34, 36, 37, 46, 47, 48, 55, 105, 109, 110, 127–8, **151**–3, 160, 167, 171, 175
  proximity, **245**, 248
  Treaty, **32**, 33, 34, 36, 39, 128, 129
acquis (communautaire) also community law, 21, 22, 23, 24, 26, 28, 30, 31, 32, 33, 37, 45, 46, 60, 106
agriculture, 21, 23, 28, 31, **33**, 37, 148, 156, 157, 158, 162, 167, 175
  agricultural subsidies, 19, 27, 33, 34, 36, 151
  Common Agricultural Policy (CAP), **33**
  Special Accession Program for Agriculture and Rural Development (SAPARD), 23
Albania, 86, 87, 88, 89, 91, 92, 94, 95, 96, 98, 99, 103, 166, 168, 174, 179
Association Agreements, 20
Austria, 39, 130, 139

Balkans, 165–70, 173, 174, 177–85
Baltic States, 14, 15, 50, 64, **187**–93, 198–200, 247
Belarus, 219
Berlin Wall, 169

Bosnia, 166
Bratislava, 115
Bucharest, 168, 170
Bulgaria, 14, 27, 28, 37, 48, 51, 52, 62, 66, 79, 86, 87, 90, 91, 96, 103, 107, 108, 166–175, 178–184, **203**–6, 208, 210, 212–16, 243, 245, 246, 249

capitalism, capitalist, 58, 61, 69, 70, 71, 76, 77, 78, 153
  capitalist democracies, 26, 31
  capitalist economies, 31, 92
China, 167
church, 133, 165, 167, 168, 200
  Byzantine Orthodox Church, 165
  Christian, 55, 56, 58, 67, 68, 69, 70, 74, 81, 91, 99, 113, 115, 153, 165, 167, 168, 187, 196, 239, 240: Catholic, 76, 122, 126, 127, 128, 130, 133, 139, 140, 166, 179, 187; Orthodox, 165, 166, 167, 179, 180, 182; Protestant, 166, 179, 187; Roman Catholic, 128
  church attendance, 200
  denomination, 165, 166, 167, 179, 180, 182
cleavages (*see also* sociodemographic characteristics), 10, 26, 44, 47, 49, 54, 58, 59, 64, 81, 95, **123**, 124, 126, 143, 199, 237, 250
Community Law, *see acquis*

consolidation, 5, 130, 148, 217, 250
constituency building, 247
Copenhagen, 128
  criteria, 21, 22, 24, 26, 27–9, 38, 75
  summit (*also* meeting), 21, 105, 128
cost mobilization, **12**, 15, 106, 119, 190, 192, 198, 199, 200, 243, 245, 247, 248
Croatia, 166, 167, 169, 180
Cyprus, 28, 39
Czech Republic, 14, 27, 28, 35, 37, 39, 48, 50, 52, 55, 58, 60, 61, 62, 64, 66, 82, 86, 87, 88, 92, 95, 103, **105–**19, 124, 125, 180, 243, 246

democracy, 15, 26, 27, 65, 75, 94, 98, **100, 102**, 103, 105, 117, 123, 129, 131, 134, 136, 137, 138, 139, 143, 147, 148, 163, 178, 179, 195, 198, 199, 201, 211, 214, 216, 220, 228, 230, 233–4, 235, 236, 237, 238
  national democracy, 178, 198
  pluralist democracy, 123, 139
democratization, 38, 61, 169
Denmark, 30, 33

Estonia, 14, 27, 28, 29, 37, 50, 51, 52, 55, 56, 60, 62, 64, 86, 87, 88, 92, 93, 96, 107, 109, 187–9, 191, 193–99, 201, 215, 243, 246, 249
Eurasianism, 219, 221, 236, 237
Euro (the), 119, 246, 249, 251
Euroenthusiasm, Euroenthusiastic, 59, 73, 107, 127, 128, 153, 154, 182
Europe
  anti-Europe *also* anti-European, 47, 50, 55, 60, 61, 62, 64, 126, 127, 130, 154, 169
  Eurobarometer, 86, 87, 102, 117, 120, 157, 160, 162, 166, 173, 181, 190
  Euroland, 175
  Europeanization, 206
  federal Europe, 61
  new Europe, 170, 184
  old Europe, 44, 173
  pro-Europe *also* pro-European, 58, 114, 116, 127, 154, 173, 179, 180, 182, 183, 192
  "return to Europe", 43, 45, 47, 49, 60, 64, 105, 121, 168, 169, 170, 172, 173, 183, 188, 199
  united Europe *also* unified Europe, 46, 170, 175, 176, 251
Eurorealist, 52
Euroskepticism, Euroskeptic, 2, 27, 38, **43–**56, 58–64, 73, 74, 76, 78, 82, 91, 107, 112, 115, 116, 121, 122, 127, 129, 130, 131, 133, 138, 140, 153, 154, 164, 176, 177
extremism, 61, 70, 73, 79, 133, 149, 155, 158, 159, 163, 164, 221

France, 36, 172
free movement
  of capital, 28, 35
  of goods, 28
  of labor, 37
  of persons, 28, 33, 34, 36
Freedom to provide services, 28

Germany, 36, 38, 86, 87, 88, 90, 91, 93, 95, 96, 98, 103, 104, 129, 132, 142, 172, 175, 187
Greece, 30, 165, 166, 173, 185

human rights, 21, 23, 26, 27, 102, 169, 189, 207
Hungary, 10, 20, 27, 28, 29, 35, 37, 39, 48, 51, 52, 55, 56, 60, 61, 63, 66, 76, 77, 80, 86, 87, 89, 90, 92, 96, 107, 108, 110, 113, 120, 125, 145–53, 155, 160, 161, 162, 163, 175, 178, 180, **203–**6, 208, 210–16, 243, 246, 249

institutional capacity, 39, 106
Instrument for Structural Policies for Pre-Accession (ISPA), 23
Ireland, 30, 140

Index

iron curtain, 169, 205
Italy, 30

Kaliningrad, 33
Kazakhstan, 219
Klaus, Vaclav, 27, 76, 82, 113
Kosovo, 89, 166, 178

labor, 9, 27, **34**, 35, 37, 39, 61, 88, 93, 110, 111, 122, 151, 170, 176
  markets, 9, **34**, 39, 88, 93, 110, 111
  mobility, 27, 35, 151
land sales, 19, 35
Latvia, 14, 27, 28, 29, 37, 48, 50, 51, 52, 55, 56, 60, 61, 63, 66, 80, 107, 109, 187–91, 195–99, 201, 215, 243, 246, 249
left/right (dimension, divide), 66, 67, 68, 69, 70, **71**, 72, 73, 74, 78, 79, 80, 210, 212, 213
Lepper, Andrej, 75
Lithuania, 27, 28, 29, 33, 37, 39, 48, 50, 51, 52, 55, 56, 63, 64, 66, 80, 82, 187–91, 193, 195–202, 215, 243, 246, 248, 249
Luxembourg, 66, 73, 80

Macedonia, 166, 174, 178, 180, 181, 184
Maghreb, 167
Malta, 28, 32, 39
market, 1–9, 12, 14, 15, 21, 26, 28, 31, 33, **34**, 37, 39, 55, 58, 65, 69, 71, 72, 73, 75, 76, 78, 80, 88, 89, 92, 93, 94, 96, 99, 100, 110, 111, 115, 123, 124, 142, 147, 148, 150, 153, 154, 155, 157, 158, 159, 160, 162, 163, 170, 172, 196, 201, 206, 209, 210, 211, 212, 215, 217, 219, 220, 221, 224, 225, 228, 229, 230, 233, 234, 235, 237, 238, 241, 242, 243, 244, 245, 246, 249, **251**, 252
  common market, 2, 9, 28, 155, 244
  internal market, 21, 71, 72, 73, 80
  market economy, 4, 7, 21, 28, 55, 69, 75, 92, 93, 94, 96, **99**, 100, 123, 124, 147, 155, 160, 162, 172, 211, 212, 215, 238
  market ideals, 211, **251**
  market values, 2, 5
  single market, 26, 31, 71, 243
Meciar, 19, 26, 105, 113, 115
migration, 3, 12, 35, 170, 187, 189, 245, 246, 248, 249, 250, **252**
  immigration, 67, 72
minorities, 10, 14, 21, 23, 26, 27, 35, 75, 118, 123, 127, 178, 180, 184, 189, 190, 192, 193, 194, 196, 198, 199, 200, 243, 245, 246, 248, 249, 251, 252
  protection, 27, 75
  rights, 27, 243
Moldova, 10, 243, 248, 249, 251
Montenegro, 166, 174, 178, 180, 181, 184

nationalism *also* nationalists, **9**–10, 11, 14, 38, 46, 55, 58, 61, 67, 72, 76, 81, 82, 88, 91, 98, 99, 114, 126, 127, 146, 149, 153, 155, 159, 164, 166, 169, **176**–8, **183**–4, 188, 189, 194, 195, 201, 205, 208, 209, 210, 212, 213, 214, 215, 222, 224, 232, 235, 239, 240
NATO, 10, 14, 15, 89, 103, 122, 173, 174, 181, 182, **203**–13, 215, 218, 220, 225, 246, 248, 249, **252**

Orbán, Viktor, 27, 37

parties
  Alliance of Democratic Left (SLD), 60, 75, 122, 125, 126, 129, 130, 133
  Alliance of Free Democrats (SzDSz), 153, 154, 163
  Association of Slovak Workers (ZRS), 116
  Bulgarian Socialist Party (BSP), 215, 245
  catch-all, 12, 26
  Centre Party (Kesk), 55, 56, 60, 63
  Centre Union (LCS), 56

parties—*continued*
  Christian Democratic Movement
    (Slovakia, KDH), 57, 113
  Christian People's Party (EKRP), 56
  Civic Democratic Party (ODS), 27, 55,
    56, 60, 63, 76, 82, 112, 113, 115
  Civic Platform (PD), 122, 126, 130
  Coalition for Bulgaria (KzB), 215
  Communist Party (Czech KSCM),
    56, 58, 82, 112, 113, 115
  Communist Party (Slovakian KSS),
    57, 76, 77, 113
  Communist Party (Ukrainian
    KPU), 215
  Electoral Action Solidarity (AWS),
    57, 122, 125, 126
  Fatherland and Freedom
    (TB/LNNK), 55, 56
  Federation of Young Democrats
    (FIDESZ), 27, 52, 153, 154,
    163, 164, 245
  Freedom Union (UW), 82, 115, 122,
    125, 126, 129, 130, 133
  Greater Romania Party (PRM), 57
  Green and Farmers Union (ZZS), 56
  Independence Party (Iseseiv), 55, 56
  Independent Party of Smallholders
    (Hungarian FKgP), 56, 60, 153,
    163, 215
  Justice and Life Party (MIEP), 55,
    56, 61, 76, 153, 155, 159, 163,
    164, 215
  Labor Union (UP), 122, 126, 129, 130
  Law and Justice (PiS), 56, 57, 122,
    126, 129
  League of Polish Families (LPR), 57,
    61, 62, 76, 122, 126, 129, 130,
    131, 133, 136, 137, 138, 142
  Lithuanian Peasants' Party (LVP), 56
  Movement for a Democratic Slovakia
    (HZDS), 57, 113, 115, 116
  Peasants Self-Defense *also*
    Self-Defense (SO *also* SRP), 56,
    63, 75, 122, 126, 127, 129, 130,
    131, 133, 136, 137, 138, 142
  People's Party (Czech KDU-CSL), 115
  Polish Peasant Party (PSL), 57, 60,
    122, 125, 126, 129, 133
  Real Slovak National Party (PSNS),
    57, 62
  Republican Party (RMS), 55, 56, 61
  Right Slovak National Party, 76
  Slovak Communist Party (KSS), 57,
    76, 77, 113
  Slovak Democratic and Christian
    Union (SDKU), 115
  Slovak Democratic Coalition
    (SDK), 115
  Slovak National Party (SNS), 55, 57,
    61, 76, 116
  Slovenian National Party, 57, 82
  Smallholders' Party (Hungarian
    MPP), 153, 154, 163, 164
  Social Democratic Labor Party *also*
    Social Democratic Workers'
    Party (LSSP), 56, 61
  Social Democratic Party (Czech
    CSSD), 115
  Social Democratic Welfare Party
    (SDLP), 56, 61
  Socialist Party (Hungarian, MSzP),
    77, 153, 154, 163
  Socialist Party (Ukraine, SPU), 215
  Workers' Party (MMP or MP), 56,
    61, 76, 153, 155, 163, 164, 215
party polarization, 119, **245**, **247**,
  248, 249
party preferences, 44, 54, 59, 125, 133,
  134, 135, 142, 155, 157, 158, 159,
  163, 164
permissive consensus, 43
Phare, 23, 24, 37, 38
Poland, 10, 20, 28, 29, 32, 35, 36, 37, 39,
  48, 51, 52, 55, 57, 60, 62, 63, 64, 66,
  75, 80, 86, 87, 88, 92, 96, 103, 104,
  110, 113, **121**–35, 137–43, 151, 179,
  180, 187, 243, 249
political affiliations, 207
political divisions, 235, 250
Portugal, 39

Index

Potsdam, 132
public
 goods, 33
 opinion, 5, 6, 15, 20, 27, 44, 45, 46, **47**, 48, 49, 50, 62, 63, **83**, 85, 105, 120, 121, 127, 128, 130, 131, 147, 150, 154, 155, 158, 159, 160, 161, 166, 168, 192, 220, 221, 231, 236, 237, 245

referendum (referenda), 14, 36, 48, 49, 75, 97, 106, 107, 108, 109, 110, **112**–20, **121**, 127, **128**–38, 140, 141, 143, 146, 149, 153, 161, 172, 179, 181, 190, **194**, 198, 202
religion, 95, *see also* church
 confessional, 70, 74, 81, 123
 Muslim, 165, 166
 religiosity, 125, 126, 127, 130, 132, 133, 134, 135, 136, 137, 138, 139, 140, 142, 193
 religious, 11, 67, 103, 125, 128, 130, 132, 133, 139, 142, 167
 secular, 67, 123, 126, 130, 140
Romania, 10, 14, 19, 27, 29, 35, 37, 48, 51, 52, 55, 57, 63, 66, 80, 82, 86, 87, 88, 92, 96, 103, 107, 108, 166–75, 178–84, 215, 243, 246, 249
rule of law, 21, 23, 27, 102, 148, 179, 183
Russia, 10, 14, 15, 33, 35, 86, 87, 88, 89, 92, 93, 96, 98, 103, 139, 165, 166, 167, 171, 172, 187, 188, 189, 192, 193, 199, 204, 207, 214, 215, **217**–40, 243, 249, 251

Serbia, 174, 178, 180, 181
Slavic, Slavophiles, 218, 239
Slovakia, 14, 19, 26, 27, 28, 35, 37, 39, 48, 51, 52, 55, 57, 60, 61, 62, 63, 66, 76, 77, 80, 86, 87, 88, 91, 92, 96, **105**–19, 167, 171, 178, 179, 180, 215, 243, 246, 249

Slovenia, 10, 28, 37, 39, 48, 51, 52, 57, 63, 66, 80, 82, 86, 87, 88, 93, 94, 96, 103, 104, 108, 120, 166, 167, 180, 215, 243, 246, 249
socio-demographic characteristics, 86, 95, 97, 115, 116, 131, 157, 158, 164, 193, 200, 201, 226
 age, 9, 95, 96, 115, 127, 130, 131, 132, 133, 135, 136, 137, 138, 141, 156, 157, 161, 164, 183, 193, 200, 209, 226, 228, 229
 class, 66, 88, 124, 125, 126, 139, 140, 172, 173, 178, 179, 226, 227, 229, 240
 class voting, 124, 125
 education, 9, 27, 28, 33, 95, 96, 110, 111, 127, 130, 131, 132, 133, 134, 135, 136, 138, 141, 156, 157, 158, 162, 164, 174, 175, 193, 200, 207, 209, 210, 211, 212, 226, 228, 229
 employment, 28, 38, 71, 72, 78, 80, 112, 117, 124, 125, 130, 131, 132, 135, 136, 138, 140, 141, 163, 193, 195, 200, 201, 224, 226, 229
 ethnicity, 9, 10, 11, 14, 35, 69, 70, 74, 81, 88, 92, 96, 123, 126, 166, 167, 168, 176, 177, 178, 184, 188, 189, 192, 193, 194, 196, 197, 198, 199, 200, 201, 204, 206, 218, 223, 226, 227, 229, 237, 240, 242, 251
 income, 34, 75, 94, 96, 99, 100, 127, 130, 131, 132, 133, 134, 135, 136, 137, 138, 141, 147, 167, 175, 193, 200, 209, 210, 211, 212, 238
 occupation, 9, 96, 127, 130, 131, 132, 134, 141, 147, 153, 156, 174, 209, 240
 religion, 95
 residence, 28, 35, 127, 130, 131, 132, 133, 134, 135, 136, 137, 138, 141, 142, 207

socio-demographic characteristics—*continued*
  sex *also* gender, 71, 79, 81, 130, 131, 132, 135, 136, 138, 193, 200, 207, 209, 226, 228, 229
  urban-rural, 69, 115, 126, 127, 130, 132, 137, 147, 167, 168, 176, 183, 207, 239
Sofia, 168, 170, 216
Spain, 36, 39
Stability Association Pacts (SAP), 169
supranational, 1, 3, 4, 5, 7, 8, 10, 70, 78, 88, 114, 188, 194, 205, 207, 244

think-tank, 171, 255
transposition of community law, 30, 38
treaties
  Accession Treaty, *see* accession
  Anglo-Irish Treaty, 140
  European Constitution, 29, 72
  Maastricht Treaty, 33
  Nice Treaty, 29, 36
  North Atlantic treaty Organization *see* NATO
  Washington Treaty, 122
Turkey, 107, 108, 166, 167, 172, 175

Ukraine, 10, 15, 35, 188, **203**, 204, 206, 208, 210–16, **217–26**, 229, 230, 231, 232, 235, 236, 237, 239, 240, 243, 248, 249, 251
United Kingdom, 30

value added tax (VAT), 33, 106
visas, 19, 29, 33, 35, 170
  policies, 19, 29, 33
  requirements, **35**
Voting behavior, 90, 124, 125, 130, 131, 132, 133, 134, 135, 139, 140, 214

welfare system, 92, 95
West, 2, 4, 5, 6, 9, 14, 15, 20, 26, 32, 35, 44, 45, 46, 58, **65**–74, 76–79, 81, 82, 85, 87, 88, 89, 91, 92, 93, 95, 96, 97, 98, 99, 103, 123, 129, 130, 132, 133, 137, 146, 147, 153, 159, 160, 163, 165, 167, 168, 169, 172–82, 184, 187, 188, 201, 204, 206, 207, 209, 211, 213, 214, **217**–27, 229–37, 240, 241, 243, 244, 245, 246, 247, 249, 250, 252
World Trade Organization (WTO), 34, 218

Yalta, 168
Yugoslavia, 10, 165, 166, 167, 168, 174, 181, 206